Felix Narjoux, John Peto

Notes and Sketches of an Architect taken during a Journey in the

Northwest of Europe

Felix Narjoux, John Peto

Notes and Sketches of an Architect taken during a Journey in the Northwest of Europe

ISBN/EAN: 9783744794909

Printed in Europe, USA, Canada, Australia, Japan

Cover: Foto ©Andreas Hilbeck / pixelio.de

More available books at **www.hansebooks.com**

NOTES AND SKETCHES
OF AN ARCHITECT

TAKEN DURING A JOURNEY IN THE

NORTHWEST OF EUROPE.

TRANSLATED

FROM THE FRENCH OF FÉLIX NARJOUX

By JOHN PETO.

AUTHOR'S EDITION, FROM ADVANCE SHEETS.

WITH 214 ILLUSTRATIONS.

BOSTON:
JAMES R. OSGOOD AND COMPANY,
LATE TICKNOR & FIELDS, AND FIELDS, OSGOOD, & CO.
1877.

PREFACE.

IT has long been thought necessary that a young man should visit foreign countries in order to complete his education, and it has also, from the earliest times, and with very great propriety, been asserted, that foreign travel is no less fitted to develop the faculties of a man in maturer life; and from these maxims, the fruit of long experience, we may confidently deduce the incontestable and undoubted utility of visiting other countries besides our own.

And yet a taste for travelling has not been very common among us. The French have a strong objection to quit "*la belle France*," — some from an unwillingness to leave their homes; others, because it is not in their power. But all are agreed on one point, that, if they do not themselves travel, they ought to profit by the descriptions given by the fortunate individuals who are able to do so.

We are therefore performing a task useful to our fellow-men, when we record the events of our wanderings. But all the readers of this class of books are unanimously agreed that those which excite the warmest interest and from which they can derive the greatest advantage and satisfaction are illustrated works, in which a great number of plates render the narrative more intelligible.

Therefore we have travelled, pencil in hand, like an architect, making sketches wherever we have taken notes, so that the illustrations and descriptions should afford each other mutual aid.

The sketches themselves, besides representing the larger public buildings erected in each country, which serve as the exponents of its greatness and of the degree of its civilization, give also, and more especially, an idea of the dwellings of private persons. They show the interiors, and the less conspicuous parts of houses which have been constructed with a view to meet the wants of the inhabitants, the local customs, and the requirements of the climate.

With this intention we have sketched the internal parts, the decorations, and even the furniture of these houses. The text itself is nothing but the explanation of the plates; it shows the relations which exist between the customs of a country, the climate, the materials employed, and the dwellings erected by the inhabitants, — dwellings adapted to the tastes and wishes of their proprietors, and in which they find comfort and delight.

The strange and sometimes grotesque aspect of the manners of a people is thus brought under consideration; while it is shown that unusual forms of construction, and the manner in which they have been worked out, have been necessitated by these peculiarities.

We have endeavored to interest the reader by describing countries but little known. Tourists occasionally indeed make excursions into Holland, but most of them are satisfied with visiting the Hague or Amsterdam, the cottage of Peter the Great at Zaandam, or the village of Broeck; and not many travellers venture so far as Hanover or Hamburg. As to poor

Denmark, the names of but few Frenchmen have been entered in the visitors' book at Helsingœr during the space of eight years.

It will therefore be a new and interesting journey which the reader may make with us, — a novel excursion among people and through countries of whose buildings he knows nothing, or which, having once seen, he may be glad to visit a second time.

FÉLIX NARJOUX.

Charly, September, 1875.

CONTENTS.

HOLLAND.

MOERDYK. — DORDRECHT.
The Country. — The Meuse. — The Town. — The Cathedral . . 21

ROTTERDAM.
The Groote-Kerk. — The Hospital. — The Museum. — The Houses. — The Delft Gate 25

THE HAGUE.
The Binnenof. — The Town Hall. — The Market. — The Houses. — The Museums 43

SCHEVENINGEN.
The Villas. — The Church 61

LEYDEN.
The Koornbrog. — The Town Hall 70

HAARLEM.
The Groote-Kerk. — The Shambles. — Head-dresses 74

AMSTERDAM.
The Houses. — The Nieuwe-Kerk. — The Oude-Kerk. — The Wester-Kerk. — The Katolik-Kerk. — The Crystal Palace. — The Amstel-Hotel. — The Montalbans-Toren 87

NORTH HOLLAND 131

UTRECHT 142

FINE ARTS. — MANNERS. — CUSTOMS 150

GERMANY.

HANOVER. — HAMBURG. — THE DUCHIES.

FROM UTRECHT TO HANOVER.

The Country, the Journey, and the Travellers 161

HANOVER.

I. General Appearance. — New Streets. — The Old Town. — The Rathaüs. — The Markt-Kirche. — The Residenz-Schloss. — The Opera-House. — The Gymnasium. — The Synagogue. — The Schools . 167

HANOVER.

II. The Houses, their Furniture, and their Inhabitants . . . 206

HAMBURG.

From Haarburg to Hamburg. — The Elbe. — Hamburg. — The Alster. — The Jungfernstieg. — The Old Town. — The Conflagration of 1842. — The New Town. — The Public Buildings. — The Houses and their Inhabitants 254

ALTONA.

A Funeral. — The Kindergarten. — Altona. — Blankenesse . . 290

HELIGOLAND 294

THE WAR OF THE DUCHIES.

Preliminary Remarks. — The Austro-Prussian Army. — The Danish Army. — The Lines of Danevirke. — Taking of Missunde. — Fortifications of Duppel. — Taking of Duppel. — The Island of Alsen. — Conditions of Peace. — The Prussians during the Campaign . 304

DENMARK.

Jutland. — The Little Belt. — A Ferry-Boat. — A Farm. — Funen. — The Great Belt. — The Island of Zealand 323

COPENHAGEN.

I. General Aspect 346

COPENHAGEN.

II. Kongens-Nytorv. — Amalienborg. — Ronde-Kirk. — Frue-Kirk. — Christianborg. — Rosenborg. — Exchange. — Crystal Palace. — Hospital. — Schools. — Frederiksborg. — The Old and New Fortifications 354

COPENHAGEN.

III. The Museums. — Thorwaldsen Museum. — The Museum of Northern Antiquities. — The Ethnographical Museum 374

COPENHAGEN.

IV. The Danes. — The Theatres. — Amusements 399

COPENHAGEN.

V. The Dwelling-Houses 409

ELSINORE (HELSINGŒR).

The Copenhagen Station. — The Country. — Elsinore. — The Town Hall. — The Kroonborg. 425

LIST OF ILLUSTRATIONS.

FULL-PAGE ILLUSTRATIONS.

Fig.		Page
65. Church of the Sacred Heart, Amsterdam	to face	108
85. Cathedral Tower, Utrecht	"	144
125. Country House, near Hanover	"	230
128. Chimney-piece	"	236
145. Ground-plan of the General Hospital, Hamburg	"	270
157. Bathing Establishment, Heligoland (Section and View of Interior)	"	300
158. Bathing Establishment, Heligoland	"	302
175. The Château of Rosenborg, Copenhagen	"	362
181 to 185. Trumpet of the Age of Bronze	"	378
209. Town Hall, Elsinore	"	428
213. The Kroonborg, Elsinore	"	436

WOODCUTS IN TEXT.

	Page
1. General View of Dordrecht	23
2. Ground-plan of the Groote-Kerk at Rotterdam	26
3. Interior of the Groote-Kerk	28
4. The Groote-Kerk	29
5. Elevation of the Hospital at Rotterdam	30
6. Ground-plan	31
7. Enlarged Plan of Sick-Ward	31
8. The Ground-plan of the Boymans Museum, Rotterdam	32
9. The Boymans Museum	33

LIST OF ILLUSTRATIONS.

10. Statue of Erasmus, at Rotterdam	34
11. House in one of the Streets of Rotterdam	37
12. Ground-plan of a House at Rotterdam. Basement	38
13. " " Ground-floor	38
14. " " First Floor	38
15. Houses on the Banks of a Canal, Rotterdam	40
16. The Delft Gate, Rotterdam	41
17. The Binnenof at the Hague	44
18. The Lottery Hall at the Hague	45
19. Ground-plan of the Senate Hall at the Hague	46
20. Section " " "	46
21. The Town Hall at the Hague	50
22. Fish-market	51
23. Ground-plan	51
24. Vehicle used by Country People	52
25. Monument in Commemoration of the Independence of Holland	53
26. View of a House in an Avenue at the Hague	54
27. Ground-plan of Private House	55
28. First Floor	55
29. Elevation	56
30. Ground-floor of Villa at Scheveningen	63
31. First Floor	63
32. A Staircase	65
33. Ground-plan of Church at Scheveningen	66
34. View of Exterior	67
35. View of the Koornbrog at Leyden	71
36. The Town Hall at Leyden	72
37. Ground-plan of the Church of St. Bavon, at Haarlem	77
38. Interior and Organ-case, at the Church of St. Bavon, at Haarlem	78
39. Stadthouse at Haarlem	79
40. The Old Shambles	80
41. The Amsterdam Gate at Haarlem	81
42. Head-dress of the Women of Zuid Hollande	84
43. Head-dress of the Women of North Holland	85
44. Dutch Head-dress	85
45. Houses in one of the Streets of Amsterdam	88
46. Elevation of a House in the Nieuwe-Mark, Amsterdam	90
47. Plan of Ground-floor	91
48. Plan of First Floor	91
49. Elevation of a House in the Calver-Straat, Amsterdam	92
50. Ground-plan of the Frontage	92
51. Plan of Ground-floor	94

LIST OF ILLUSTRATIONS.

52.	Plan of First Floor	94
53.	Geometrical Elevation	95
54.	Houses of Business at Amsterdam. Basement	96
55.	" " Ground-floor	96
56.	Geometrical Elevation	97
57.	External View of the Royal Palace at Amsterdam	100
58.	Ground-plan of the Oude-Kerk at Amsterdam	102
59.	View of the Interior of the Oude-Kerk	103
60.	Ground-plan of the Nieuwe-Kerk at Amsterdam	104
61.	Section of Aisle	105
62.	Ground-plan of the Wester-Kerk at Amsterdam	106
63.	View of the Wester-Kerk at Amsterdam	107
64.	Ground-plan of the Church of the Sacred Heart at Amsterdam	108
66.	Tranverse Section of Arches of the Aisles	111
67.	Details of the Timber-work of the Spire	113
68.	Ground-plan of the Crystal Palace at Amsterdam	116
69.	View of Exterior of Crystal Palace	117
70.	View of the Interior	118
71.	Amstel Hotel. Ground-floor	119
72.	First Floor	119
73.	General View of the Amstel Hotel and Neighboring Buildings	120
74.	A Movable Bridge at Amsterdam	122
75.	Offices of Inspector of Weights and Measures, Amsterdam	123
76.	The Montalbans-Toren, Amsterdam	125
77.	Reception-room in a Farm-house in North Holland	133
78.	View of the Exterior of a Farm-house in North Holland	134
79.	Ground-plan of a Farm-house	134
80.	View of a large Farm-house	136
81.	Ground-plan	136
82.	Elevation of Artisans' Houses at Enkuisen	140
83.	" "	140
84.	Plan of the First and Second Stories of the Tower of the Cathedral at Utrecht	143
86.	Canal at Utrecht	147
87.	Windmill	148
88.	Railway-station in Germany	164
89.	A Corner-house in Hanover	171
90.	House in Hanover	172
91.	View of a House in a Square	173
92.	Corner-house in Hanover	175
93.	Ground-plan of angular Portion	176
94.	House with ancient Gables in a Street in Hanover	178

LIST OF ILLUSTRATIONS.

95. The Rathaüs, Hanover	179
96. Ground-plan of St. George's Church, Hanover	182
97. View of the Church of St. George and its Surroundings, at Hanover	183
98. The Opera-House, Hanover	186
99. Ground-plan of Opera-House, Hanover	189
100. The Gymnasium, Hanover	190
101. Ground-plan of Gymnasium	191
102. Plan of the First Floor	192
103. Section and View of Roof of Gymnasium	193
104. Interior of a Church in Ægidien-stadt, Hanover	196
105. Ground-plan of the same	196
106. Ground-plan of Synagogue, Hanover	198
107. Transverse Section	200
108. Exterior, with principal Entrance	201
109. Plan of Ground-floor of Private House	212
110. Plan of First Floor	212
111. Semi-detached Houses, Hanover	214
112. Ground-plan of Private House, Hanover	215
113. View of Interior	217
114. Decorative Paintings	218
115. Ground-plan of a Mansion, Hanover	219
116. Plan of First Floor	220
117. Hall, with Staircase	221
118. Geometrical Elevation of the Façade of a Private Mansion, Hanover	222
119. Country House, Hanover	223
120. Plan of First Floor of Public Hotel, Hanover	225
121. Ground-plan	225
122. Interior of large Dining-room	227
123. View of the Façade	229
124. Ground-plan of a Country House in the Environs of Hanover	230
126. Surface and Section of a Panelled Ceiling, Hanover	231
127. Surface and Section of Panelled Ceiling	236
129. Sofa Table	240
130. Table with Cupboard below	241
131. What-not	242
132. Pine-wood Bedstead	243
133. Walnut-wood Cupboard	244
134. Walnut-wood Bureau	245
135. Bookcase	246
136. Arm-chair	247

LIST OF ILLUSTRATIONS. 17

137. Chair	248
138. Chair	249
139. Bracket	250
140. View of the Alster Quay, Hamburg	257
141. An Old Street in Hamburg	261
142. Flower-girl	264
143. Ground-plan of the Museum at Hamburg	267
144. Elevation of Museum, Hamburg	269
146. Ground-plan of Roman Catholic Church at Hamburg	276
147. View of the Interior	277
148. Exterior of New Roman Catholic Church at Hamburg	278
149. Ground-plan of Lodging-house	284
150. Plan of First Floor	284
151. Exterior and Section	285
152. Ground-plan of Private House, Hamburg	288
153. Plan of First Floor	288
154. View of Exterior and Section	289
155. View of Heligoland	297
156. Ground-plan of Bathing Establishment at Heligoland	299
159. Blindage in the Lines of Danevirke	308
160. Improved Blindage	310
161. A Peasant-Girl, Jutland	324
162. Pier and Ferry on the Little Belt	325
163. Section of the Movable Pontoon	327
164. General Plan of a Farm in the Island of Funen	333
165. General View of a Farm	334
166. Exterior of Farm-house	335
167. View of Interior	336
168. Ground-plan of the Cathedral at Roeskilde	342
169. Geometrical Elevation of the Façade of the Transept	343
170. The Kongens-Nytorv, at Copenhagen	347
171. The Palace of Amalienborg	356
172. Plan of the Amalienborg-Slot	357
173. Runde-Kirk, Copenhagen	358
174. Ground-plan of the Rosenborg	361
176. The Exchange, Copenhagen	365
177. Ground-plan of the Exhibition Building	366
178. Transverse Section of the Exhibition Building, Copenhagen	367
179. General View of the Industri-borg	368
180. Ground-plan of Communal Hospital	370
186. Handle of Drinking-vessel	382
187. Bronze Pin	383

LIST OF ILLUSTRATIONS.

188. Bronze Pin	384
189. Bronze Pin	384
190. Bronze Cup	385
191 and 192. Harness found in a Tumulus in Funen	386
193. Granite Tomb. Front View	387
194. Opposite Side of Tomb	387
195. Granite Font	388
196. Chancel Candlestick	389
197. Terra-cotta Taper-stand	390
198. Modern Gable, Copenhagen	410
199. Elevation of a Lodging-house	411
200. Plan of the Ground-floor	412
201. Plan of First Floor	412
202. Ground-plan of Private Residence	415
203. Plan of First Floor	415
204. Interior of two Rooms	417
205. External View	418
206. Ground-plan of a Private Mansion	421
207. Plan of First Floor	422
208. Interior of Drawing-room and Anteroom	423
210. Ground-plan of Town Hall, Elsinore	431
211. Town Hall, Elsinore. First Floor	432
212. Interior. First Floor	433
214. Life-boat Station, Elsinore	441

HOLLAND.

"Hollande ; canaux, canards, canailles." — Voltaire.

"La Hollande est le pays le plus charmant, le plus lointain qu'on puisse parcourir sans sortir d'Europe." — Maxime Ducamp.

MOERDYK. — DORDRECHT.

THE COUNTRY. — THE MEUSE. — THE TOWN. — THE CATHEDRAL.

THE Belgian Railway terminates at Moerdyk;[1] at this point the traveller who is going to Holland ought to embark on the Meuse, and ascend it as far as Rotterdam, if he desires to have vivid impressions of the country, and to grow accustomed to it by degrees as he proceeds.

The river is as wide as a sea: its gray, muddy, thick waters, glittering with reflections of yellow light, are covered with vessels from every port and bound to every destination. The mudbanks on each side rise above immense meadows intersected by canals, streaked with long lines of poplars, and enlivened by large herds of black or white cows, which feed there during the whole year, finding a plentiful supply of pasture, and yielding abundance of meat and milk.

In the midst of these meadows boats or steamers appear to be passing over dry land, for the canals along which they go are enclosed between two artificial banks rising above the level of the surrounding soil.

The sea-breeze gently stirs the leaves of the trees, brings flocks of herons or storks, and turns the gigantic sails of windmills, whose cheerful click resounds on all sides.

A slight mist, a bluish haze, rises from the soil; if a gust of wind dissipates it for a moment, it returns immediately afterwards more heavily and densely; it tones down the outlines, and rounds off the forms of objects, so that they appear soft, and

---

[1] It is now continued as far as Rotterdam.

as if they had been steeped in water. There is nothing to arrest or fix the eye as it glances around and passes from one object to another without resting on anything or feeling any desire to make a choice; all nature is seen through a thin veil. The herdsmen who tend the flocks, the peasants who till the ground, the girls who milk the cows, move but seldom, and with a heavy step; they utter no shouts or songs, and are not easily induced to do anything hastily; the animals, tied to painted stakes placed at regular intervals, seem more calm and peaceful than in any other country. Here and there, nearer the environs of towns and villages, are country-houses, built of wood or brick, more grotesque than original, souvenirs of Java or Japan. In front of each there is a little garden, planted with gaudy flowers, especially bright-colored tulips; instead of being enclosed by a wall they are surrounded by a ditch full of water. The buildings are neat, though low, contracted, and of small size, painted with vivid and monotonous colors, and always detached from each other, in order not to shock the unsociable tastes of their inhabitants. Behind is the inevitable windmill, which pumps out the water in case of an inundation, fills the ditch in dry weather, supplies the house, waters the garden, saws the wood, and makes a slight noise in the midst of this deep silence. The whole scene is strange; the perfect calm astonishes and soothes us at first. It is an entirely new country which unfolds itself before the spectator.

We give a representation of Dordrecht or Dor, as it is called in the neighborhood. The new-comer, as yet little accustomed to the solitude, the monotony, and the scrupulous cleanliness of the Dutch towns, finds here the first cause for astonishment. The effect produced by this small town is unexpected and charming; almost lost in the river, and confounded with it, half hidden by a curtain of verdure, it shows only as much as it cannot conceal of its singular houses, so brightly colored, so neat and uniform, and grouped so regularly around the Dom-Kerk, which dwarfs them by its size and its height.

In the harbor vessels of every form and size pass to and fro, either going up or down the river. This continual incessant movement on the water forms a striking contrast with the calmness which reigns on dry land.

As we enter Dordrecht we are struck with the quiet which surrounds us. The sound of our footsteps awakes no echo;

Fig. 1. — General View of Dordrecht.

scarcely does it attract any curious fair-haired woman to the diagonal mirror of her ever-closed window. We pass through one street, a second, and a third, and we imagine that we have retraced our steps, so much does the third resemble the second, and this again the first. The houses are identically the same everywhere, the same not only in their general arrangements and their outlines, but in their details; all are built of brick more or less unfaced; they have the same appearance, the same form. The frames of the windows and doors are of wood, all of the same dimensions, and of a similar color, and, what is more, of the same tone of this same color. Thus Dordrecht prefers yellow, and all is yellow, and the same yellow.

The public buildings of Dordrecht are soon seen; indeed, we might dispense with the sight of them. The Dom-Kerk, an ancient cathedral, which has been turned into a Protestant place of worship, was built in the fourteenth century; before it stands an enormous brick steeple, which has been several times altered and mutilated, so that its original proportions cannot be ascertained. The Town Hall is common and unworthy of notice; the pier and the harbor are uninteresting, and — that is all.

ROTTERDAM.

THE GROOTE-KERK. — THE HOSPITAL. — THE MUSEUM. — THE HOUSES. — THE DELFT GATE.

AFTER leaving Dordrecht we soon come to Rotterdam. Landing at the quay of Bompjes, an architect may for a considerable time imagine himself still on board ship, for the houses appear to him to be dancing a saraband, which disturbs their equilibrium. The symmetrical gables advance, retire, lean to the right or the left, backwards or forwards; not one has maintained its perpendicularity. This may, however, be easily understood when we consider that the town was built on piles driven into the subjacent marshes that have been disturbed and shifted by frequent inundations; still, if the equilibrium has been affected, the stability has not been impaired; the fall of houses is not more frequent at Rotterdam than elsewhere, and one may venture to walk through the city without any danger.

The most important structure in Rotterdam is the Church of St. Laurence, better known by the name of the Groote-Kerk (the great church). Like all other ecclesiastical buildings in the Netherlands, the Groote-Kerk, originally intended for Roman Catholic worship, has been subsequently turned into a Protestant church.

Holland is Protestant; and when, after the excesses of John of Leyden and the Anabaptists in the sixteenth century, the Reformation was firmly established in the Netherlands (1536), the Roman Catholic churches became places of worship connected with the new faith; but, not having been constructed for that purpose, this transformation was not easily effected. We can clearly understand that, of all ecclesiastical edifices, Gothic churches are, less than any others, suited to the requirements of the Protestant religion.

Nothing is needed for the reformed *temple* but a large hall;

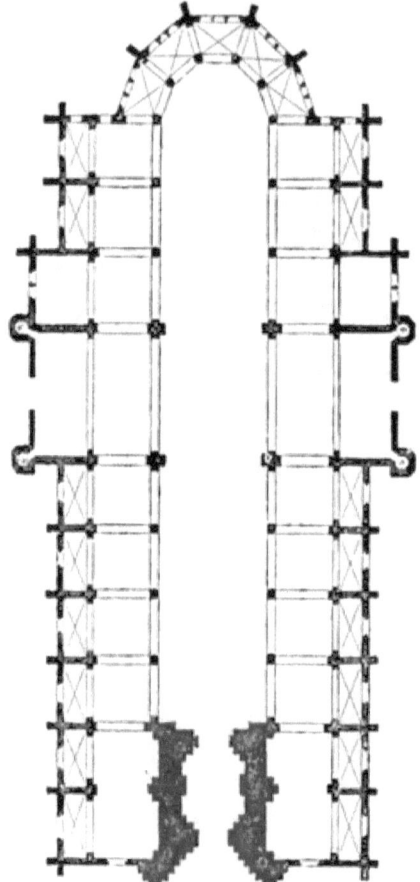

Fig. 2.—Ground-plan of the Groote-Kerk at Rotterdam.
(Scale, .009 inch to the yard.)

it is unnecessary to have side aisles for Catholic processions, a vast choir to accommodate a great number of priests, spacious chapels where divine service may be celebrated in many different functions, and ornaments of all kinds, which give such effectual aid to the pomp of ceremonies. The minister and the priest cannot officiate in the same sanctuary; the building which is adapted to the one is unsuited and inconvenient for the other.

The Groote-Kerk has passed through these various transformations. Its naked walls, of a uniform tint of coloring, present a cold and sad appearance; the choir and the chapels are closed; the windows have been despoiled of their colored glass; the transept and nave are filled with seats placed as in an amphitheatre, which hide the arcades, the bases, the shafts, and even the capitals of the columns of the side aisles. The ancient edifice can no longer be recognized; it is degraded and mutilated, and the effect which it might otherwise produce is completely destroyed.

Yet, even such as it is at the present day, it deserves examination, and attracts attention; its ground-plan (Fig. 2) shows a certain kind of grandeur and much unity in the arrangements of the nave, transept, and choir, but the apse is poor, and the aisles surrounding the east end correspond badly with the rest of the building. The most curious part is the timber-vaulted roof which covers the nave, the weight of which rests on the ends of enormous bare tie-beams, which also serve to buttress the walls. The transverse ribs of the roof extend from aisle to aisle, and support the boards which form its framework; each of these ribs springs from a slender column or pilaster, also of wood, which extends down to the chapiter of the column, and is supported by it, its bearing being sometimes strengthened by a brace placed below.

This very homogeneous structure is entirely independent of the main masonry; the profiles of the arches resemble those of stone voussoirs; they are composed of small pieces of wood indented together, thus forming a rigid system, but possessing sufficient elasticity to yield without breaking, and without losing their shape in consequence of the movements communicated to the whole building by an unstable soil.

Constructions of this kind are very frequent in the ecclesiastical buildings of the Netherlands. This is explained by the double advantage which they offer: first, in not imposing too great a weight on walls erected on a bad soil, and also in allowing

Fig. 3.—Interior of the Groote-Kerk.

architects to make use of those materials which, at the time when the churches were erected, were found abundantly in the country, then covered with forests which have since disappeared. It is true that a fire — and they are frequent here — would soon have destroyed the whole. The timber roofs of the Groote-

Kerk are in good preservation; they are of no older date than
1513; they are not so well constructed, and are certainly less
interesting, than those of other buildings of which we shall
have occasion to speak. The architect made his wood-work too

Fig. 4.—The Groote-Kerk.

massive for the purpose for which it was intended, and therefore the whole looks heavy and almost clumsy. This exaggeration of necessary solidity is, indeed, a general fault in Holland,
where, less than elsewhere, we meet with delicacy and gracefulness.

We see, at the entrance of the choir, an open screen in copper, of the Louis Treize style, of very remarkable workmanship, and with exceedingly rich decorations; there is also in one of the chapels another communion screen in copper, the tracery and sharp edges of which are in a perfect state of preservation.

The building is entirely of brick, except the points of support and some courses placed on the external façades, which are of stone (Fig. 4), the white color of which contrasts strongly with the deep red of the bricks. The tower above the entrance was not erected till the seventeenth century; a wooden spire was then placed upon it, which was afterwards destroyed, and replaced by the tower of several stories which we see at present.

We must remember, in order to explain the date assigned to the erection of the Church of St. Laurence, that in the Middle Ages the North of Europe was far behind our French provinces, and that in the thirteenth century admirable cathedrals had already been erected in the Ile-de-France when the German races were only just beginning to construct equilateral arches.

Fig. 5. — Elevation of the Hospital at Rotterdam.
(Scale, .039 inch to the yard.)

We must not, indeed, expect to find in Holland ecclesiastical edifices such as have been so much admired in France, Italy, Belgium, or Spain. Nothing is to be seen there in the least degree approaching those admirable churches in which a religion which appeals to the eye and the imagination has collected artistic treasures which every one can now see and admire.

On the right hand rises, high above this part of the city, a vast building, — the hospital, which was begun in 1844. In consequence of their not having taken the precautions which were

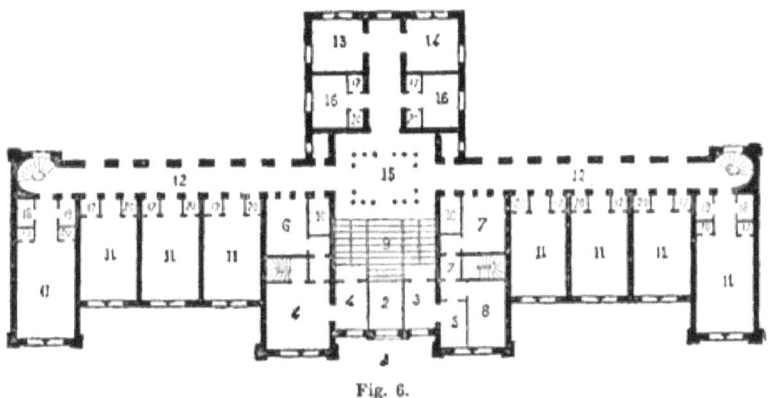

Fig. 6.
(Scale, .039 inch to the yard.)

1. Principal entrance.
2. Entrance-hall.
3. Board-room.
4. Director's apartments.
5. Physician's room.
6. Bath-room.
7. Vapor baths.
8. Drawing-room.
9. Staircase.
10. Lifts.
11. Sick-wards.

12. Corridors.
13. Library.
14. Theatre for operations.
15. Principal hall.
16. Wards for patients who pay for attendance.
17. Water-closets.
18. Nurses' apartments.
19. Store-rooms.
20. Dressing-rooms.

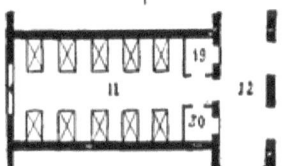

Fig. 7. — Enlarged Plan of Sick-Ward.
(Scale, .078 inch to the yard.)

rendered necessary by the nature of the soil, the works were interrupted for four years, and completed in 1850 (Fig. 5). This hospital is therefore one of the modern benevolent establishments constructed in Europe. The praise which has been bestowed upon it is doubtless somewhat exaggerated, for we shall see that the arrangement of the sick-wards, an essential part of such a building, is not free from blame.

The hospital at Rotterdam is capable of containing from 260 to 280 beds. It is three stories high; on the ground-floor are the surgery, the kitchen and its offices, the steam-engine, and other necessary appendages. The central part is reserved for the officers of the institution. The two wings are devoted to the patients, and are divided into small wards, each containing only twenty beds, which is an excellent arrangement. But the dimensions of these rooms, 6,5 × 11 × 4,6 metres = 328,9 cubic metres (about 430 cubic yards), only allow each patient 33 cubic metres (about 43 cubic yards), which is very insufficient.[1]

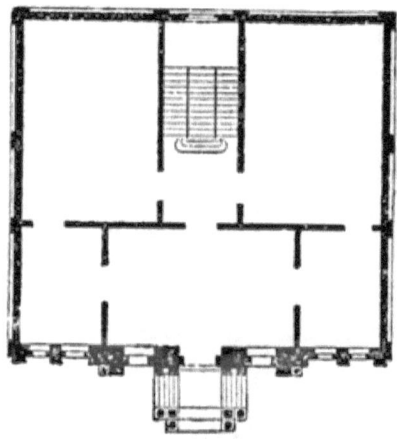

Fig. 8. — The Ground-plan of the Boymans Museum, Rotterdam.
(Scale, .039 inch to the yard.)

In addition to this, the wards are lighted and ventilated merely by a window and a half-glass door opening on a common

[1] The quantity of air to each bed, in the Hôpital Lariboisière at Paris, is from 50 to 60 cubic metres (65 to 78 cubic yards).

corridor perfectly closed, and therefore a constant cause of insalubrity, especially during epidemics (Figs. 6 and 7).

Each ward has a dressing-room and water-closet, the walls of which are covered with glazed tiles, and which are ventilated only by means of the corridor common to all the wards. The

Fig. 9. — The Boymans Museum.

floors of the latter are of deal, and are washed every day, so that they are perfectly clean, but at the same time constantly damp.

The patients are raised to the upper floors by a lift, so as not to expose them to any inconvenience from jolting, and this also spares the attendants the fatigue of carrying up heavy and cumbrous packages.

The Boymans Museum was one of the glories of Holland. It was burnt in 1864. This building, which contained the masterpieces of the Dutch school, has been re-erected, but unfortunately it has not been so easy to replace the pictures that were destroyed.

Fig. 10.—Statue of Erasmus, at Rotterdam.

The new museum is not faultless. Detached on three sides, it is in the form of a rectangle, and contains two vast halls, lighted from the ceiling, for the reception of pictures of large size, and three smaller rooms for drawings, medals, etc.; the ground-floor contains sculptures and more unimportant works. The façades, constructed of stone brought from Belgium, at great expense, are well proportioned and highly decorated, but have no originality. However, the building is far superior to the museums of the Hague and Amsterdam.

The statue of the magistrate Gysbert Karel has been lately erected behind the Museum. This personage is seated in an arm-chair, and clothed in a robe, the folds of which conceal the details of the seat; the sculptor has given to the figure the simplest position possible. The body is leaning backward, and the legs are crossed in a careless and natural manner, perhaps rather too realistic; but this will be readily pardoned, as there is an entire absence of studied effect and pretension.

The bronze statue of Erasmus stands on the Groote Mark (Fig. 10); it was cast in 1622, and is very celebrated in the North, and considered as the masterpiece of the sculptor Keiser. Erasmus is represented as standing, draped in a long doctor's robe, the folds of which cover his feet; he holds in his hand an open book, which he is reading. This figure has been alternately much praised and greatly decried; it certainly deserves " neither this excess of honor nor this indignity." It is a mediocre work, but it has the merit of representing a person who really seems to live, to read, and to walk.

The bases of these two statues are equally common and worthless.

The Dutch think a great deal of their primary schools; but there was nothing in their contributions to the Universal Exhibition at Paris in 1867 which seemed to justify their pretensions, and the schools which we visited did not induce us to change our opinion. The buildings, both in their external appearance and internal arrangements, are far inferior to ours. As to the boasted neutral schools, in which children of every sect receive necessary instruction without any interference with their religious tenets, it is easily understood that they are indispensable in a country whose inhabitants are unwilling to admit any variety or fancy except in their religious notions; in a country where a city of 100,000 souls, like Rotterdam, has seventeen different sects of almost equal importance, — Roman Catholics, Jansenists, Remonstrants, Mennonites, Reformed, Lutherans, Anglicans, English Presbyterians, Scotch, Jews, Greeks, etc.

We readily acknowledge that neutral schools might be useful in France, especially in certain provinces; but in most cases the uniformity of religion amongst us renders them superfluous, while, on account of the excessive division of religious sects, they are indispensable in Holland.

The Exchange is an edifice of the eighteenth century, possessing no architectural interest. This large block of buildings surrounds a vast enclosure covered with glass, the metallic framework of which is supported by enormous cast-iron columns, painted to imitate stone.

The whole is surmounted by a campanile, which was, at the time of our visit, surrounded by scaffoldings made of small pieces of rough wood with the bark on; and this excessively light construction reminded us of those which we see in Rome at the present time,—a circumstance which strikes one more forcibly, since the Dutch do not generally excel in the economical use of materials.

Holland extends her commerce over the whole world: she has factories at the North Cape, and others in Oceania; her numberless vessels bring into her ports the riches of the globe, to be conveyed over the Continent by railways and canals.

Rotterdam is the second, and will, it is said, soon be the first of her ports. The productions of the farthest East are brought thither by the mercantile genius of its inhabitants. Regular lines of sailing vessels and steamers constantly make the long voyage of six thousand leagues which separate Batavia from the North Sea. We see them, full and heavily laden, enter the deep canals of the interior, along which they pass to the very houses of their owners, to discharge their freight.

This exceptional circumstance, resulting from local arrangements, converts the whole city into a port, instead of limiting it to that portion by the side of the river; and this renders unnecessary at Rotterdam those immense warehouses which we see in London, Marseilles, Genoa, etc. But although each ship-owner has his private warehouses and depots of merchandise, there are some general establishments of this kind at the extremity of the Bompjes. But these dark and gloomy buildings are very badly placed; the usual Dutch cleanliness is wanting, and the architect can find nothing to admire in their construction.

The private dwellings of Holland differ essentially from those

Fig. 11. — House in one of the Streets of Rotterdam.

of France, which would suit neither such a climate nor habits so different from ours; but, on the other hand, they are perfectly adapted to the wants, the manners, and the tastes of their inhabitants; and in this respect the practical disposition of this nation of merchants is especially manifested.

The Hollander is not very sociable; it is difficult to form

any intimate acquaintance with him; his house, closely shut up, is but rarely, and only under certain circumstances, open to the members of his family. As soon as his business is over at his warehouse or his office he goes to a club, where he passes many hours smoking and drinking beer; he speaks but little, unless he has some direct motive for breaking the silence. His wife keeps the house, and brings up the children. The pleasures of the understanding and the mind, the love of art, are not so much

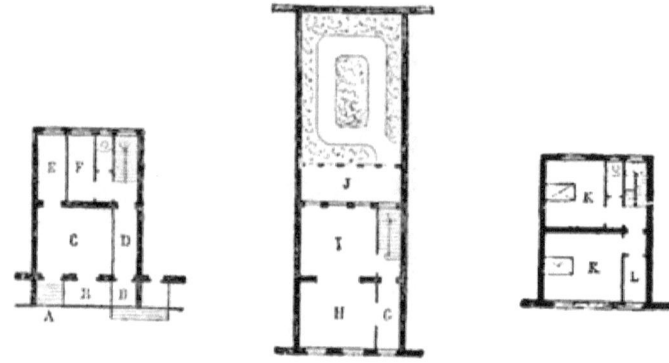

Ground-plan of a House at Rotterdam.

Fig. 12.—Basement.   Fig. 13.—Ground-floor.   Fig. 14.—First-floor.

(Scale, .039 inch to the yard.)

A. Kitchen entrance.
B. Area.
C. Kitchen.
D. Coal-hole.
E. Wine-cellar.
F. Bath-room.
G. Hall.
H. Drawing-room.
I. Dining-room.
J. Greenhouse.
K. Bedrooms.
L. Dressing-room.

cultivated in Holland as among ourselves. Thus Rotterdam, a town of 100,000 souls, has no theatre; and at Amsterdam, which contains 300,000 inhabitants, there is no opera-house.

The love of flowers, carried to such an extent in some cities as to become a mania, may, however, be accounted for by the very natural desire which these people must feel to see here and there around them some brilliantly colored spots breaking their gray and misty horizon. This desire, perhaps, justifies their exaggerated taste for tulips of the most gaudy colors, and for pink or blue houses, and induces them to paint the trunks of trees white and the wooden shoes of the peasants red.

In order to satisfy these tastes and habits — which, as we have seen, must leave the mind and the imagination perfectly calm — the Dutchman, who loves neither change nor variety, who can comprehend nothing but symmetry and monotony, who seeks neither society nor intercourse with his neighbor, constructs for himself dwellings arranged exactly on a uniform plan, with scarcely even a variation in size; the only difference which exists in the front of their houses is in the shape of the gables, which, according to the period of their construction, and the taste of the day, are more or less strange; and nothing can, in every case, justify their grotesque forms (Fig. 11).

The ground-floor (Figs. 12, 13, 14) is composed of two rooms of equal dimensions, separated by a partition formed of panels, so as slide upon each other by means of rollers, which renders it easy to throw both into one. Opposite to the street-door is the staircase leading upwards to the first floor, and downwards to the basement, where are the kitchen, the room for coal or peat, the cellar, a bath-room, and closets. There is direct access to this underground portion from without, and, in order to give all the air and light possible, an area of from 3 ft. 3 in. to 5 ft. wide separates the front wall from the public way, and keeps the passer-by at a distance. The upper story comprises two apartments similar to those on the ground-floor, a dressing-room over the hall, and a closet. If the house is of greater importance, there is another story or even two or three above it, but the latter case is very rare. The attics are used for stores, and, in order to avoid anything being carried up or down the staircase, a pole with a pulley attached is fixed on the outside, by which all packages can be raised or let down.

When the fronts of the houses abut on a canal, they are sometimes covered with enclosed or sheltered balconies, or large projecting bay-windows, which produce a picturesque effect (Fig. 15).

The rooms on the ground-floor are intended to be seen by the public who pass along the street, but do not enter: the windows of these rooms have their sill very low, and are ornamented within by stands full of flowers. The furniture can thus be seen from without, and is almost always composed of the produc-

Fig. 15. — Houses on the Banks of a Canal, Rotterdam.

tions of Java, China, or Japan, of objects of art or *vertu*, of strange forms, but of an inappreciable value and rarity; immense jars, hideous Bouddhas, jade vases, and unsightly bronzes are seen in abundance. Nothing interferes with the view of the back room, and the rare plants and choice tulips arranged on the floor of the conservatory. A very simple contrivance serves to bring the flowers nearer to or farther from the window.

All the windows are hung with sashes, — an excellent plan for enabling them to be securely closed without any inconven-

Fig. 16 — The Delft Gate, Rotterdam.

ience, in a country where there is no necessity to renew the air of the apartments frequently, and where it is not only contrary to the usual custom to look out of the window, but even to open it.

To atone for this imprisonment, the women, who always live in the upper story, have adopted the Belgian or Swiss *spy mirror*,[1] by means of which they can, while seated within the room, notice all that passes in the street. But in rigid families this mirror is prohibited, and the women live in the rooms which look into the back garden.

[1] A diagonal mirror on the outside, so placed as to reflect all objects in the street below. — Tr.

The use of outer blinds is a rare exception; they are replaced by inner shutters or double windows. When they wish to prevent passers-by or neighbors seeing what takes place within, they put before the windows, on the inside, small fine wire-work screens, painted blue or rose-color, called *Horren*, which allow them to see without being seen.

These houses are entirely constructed of brick: the floors and timbers are of deal, as well as the internal wood-work, and the doors and window-frames. The roofs are covered with curved tiles, slightly differing in form from ours; the bricks, which are generally of a deep color, measure about $8\frac{1}{2}$ in. $\times$ 4 in. $\times$ 2 in.; they are employed in the most primitive manner, without any attempt at combinations which might offer any advantages in the construction, or present forms pleasing to the eye.

The highway regulations, which, with us, restrict in so many ways both architects and their buildings, do not appear to be very rigorous in Holland. Each person builds his house in a certain given line; he constructs it solidly, because it is his interest to do so; he renders it convenient and healthy, because otherwise he could neither let, sell, nor inhabit it; but he attains this end without being subjected to our many regulations, which are difficult in application, variable, and often doubtful in interpretation.

When we leave Rotterdam we pass through the Delft gate (Fig. 16), built in the last century, which is considered an important structure in a city where there are so few. Then we arrive at a modern *Gothic* building — and *such* Gothic! — which is the terminus of the Hague Railway.

As soon as we lose sight of the last houses in Rotterdam, we find the country just as we left it on the other side before we entered the towns. The canals, the meadows, the flocks, the windmills, the roads paved with brick, return incessantly, and succeed each other in such a regular and uniform manner that one is afraid after a while of being the victim of an illusion, and is tempted to rub the window of the carriage in order to be assured that this invariable image is not engraved upon it.

THE HAGUE.[1]

THE BINNENOF. — THE TOWN HALL. — THE MARKET. — THE HOUSES. — THE MUSEUMS.

IF the terminus where we start for Rotterdam is Gothic, that, on the contrary, at which we stop at the Hague is Grecian. One is as good as the other; indeed, it is almost impossible to choose between them.

The Hague (St. Gravenhage) is more unlike a Dutch town than any other in Holland; it has no decided character, no original personality; it is the capital of the kingdom, the residence of the Court, a fashionable city, a favorite abode of that nomadic crowd, without fixed habitation, who look upon Europe as their dwelling-place. It has constantly offered an asylum to exiles of all nations; you find there enlightened, learned society, beautiful fine-art collections, and all kinds of intellectual resources. The natural productions are rich, and the sea is close at hand.

The appearance of the city corresponds very well with the idea which one would form of it. The streets are straight, and there are wide avenues and squares planted with trees; and also — a noticeable thing in a Dutch town — no internal canals; they have all been restricted to the harbor. A single piece of water has received the freedom of the city, the Vivyer, whose dimensions are those of a lake, and which, occupying the side of a vast square, bathes the walls of the Binnenof.

The Binnenof (Fig. 17) is a palace, or rather an assemblage of buildings fulfilling the same purposes as that *degli Uffizi* at

---

[1] The Hague is the town where the Dutch nobility reside; there is scarcely any place more agreeable in the world. — REGNARD, 1681.

Florence. It is the ancient palace of the Stadtholders, and the cradle of the Hague, and was formerly a fortress surrounded by trenches. There is still no communication between it and the city, except by three bridges.

Installed in this vast building there are a chapel, the Treasury offices, the Senate, the Museum (a little beyond the ancient

Fig. 17. — The Binnenof at the Hague.

buildings), two offices of the Ministry, and those of several other branches of public administration. In the midst of the court stands a building of the thirteenth century, intended originally as a chapel, but now used as a place where the public lottery is drawn, and for the exercises of the civic guard, who thus perform their manœuvres sheltered from the sun and rain (Fig. 18).

The whole of the Binnenof has been several times altered and modified. The original buildings, which are to be seen around the inner court, are composed of a ground-floor before which is a portico, and two upper stories of a square form.

The materials employed are stone and unfaced brick. It has been very carefully constructed, so that, in spite of time, and foundations resting on a movable and compressible soil, the general mass of the building has stood well, and no deterioration is perceptible to the eye; but the appearance of the edifice is not cheerful, and it gives one the idea of a barrack or a prison rather than of a palace.

Fig. 18. — The Lottery Hall at the Hague.

The Lottery Hall alone relieves the whole structure. This little Gothic building makes an agreeable break in the monotony of the cold and symmetrical lines which surround it.

The two turrets, the object of which is not at once evident, were formerly watch-towers, commanding the flat and level country all around. The campaniles which are above them are modern.

The interior of this hall has a bare wooden roof, said to be of cedar; but we could only examine it through a broken pane of glass, all our attempts to penetrate farther having been ineffectual.

The discussions which lately took place in France, when it was proposed to install the Municipal Council of Paris in the Luxemburg and in the projected Hôtel de Ville, give a certain

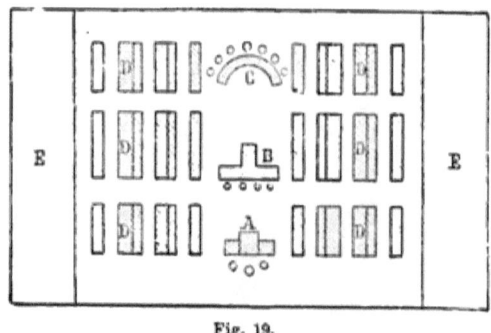

Fig. 19.

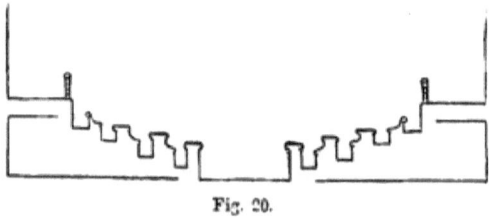

Fig. 20.

Ground-plan and Section of the Senate Hall at the Hague.
(Scale, .078 inch to the yard.)

A. President's seat.
B. Secretaries.
C. Seats of ministers.
D. Seats of senators.
E. Gallery for the public and the press.

amount of interest to the arrangements adopted at the Hague in order to seat the members of the Senate.

The hall of assembly, of which we give a ground-plan (Fig. 19), and a section (Fig. 20), has nothing remarkable in itself, but its arrangement deserves to be noticed. On the right and left are the seats of the great dignitaries of the kingdom, the representatives of foreign Powers, and the public; below, the senators, thirty-nine in number, are seated three by three on benches with alternate desks; these benches are placed in six rows opposite to each other. In the intermediate space are the president's arm-chair, and the seats of the ministers and secretaries. This is, in principle, almost the same arrangement as that adopted at the House of Commons in London. There is no tribune; the members speak from their places; each one rises to ask a question or to reply, without making a formal speech. The senators engage in conversation or discussion, rather than in an oratorical tournament, and the affairs of the country do not suffer in consequence.

The Dutch do not seem to value the works of art which they possess, so much for the pleasure which they may afford, as for the profit which they may derive from them. The museums of the Hague and Amsterdam are badly placed in third-rate buildings, and the public are not admitted, except on payment, — a custom which is observed in no part of Europe except in Belgium and the Netherlands.

The Museum at the Hague contains on the ground-floor a collection of Chinese and Japanese curiosities of an exaggerated reputation; and, on the first floor, a gallery of paintings containing about three hundred pictures. The greater part of these belong to the Dutch school, among which are found Paul Potter's "Bull," and Rembrandt's "Lecture on Anatomy."

Although the numerous copies of the masterpiece of Paul Potter have rendered it so well known, the impression which it gives us is new, because none of its reproductions have given the exact proportions and the scale of the original, which is of the natural size; to this striking peculiarity we must add the excessive study of detail, and a minute care to reproduce the slightest accessories. Thus the spectator feels more surprise than admiration; he counts the flies scattered over the animal's back, and the roughened parts of the horns, and remains almost unmoved before such an exact and rigorous copy of nature.

The "Lecture on Anatomy" is a work of a different character.

The spectator cannot avoid feeling a certain emotion when studying the scene which the painter places before him. A dead body is lying extended, the students surround it, listening to the lecture delivered by Professor Tulp, *in corpore vili*. This is the subject, which is not in itself very attractive; but the body is unmistakably a dead body; the head of the professor and those of the physicians are portraits; each is represented with his natural characteristics, his usual gestures, his peculiar temperament, expressed in such lively though apparently insignificant detail, thanks to the genius of Rembrandt, as clearly to show the impression made on each person present at this dismal scene, the points in which they differ, and those in which they resemble each other.

Many other works at the Hague Museum are as remarkable as the preceding, without being so well known. They all have the same character peculiar to the genius of this people and this school of artists, the last which has appeared in the history of art. In the "Woman at the Window," and the "Woman with the Lamp," by Gerard Dow, the "Herb-Market at Amsterdam," the "Musicians," and the "Huntsman," by Metzu, in the "Painter and his Wife," and the "Soap-Bubbles" of Mieris — in all of them, in fact — we constantly find the same representation of the actions of ordinary life, and of facts patent to every one, there is nothing ideal or elevated, nothing which strikes us as great. Contemporary history, the remarkable deeds of heroes, love, religion, or the glory of one's native country, have only inspired these masters with citizen scenes, treated in a citizen-like manner. They have felt only the material side of life and nature; dreams and imagination have evaded their genius, which only shows itself in conscientious studies of subjects, at times the most vulgar and grotesque, in copies of common models, without grandeur or elevation, in which there is nothing to awaken the vibration of those noble sentiments which Art is destined to arouse in the heart of man.

We shall have again to return to this subject when visiting

the museum at Amsterdam, and shall then describe more fully the characteristics of the Dutch school of painting.

Prince William proposed, about the year 1840, to have a palace built for him by an English architect, — the most absurd palace that ever excited the mirth of an architect. It is said to be Gothic; but we cannot tell why. It is in every respect a work of folly, and beyond the bounds of reason: its turrets, machicolations, and half-hidden apertures cannot be described. The strangest thing of all is, that this grotesque assemblage is only an outward show, a mere decoration. Behind it is the veritable palace, with real walls, real windows; a palace in which it is possible to live and to endure life.

In front of William's palace is a Neo-Grecian edifice, which is the royal residence.

One who was fond of finding fault with the architecture of the Middle Ages said one day, as he showed us a stonemason's shop near one of the cemeteries of Paris : " See how easy it is to *make* Gothic architecture; it is within the reach of every mind and every workman." This simpleton considered funeral monuments as types of Gothic architecture. He might have repeated his tirade before Prince William's palace. Instead of entering into a long discussion we should then have asked him to " face-about" towards the royal palace, and should have cried in our turn: " See, then, how easy it is to construct Grecian architecture."

This simple story shows that neither good Gothic nor good Grecian architecture is easy, and that we ought not to employ either one or the other indifferently; that, on the contrary, each has its *raison d'être* and its conditions of existence; that, indeed, at the present day, a supposed Grecian palace ought not to have been built at the Hague opposite to one pretending to be Gothic.

The churches of the Hague possess little interest. The Groote-Kerk dates from the fourteenth century; it has lost its first character, and there remains no trace of the original plan except the large tower at the entrance.

The Nieuwe-Kerk is built entirely of bricks of different forms and dimensions; all the plain mouldings, fillets, small columns, and mullions are constructed of bricks of the requisite shapes; these bricks are not faced, and are simply jointed together, — a logical and reasonable process, far preferable to that which consists in covering brick walls with a sufficiently thick coat to

Fig. 21. — The Town Hall at the Hague.

obtain in plaster the desired forms. We see, also, in Germany the former process prevalent and in constant use.

The Town Hall (Stadhuis) is of the sixteenth century, and underwent important modifications about 1730. It is placed at the corner of two streets, and shows the traditional belfry still intact, and the flight of steps, from the top of which orators used to address the people.

The architectural details are excessive and somewhat exaggerated; this defect, however, does not entirely destroy all interest in this little edifice (Fig. 21).

Fig. 22. — Fish-market.

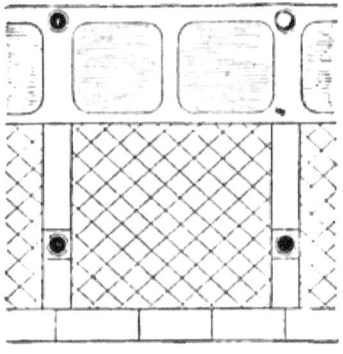

Fig. 23. — Ground-plan.
(Scale, .039 inch to the yard.)

Near the Town Hall stands the fish-market, sheltered above, but open to all the winds, an arrangement not conducive to comfort, but evidently favorable to cleanliness and the avoidance of unpleasant odors. This market is covered with a sloping platform roof; the fish-woman stands at the lower side, behind a trough in which are the fish; the customer, protected from the rain and the drip from the roof, walks round under the projecting part. This market, represented in perspective in Fig. 22, and in ground-plan in Fig. 23, is very economical, but inadequate for a large city, and yet far superior to those we find in many of our provincial towns.

Fig. 24. — Country Vehicle.

The country people who come to the city use curious vehicles of varnished deal, ornamented with carving. When the weather requires it, these carriages are covered with a linen tilt. The driver sits on the single seat in front, the rest of the vehicle being intended to receive packages (Fig. 24).

The Hague has erected a statue to King William II. and two to William the Silent. With the exception of the rider in the equestrian statue of the latter king, which is well executed, the three works are but mediocre. The monument erected to perpetuate the remembrance of the day when the independence of Holland was proclaimed possesses no very great interest; but it is the most important of its kind, and on this account we give a sketch of it (Fig. 25).

Fig. 25. — Monument in Commemoration of the Independence of Holland.

Another building also awakens political recollections, but such as are written in characters of blood in the history of the Hague. This is the prison which served as the last abode of Barneveld Olden, the chief of the republican party, who was assassinated in 1617; and of the two brothers De Witt, the grand pensionaries or prime ministers of Holland, at first the idols and then the victims of the people.

Places that have witnessed gloomy tragedies of this kind have usually changed their character and appearance, and the traveller cannot find in them the traces of the past. The hall in the Château de Blois, where the Duke of Guise was assassinated, now richly painted and restored, certainly inspires us with no melancholy ideas; the old prison of Cardinal la Balue, where he

Fig. 26. — View of a House in an Avenue at the Hague.

was shut up in his celebrated iron cage, serves at present as a bedroom for a pretty Touraine peasant-girl; the Castle of St. Angelo, at Rome, is covered with the joyous inscriptions of our French soldiers; in the Tower of London delicate fair young English ladies gayly lay their heads on Anne Boleyn's block, while the attendant touches their white necks with the edge of a tin sabre. The prison of the Hague, on the contrary, yet remains a gloomy and desolate place; it is still the prison in all its horrors; a staircase of worn stones, fortress walls, cells insufficiently lighted by narrow windows so high that the hands cannot reach them, and defended by iron bars and gratings; heavy thick doors, studded with large-headed nails, and closing with enormous bolts which slip into their sockets with a dismal sound; and on the walls words of hatred and vengeance, and traces of the bloody hands of the wretched men who sought to defend themselves in the last convulsions of terror and despair.

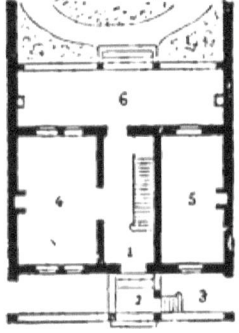 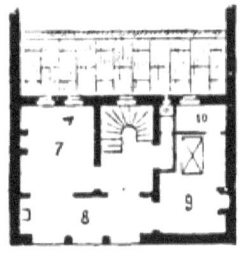

Fig. 27. — Ground-plan.   Fig. 28. — First-Floor.

(Scale, .078 inch to the yard.)

1. Hall.
2. Porch.
3. Area.
4. Drawing-room.
5. Dining-room.

6. Winter garden.
7. Morning-room.
8. Enclosed balcony (Loggia).
9. Bedroom.
10. Dressing-room.

The dwelling-houses of the Hague differ from those which we have seen at Rotterdam, and those which we shall see at Amsterdam. The Hague, as we have said, is a city of pleasure. The stranger who pitches his tent there thinks only of the means of passing his time agreeably. The Dutchman, who retires there after having made his fortune by selling for seventy-five francs in Europe the *picol* of sugar or of coffee which he bought in Java for seven francs, has no other care than to enjoy the riches which he gained so rapidly by such a lucrative trade. It is interesting to observe how, without renouncing entirely the habits inherent in his race and the usages which belong to his nature, he passes from the sombre houses of the Hoog-straat or the Kalver-straat, from the fetid canals of the Rokin or the Amstel, to the cheerful

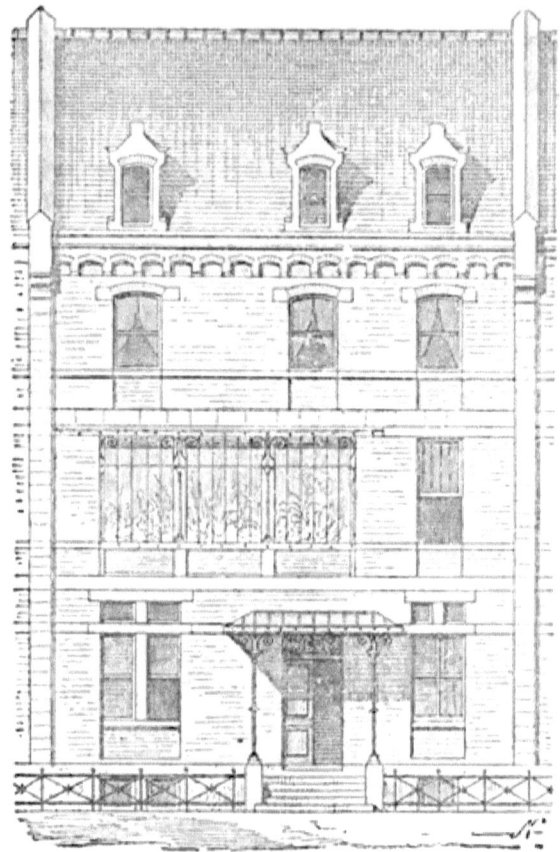

Fig. 29. — Elevation.

(Scale, 1_5 inch to the yard.)

dwellings of Langevoorhout or of Princessgratch, to the gay villas of the Wood or of Scheveningen.

The houses in the luxurious quarters of the Hague are large

and conveniently situated, always surrounded by gardens filled
with brilliant flowers, and, in proportion to the means of the
proprietor, adorned with external conservatories and glazed porticos, forming an outer saloon (Fig. 26). We no longer meet
with façades of such monotonous and frightful uniformity as are
seen in all other Dutch towns : the height, the dimensions, and
even the *color* of almost all of these vary.

Still the true Dutchman, even at the Hague, cannot renounce
the traditions of his whole life ; and here we give, as an example
of this transformation, a house in which he has endeavored to
reconcile his old recollections with his new aspirations (Figs. 27,
28). He always separates it from the public road by an area,
which gives access to the kitchen and offices ; a covered entry
above leads to a hall, which opens, on the right, to the dining-
room, and on the left to the drawing-room. Behind these rooms
is a conservatory or winter garden ; on the first floor are the
dwelling-rooms of the family ; the principal bedroom is, as a
concession to modern ideas, ornamented with a balcony, but this
balcony is enclosed on all sides, and is always kept shut, so that one
can, without being seen, notice all that passes without (Fig. 29).

Environs of the Hague. — Close by the gates of the city is the
celebrated promenade called the Wood, for which the whole of
Holland professes the warmest admiration, and which Gérard de
Nerval once asserted to have been raised on piles and subsequently planted.

When the sky is clear, and the sun shines, which seldom
occurs in Holland, this park is on *fête* days the rendezvous of
the whole population of the city. Rich citizens, workmen in
their Sunday clothes, and paupers in the livery of their asylum,
come here to listen to concerts in the open air, given gratuitously
by the military bands, which are stationed on a small island,
around which the promenaders pass, always going methodically
in the same direction, without interfering with each other, and
especially without any haste. Carriages are rarely to be seen ;
we remember that one day we met but two. In one were the

Queen-Dowager and the King; in the other, an odd coincidence, was a Frenchman who acquired a sad notoriety at the time of our last civil discords.

As the royal personages passed, there was no cry, no noisy demonstration; every one uncovered at their approach, whilst they themselves saluted the crowd with that automatic movement peculiar to crowned heads. The presence of their king awakened neither transports nor enthusiasm in those who were present, but only simple marks of regard, the testimony of the respect which is due to the representative of a government freely accepted by the nation. This attitude, however, was very noble, and presented a striking contrast to the silly manifestations which are seen elsewhere under similar circumstances.

It would be wrong to compare the Wood at the Hague with our Bois de Boulogne, since there could be no points of resemblance between them. They present two entirely distinct aspects, each having its own merit, but different. The soil in the Wood is perfectly flat and level; water is abundant; a hole made with a walking-stick in the ground would become a small well. The walks are bordered with superb trees; the roots of the beeches passing down into a damp soil give to the bark and foliage a whitish tint, to which the rays of the sun communicate a quasi-metallic glistening, which is represented in the landscape of the national painters.

In the midst of this park stands the royal palace called the "House in the Wood," a rich, citizen-like habitation, dating from the seventeenth century; it contains a certain number of pictures and works of art of secondary interest.

Different avenues extend from the park, and are for a considerable distance bordered with villas and country houses, in which the rich Dutchmen of Holland or Java come to retire and enjoy themselves after their fashion. For the love of their native land is so great in these natures otherwise so calm and cold, that whatever may be the position which they have acquired, the distance they may have to traverse, the hopes which have been

realized or disappointed, they have always a tendency to return
to the home of their childhood. They resemble in this respect
the Chinese coolie, who is content to remain for five years among
the guano heaps of Peru, in order to gain enough for a burial-
place in the soil of the Celestial Empire.

We had an introduction to the proprietor of one of these
houses, and we went with him to inspect it. The richness of
the furniture and the objects of Oriental art which filled it
astonished us, and our admiration made him smile. He then
showed us some large colored photographic views representing
his habitation at Samarang, — a veritable palace entirely of marble, surrounded by a veranda of teak-wood. Three distinct
buildings, protected from the sun by a double roof, are connected
together by long galleries supported by pillars of carved wood;
these pavilions contain a dining-room, an immense vivarium,
and a drawing-room. In each apartment there was a ventilating
apparatus of a somewhat primitive kind, — gigantic fans, which
a Malay, dressed in a blue robe, worked by means of a string
passed round a roller, and which were sufficient to keep these
vast rooms cool, whether they were open or closed on two or
more sides, according to the hour of the day. Then there were
immense gardens filled with the productions of the exuberant
vegetation of the tropics, — fruits whose juices are deadly, plants
whose perfume is poison. And, to complete this establishment,
stables for four-and-twenty horses, and rooms for eighty servants,
whom you might see dressed in the richest costumes, and performing their various functions.

The dwelling at the Hague must have appeared poor and mean
to this man, habituated to the luxury and splendor of the East;
and yet this nabob feels occasionally that it is necessary for him
to abandon for a while the princely life that he leads there. He
quits his palace, the dazzling sunshine, and the natural luxuri-
ance of Java, and returns with delight to revisit his little villa,
and the fogs and tulips of his beloved Holland. He forgets his
riches and his power, and becomes again a simple citizen, the

modest proprietor of a little house at the Hague, in which he resumes the habits of his race and the recollections of his childhood.

"Have you any architects at Java?" we asked our host, as we took our leave of him.

"Yes, certainly. We have, first, the European architects who, imbued with the traditions of the West, come to construct there houses on the models which are seen everywhere in Holland or elsewhere; they endeavor to recall in Java the remembrance of Grecian, Roman, or Gothic buildings which they have more or less understood.[1] The result attained is what you may suppose. Besides these, we have the Chinese, who do not strive to give the predominance to their personal tastes and their own manner of looking at things, but who have, on the contrary, a remarkable talent for assimilation; they are, at the same time, to a great extent architects, engineers, and contractors. A Chinaman becomes whatever he wishes; they listen attentively to the directions of their employer, speaking not to give him new ideas, but only to induce him to develop his own. A sketch, often a mere tracing on the ground, is sufficient, and they produce immediately all that you wish. Here are buildings in wood and in marble. Notice how thoroughly the architects have understood, according to their destined use, both the materials which they have employed and the position which they should occupy. It is impossible not to distinguish, at first sight, that this compartment contains the aquarium, this the drawing-room, the other the family sitting-rooms, and the fourth the secondary apartments. As to the marvellous decorations and the infinite variety of internal arrangements, it is the result of Chinese and Hindoo art united with the effects of that dazzling light which gilds, animates, and throws into relief the simplest objects.

"It is wonderful, in fact; and to think that such results have been obtained by people whom we consider barbarians."

The Chinese, barbarians? Ah! well.

---

[1] Let us not be accused of exaggeration, since we Frenchmen have built a Neo-Grecian palace for the Governor of Saigon, and a Gothic cathedral at Shanghai.

SCHEVENINGEN.

THE VILLAS. — THE CHURCH.

"ONE can go from the Hague to the sea in less than half an hour by a very pleasant road. We saw on our way a carriage driven by sails." — REGNARD.

A PASSAGE in a *tresckuit* is a mode of travelling still held in honor in Holland, and it is well to describe it to the reader, in order that he may avoid it. One must be possessed of Dutch calmness of disposition to be able to endure a trip, however short, in those heavy, flat, and narrow boats, towed by a horse along canals of thick and greenish water. You can see nothing, for the canal is enclosed within two very high banks; nothing can be heard, for there is no noise; your travelling companions, usually inhabitants of the neighboring villages, are motionless, fixed to their seats; they have nothing to say to each other, and, certainly, not much more to think about. The men smoke, the women knit; their heavy countenances, unvarying and without expression, show no traces of any impression or emotion whatever. Sometimes the boat stops, and draws up to the side; another tresckuit is coming in the opposite direction. It is more than a hundred yards off, and there is ten times as much time as would be required to get out of its way, and to avoid delay; but it would never come into the mind of any person in this country to do anything in a hurry. We must therefore bear the inconvenience with patience, thinking with regret of the tramroad carriages which perform the journey from the Hague to Scheveningen in a quarter of an hour, and of Regnard's carriage with sails, which is no longer in use except on the plains of Hong Kong; but still, at last, we arrive at our destination.

But to do justice to the tresckuit, it gives us one moment of solid satisfaction, and that is when we leave it.

That which most astonishes a traveller when he first lands at Batavia is not the brilliant shells or the fan-palms, the marble verandas or teak-wood kiosks. Nothing of this kind seems to impress a stranger so strongly as to see under this burning sky, and surrounded by such luxuriant vegetation, narrow and mean brick houses with fantastic gables, built on this new soil by Dutch colonists, in remembrance of the mother country.

A similar, though contrary, impression awaits the traveller who passes through certain environs of the Hague, and goes to Scheveningen or Woorburg. In the midst of clumps of shrubs and groups of tropical flowers, raised in hot-houses and brought out on grand occasions, may be seen houses open to the winds of heaven, showing nothing but verandas, porticos, and enclosed or open balconies. We ask with astonishment how such buildings can be habitable under this gray and misty sky. They are doubtless very uncomfortable; but when, by chance, a bright ray of sunshine lights up the landscape, the eye can see it and rejoice.

We give the plan of one of these dwelling-houses, which is in process of construction. All of them have not been erected with the same care as this, and with so much attention to detail. Very often recollections derived from a distant country are not so happily carried out, and in every case this mutual transference of works adapted specially to climates and necessities so opposite to each other is not precisely satisfactory, either to logic or reason.

This villa (Figs. 30 and 31) has a north and south aspect, with a view of the sea. On that front it has a large loggia, — a kind of conservatory, — communicating with the open galleries on the lower floor; a veranda, which establishes a communication between the apartments on the ground-floor, shelters the south front from the sun. On the opposite side of the house there is a porch, serving as a covered entry for carriages. On

the first floor are the family rooms, all having balconies either
enclosed or open. The two principal bedrooms show in their
arrangement a great knowledge of the art of comfort; each is
provided with a dressing-room; the beds are placed on an elevation in a recess formed by the projection of the partition wall,
thus leaving a wide empty space in the room; they are also
completely sheltered from draught, or from the too bright light,
which, when reflected from the water, is rather fatiguing to the
eye. If it is fine, the occupier may, without leaving his apartment, go out into the enclosed balcony to breathe the fresh air

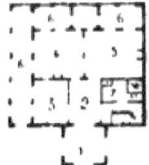

Fig. 30. — Ground-floor.

Fig. 31. — First-floor.

(Scale, .039 inch to the yard.)

1. Porch.
2. Antechamber.
3. Morning-room.
4. Drawing-room.
5. Dining-room.
6. Open gallery.

7. Closet.
8. Bedrooms.
9. Enclosed balcony.
10. Dressing-rooms.
11. Water-closets.

from the sea; if it is wet, he can sit at his fireside, sheltered
from the rain and wind, and enjoy the prospect to be seen
through his wide sash windows, which are securely closed.

The inferior apartments and the offices are placed on the opposite side of the house, where the view is less interesting. The
side facing the north has no opening, but is a dead wall, solidly
constructed, for it was necessary on this aspect to be more completely protected from bad weather. Instead of an ordinary wall
of one thickness, the builder has erected two; that on the outside is about 1 ft. 8 inches in thickness, and the inner wall,
formed of bricks placed lengthwise, is about $4\frac{1}{2}$ inches wide.

These two walls are separated by an interval of 4 inches; they are connected only by cross-pieces of iron placed at the level of the floors, intended to bind them together, without, at the same time, allowing any damp to be communicated from one to the other; the floors being supported by the inner wall, the outer has only its own weight to sustain. Four narrow openings are made in the outside, so as to keep up a draught, and at the level of the ground is a small channel, hollowed like the stones of a gutter, which receives all the water produced by fog, and any damp that may have passed through the outer wall; the paper-hangings of the internal wall are thus protected from all external influences, and remain perfectly dry.

This system of double walls is frequently employed in Russia, and the hollow space between the two serves to conduct the heat supplied by warming apparatus, which thus raises the temperature by warming large surfaces, instead of introducing heated air by a single opening, the neighborhood of which is often disagreeable.

The decoration of the interior of this villa is not less deserving of attention than the external arrangements. Deal is the only wood employed; but, notwithstanding such simple materials, the result obtained is excellent, and unquestionably superior to that produced by the use of imitative marble and papier maché so much in fashion with us.

The joists of the ceiling are left uncovered; there is a moulding on their edges, relieved by stripes of color; other bands of very bright tint, traced on the joints of the boards, serve to form regular compartments, relieving the bright and uniform ground of the deal, which glistens with a thick coat of varnish. All this is very simple, but free from pretension and vulgarity.

Fig. 32 shows the general plan adopted for the construction and decoration of the principal staircase leading to the first floor. The steps, string-boards, supports, and even the balustrades themselves, are entirely made of deal; some parts are simply moulded or carved in the solid wood.

The details bear the impress of Gothic ideas, and have been

Fig. 32. — A Staircase.

very carefully studied; the materials employed are only brick and wood, with the exception of a few pieces of Belgian stone.[1]

[1] For further details, and the drawings to which we have alluded in our descriptions, see "Habitations Modernes, par MM. Viollet-le-duc et Félix Narjoux, architectes." — Ve A. Morel et Cie, éditeurs, Paris.

The village of Scheveningen, which is the Dieppe of Holland, contains nothing interesting except its country houses. There is, however, in the part inhabited by fishermen, a church (Fig. 33) which was built in the fourteenth century; the choir was erected in the fifteenth; the nave and the side-aisles are covered with the same roof. This church is, at present, devoted to the Protestant form of worship, and has lost much of the interest which it must have formerly possessed (Fig. 34).

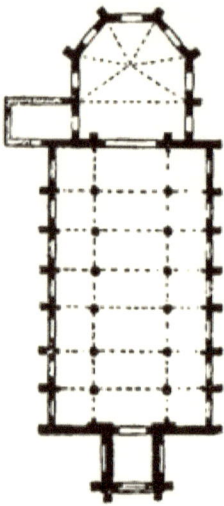

Fig. 33. — Ground-plan of Church at Scheveningen.
(Scale, .029 inch to the yard.)

On a dune, the base of which is consolidated by a brick wall, are arranged three hundred boats which the fishermen drew up for shelter from a storm of wind last night. They are lying there in quiet, in perfect order, and ready to put again to sea. These boats are heavy, thick, and massive, and are very unlike any that you may find elsewhere. Leeboards, fixed on the gunwales by a screw, hang over the sides during rough weather, in order to lessen the oscillation caused by the waves. Whether this plan is efficacious, or likely to be advantageous to boats intended for such service as these fishing-smacks, is very questionable; at all events, it appears to us that this contrivance must interfere with the management of the boats, and when the sea is rough prevent their rising easily over the waves.[1]

Fig. 34. — Church at Scheveningen.

The sea-shore at Scheveningen is very curious: there is an immense extent of fine, soft, level sand, which you reach, not by

---

[1] These boards are, more probably, used to prevent the boats making leeway while fishing. — Tr.

going down, but up, for the sea here is not below, but considerably above you. The depth of water is so slight, that bathers make use of machines on four wheels, and drawn by a horse. Before the vehicle stops, you have had time to undress; the door is then opened, and you plunge into the water in a narrow space protected from prying eyes by sail-cloth. You may, indeed, by raising this screen, swim out into the open sea, if you wish to do so. When you have enjoyed your bath, you re-enter the machine, the horse starts afresh, and you have time to dress as you return.

While speaking of Scheveningen, we may mention some traits of Dutch life and manners which are obvious, yet worthy of notice. The roads or canals from the Hague to Scheveningen are, during almost their whole length, bordered by villas, the form or the good taste of which we do not now discuss; but their appearance is cheerful, smiling, and very agreeable. In front are hedges, flowers, grass-plots, borders filled with richly colored plants carefully cultivated. From the midst of these flower-beds the eye is charmed by the sight of the country, the beauties of the neighboring landscape, the pedestrians and the carriages that pass along. Behind these buildings is usually found a confined, enclosed space, very dull and uninteresting, with a ditch of stagnant water, and the unfailing windmill. Ah, well! this is the spot which the Dutchman has reserved for his own use; here he feels at home and united with his family; this ditch, this windmill, are a source of enjoyment to them all; they neither see any one nor are themselves seen, and they are happy. As to that part of the dwelling left exposed to the public, it is entirely sacrificed to show. The Dutchman there makes an exhibition of his fortune, and of the enjoyment that it is capable of affording to him; he satisfies in this manner his vanity and his love for seclusion; for if he were actuated solely by this latter feeling, nothing would prevent him from concealing and at the same time enjoying the riches which he now exhibits to the eyes of others.

We have another instance of this. The sea-shore at Scheveningen is frequented during the season by elegant people. The women, instead of showing themselves and making a display as they do in other countries, install themselves in small huts or summer-houses, which conceal them. They do not mix with each other; there is no exhibition or competition in dress, but they live retired and by themselves. Yet they are all rich; many are very rich. They often possess a peculiar beauty, produced by the union of the Javanese and Dutch races, — a type full of contrasts: a fair and brilliant complexion with black hair, a dark skin with blue eyes, a *nonchalant* gait allied with expressive gestures. But their riches, grace, and beauty, all are concealed, and are never shown to the outer world. These are pleasures and charms reserved for the family circle. Social life is reduced to that of the family. In this respect, more than in many others, the Dutch do not resemble ourselves.

LEYDEN.

THE KOORNBROG. — THE TOWN HALL.

"THE city of Leyden is the Versailles of Holland, by its air of decayed grandeur, its perfect sadness, and its imposing solitude." — ESQUIROS.

AT the Dutch railway-stations there are no locked waiting-rooms, unfortunately so common among ourselves. We rejoiced, therefore, as we started on our journey from the Hague, to be able to go in or out of the refreshment-room as we pleased. A grave Dutchman, our fellow-traveller, explained to us, with the utmost seriousness, that such liberties could not be allowed to travellers in our country without exposing the French to great danger of accident, on account of our natural impetuosity!

It is indeed true that the inconceivable calmness and placidity with which a Dutchman enters or quits a railway-carriage is a striking contrast to our haste and vivacity. But this slowness does not accelerate the journey; and as the country to be passed through is identically similar to that which you have already traversed, and as the most frightful monotony reigns all around, in nature as well as in the works of man, a journey through these interminable meadows, filled with the same black or white cattle, watered by the same canals, interspersed with the same windmills, soon becomes very tedious.

Here we are at Leyden at last, with its encircling canals, its green houses, its *burg*, and its souvenirs of the Anabaptists, the Elzevirs, and the famous siege of 1574, during which the besiegers employed pigeons to convey news.

When we first saw Leyden we thought it dull and solitary;

but afterwards we visited Utrecht, and now Leyden seems in our recollections full of life and animation. It is indeed an interesting town, commanded by a ruined fortress, which is coeval with its earliest days. These ruins are all that remain of the old burg, the foundation of which is attributed to the Romans, and which, on the top of a hill fifty feet high, — one must be in Holland to call such a mole-hill a hill, — commanded a very

Fig. 35 — View of the Koornbrog at Leyden.

strong position on the Rhine; a position unimportant at the present time.

We expected to find in the "burg" of Leyden some souvenirs of the castles on the Rhine, and some resemblance to them; but these ruins are not very interesting, and are now converted into a café and refreshment-rooms. The keep, which is still standing, has just been repaired, and from its battlements you can see the city and the environs.

At the foot of the castle is the Koornbrug (a covered bridge), in which we do not find the character and originality seen in buildings of the same kind in Switzerland and Italy (Fig. 35).

Fig. 36.—The Town Hall at Leyden.

The Town Hall is the most ancient building in Leyden. It is a large edifice of the sixteenth century, and has a high flight of steps, which serve as an extemporaneous tribune for popular orators. The details of the façade are bad; the statues, pinnacles, balustrades, and other forms of decoration affect grotesque, distorted, and exaggerated shapes (Fig. 36), which show what kind of buildings were erected there at the time of our "renaissance."

Beyond Leyden the road crosses a bridge over a yellow and muddy stream, — the old Rhine (the Oude Rijn), as the Dutch call it. Poor noble river, which, after having rushed over the rocks of the Grisons, formed the cataracts of Schaffhausen, and extended itself in all its majesty at Cologne, finishes its course sadly between the two walls of the quay of a canal, or disappears amongst the mud-banks of Northern Holland.

HAARLEM.

THE GROOTE-KERK. — THE SHAMBLES. — HEAD-DRESSES.

"In the very place where you now see a village ships of considerable burden used to sail, scarcely twenty years ago."—Van Ostade.

BEFORE we reach Haarlem we pass by the "polders," the former site of the lake of Haarlem. This inland sea, eleven leagues in circumference, with difficulty protected from the North Sea by dunes insufficient to resist stormy weather, was subject to real tempests, to terribly high tides, which more than once threatened Amsterdam itself. It was therefore necessary to restrain this dangerous neighbor, and this was no trifling matter. The first proposals of this project were made during the sixteenth century. After having been long abandoned, it was reconsidered subsequently to the terrible inundation of November 9, 1836, but not undertaken till 1840.

This gigantic enterprise included, not only the draining of the lake, but the execution of many preparatory works of almost as great importance as the principal operation.

It was first necessary to throw up round the lake or sea of Haarlem a double dike, inclosing a ring canal with a towing-path, and a weir, emptying itself into the North Sea. The water pumped out was poured into this canal, and thence ran into the sea. Locks constructed in the canals prevented the return of the sea at high tides, and kept it in stormy weather from filling the channels and flowing back into the lake.

Having ascertained by repeated soundings that the mean

depth of the lake was about thirteen feet, they calculated that the quantity of water which it contained might be estimated at 947,000,000 of cubic yards. It was necessary to add to this large amount the water brought by rain or by infiltrations from the soil, — about 47,000,000 of cubic yards, — deduction having been made of the loss by evaporation, which is not very considerable in a country where the atmosphere is constantly saturated with vapor.

Three steam pumping-engines were employed, and were sufficient for this work, which only lasted three years and three months, in spite of unforeseen difficulties, and complications inseparable from the execution of such an undertaking.

The most important of the machines used for this purpose was the Leeghwater, which is still at work, and which, by means of eleven lifting tubes, raised at once, at each stroke of the piston, the enormous weight of 145,200 pounds of water.

The expense of this enterprise comprised, first, the actual expenditure for the drainage itself, and then that of keeping up and repairing the dikes, canals, and draining-engines still necessary in order to insure the wholesome condition of the land. The practical turn of mind of the Dutch succeeded in covering the first outlay by the sale of the land reclaimed from the sea, and in reducing the second so as not to exceed the sum allotted previously every year for the construction and repair of dikes intended to protect the province from the encroachments of the sea of Haarlem.

The surface of land devoted to agriculture by this operation is about 44,480 acres, now in full working order, and remarkably fertile. Villages have been built on this reclaimed land. Instead of liquid plains, we see solid green meadows; trees, houses, and churches now rise where formerly ships floated.[1]

But every medal has its reverse. When the traveller passes, on a hot day in summer, and looks on what was formerly the

---

[1] A similar, but much less important, work is on the point of being executed in France, at St. Louis du Rhône.

lake of Haarlem, he sees heavy vapors rising from the soil, marshy exhalations issuing from this muddy land; and if he should linger, he will soon feel the sad shivering fit which is the precursor of fever. Nature seems to try to make man pay for his victory, and to take revenge for the struggle in which she has been conquered.

This strife is without any truce; and in order to understand that such must be the case, we have only to remember that almost all the soil of Holland is below the level of the sea. Thus, taking the level of Amsterdam as a base, — an assumed line to which the situation of other cities may be referred, — we find that Rotterdam is ten feet and a half below the level of the surface of the Meuse at high water, and the environs of Leyden and Haarlem are more than eleven feet below the level of the North Sea. The only aim of the Dutch must therefore be to "bridle the fury of the waves"; and one of the characteristic traits of the persevering and industrious disposition of this people is that they have raised immense dikes to protect all the most threatened parts, and constructed them in wood and in granite, in a country which possesses neither quarries nor forests.

Haarlem is especially distinguished for its love for tulips, and for the large organ in the church dedicated to St. Bavon.

The rage for tulips has somewhat subsided. A bulb which formerly cost five thousand florins may now be bought for two hundred, which is still a considerable price. But the love of flowers has not diminished at the same time as their value, and the gardens in the environs of Haarlem are still the most beautiful that can be seen. Gardeners go thither from nearly every part of Europe to supply themselves with rare plants, and the flower-beds round the city form a brilliant border full of brightness and perfume.

The church of St. Bavon, or the Groote-Kerk, which contains the organ, the great curiosity of Haarlem, is a building especially remarkable for its great dimensions (Fig. 37). The nave and the choir were built in 1472 by Albert of Bavaria, Duke of Holland. The spire is not so old; it was not erected till 1516.

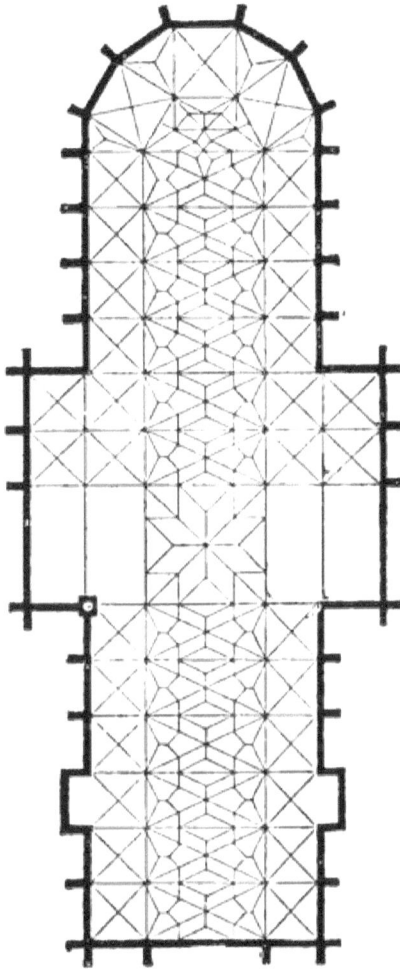

Fig. 37.—Ground-plan of the Church of St. Bavon at Haarlem.
(Scale, .039 inch to the yard.)

When we compare this church, one of the most important in Holland, with those constructed in France at the same period, we see what progress we had already made, and what results we had obtained, while our neighbors, gaining hints from our works, were only feeling their way by copying us unskilfully.

A special arrangement in the churches of Holland — and on

Fig. 38. — Internal View and Organ-Case, at the Church of St. Bavon at Haarlem.

which we must dwell, as it gives them a character entirely different from ours — is the substitution of a timber-vaulted roof for those built of stone or bricks, without any other modification than that which the suppression of flying buttresses may have caused in the lower parts of the structure; while the ground-plan, the section of the pillars, and the nature of the materials, have the same conditions of resistance as if they had been intended to support heavy roofs of masonry.

One might be induced to suppose that the Dutch architects had taken the idea of their buildings from those of other countries, or rather that they had copied them as far as the spring of the vault; but that, having arrived at this point, fearing, on account of the nature of the soil, the heavy weight of stone roofs, they had substituted for them vaulted roofs of wood.

Fig. 39. — Stadthouse at Haarlem.

The organ of the church of St. Bavon at Haarlem is enclosed in a very rich case, of which Fig. 38 will give some idea. It was built about the year 1736, and it enjoys a celebrity which may be justly rivalled by the perfection of our modern instruments. A simple remark, however, will show its importance. The organ of the Abbey of St. Denis, built in 1841, and which is well known throughout France, contains only 4,500 pipes, while that of Haarlem has 5,000.

The copper chandeliers at St. Bavon are Flemish. They have been wrought with the greatest care, and the style is very simple; but the thickness given to the metal scrolls injures the effect of the whole, and gives them a heavy appearance (Fig. 38).

Before the Groote-Kerk stands the statue of Laurence Coster, who is said by the inhabitants of Haarlem to have anticipated

Fig. 40. — The Old Shambles.

Gutenberg in the discovery of printing. Close by is seen the Stadthouse or Town Hall (Fig. 39), built of brick, about the year 1630, if one may trust to the date inscribed above the door; but the style of architecture seems to indicate an earlier period. This edifice has undergone modifications and additions which have altered its original form. The principal building, standing behind the more modern erections, has in front a very elevated flight of steps. The façade, having an open balcony, shows a simplicity rare in Holland, and contrasts strongly with the neighboring structure, the Old Shambles (Fig. 40), a Spanish and Hindoo edifice of a most grotesque appearance. The swollen pyramidal turrets, the frieze, ornamented with the heads of ani-

Fig. 41. — The Amsterdam Gate at Haarlem.

mals, the red color of the bricks, and the white tint of the stone or of the parts covered with plaster, produce altogether an effect which is characteristic, but only moderately pleasing.

The ramparts which formerly defended the town are now nearly demolished. One of the gates is still standing. It is a solid structure of the fifteenth century (Fig. 41).

When we had gone over the city, we were invited to attend a

very curious meeting, of which the reader will be glad to hear some particulars, for it was called for the purpose of deciding on a competition for the plan of a building, and there never was in France among architects a more *bonâ fide* competition.

A neighboring town, wishing to erect an elegant fountain in a public square, asked for plans and tenders for the work. Several architects and sculptors answered this appeal. The decision was made. Of course, every one was very discontented except the successful candidate; but this was not all. Each of the others declared that the judges had not adhered to the conditions of the plan laid down, and that he had fallen a victim to the strictness with which he had observed the required conditions, etc., etc., — such protestations and complaints as are always sure to be made in case of a competition, whether it takes place in Holland or in France, and which we have always known to recur on every occasion. Thus far there was nothing new; but at this point the novelty commences; for, after the decision, the judges are expected to give a public account to the competitors of the motives which decided them, and which caused them to incline to the right hand or the left.

This account was to be given at the meeting to which we were invited.

It was a very interesting occasion. The competitors were numerous. Each one claimed the right of putting two questions to the foreman of the jury, who replied, after having consulted with his colleagues. There could, therefore, be no decision with closed doors, no influence of party or position. A therefore could not give his vote to the son of B, on condition that B should, on the next day, vote for A.

The questions proposed were of course clear, precise, expressed in very good terms, and with the calmness and good temper which a Dutchman always displays, and which require a categorical answer, free from circumlocution and subterfuge. It was not sufficient to say to an unsuccessful candidate, "I consider your plan a bad one"; for he demands immediately why and in what respect this judgment has been formed, and he has the right to expect an answer.

Thus, having been closely pressed by one of the candidates, the president made the following reply: —

"A programme cannot always be literally carried out; we must interpret the spirit of it. This is a matter of tact and judgment. Suppose, for example, it was proposed to study the arrangement of a floor of a building consisting of four rooms. Among those who send in plans, the first places his apartments behind each other. He fulfils the conditions, but the arrangement is bad. Another divides a rectangle into four parts. He also fulfils the programme; and yet his solution is no better than the former. A third, however, makes his four rooms independent of each other, by means of a hall. His project is a good one. Would you accuse him of having violated the conditions because he has introduced another element, the hall, which was not specified? For my part, I should not hesitate to give him the preference; and it is a consideration of this nature which has caused the rejection of your plan. You have complied faithfully, but in a servile manner, with the conditions imposed. Another has understood and interpreted them better; he has been more intelligent and skilful, and has justified the preference which has been given to him."

There was no replying to this argument, as it was stated in so simple and moderate a manner; and, indeed, this mode of discussion, by immediately adducing an apposite example in order to render the demonstration more striking, is quite in keeping with the upright and practical disposition of the Dutch people.

Why could not we follow this example? Is it not in accordance with our disposition? I see no reason, at least, that we should not try it; and if it should become a regular custom among ourselves for architects to be called upon to compete with each other, by supplying designs for public works, a plan much to be desired, it would be necessary, in order to encourage this innovation, to surround the decision with every possible condition of impartiality; and, unquestionably, the best means of effecting this is to give each candidate an opportunity, on the day following the decision, to ask the judge the reasons for his preference without its being possible for him to refuse to reply, or to shelter himself behind the opinions of his colleagues, as was the case at ——, where an unfortunate competitor showed, one day, letters of condolence received from his four judges, each throwing upon the others the responsibility of the decision at which they had arrived.

On the walls of the hall in which we were assembled hung

Fig. 42.— Head-dress of the Women of Zuid Hollande.

some pictures, bad enough in themselves, representing the different types of head-dress of the Dutch women, — fashions which have already become obsolete in towns, but are still preserved in the villages in certain provinces. Our sketches (Figs. 42, 43, and 44) may give an idea of some of them.

The women of the southern part of Holland (Fig. 42) ornament the head with bands of gold and silver, secured under their caps, and terminating in a kind of spiral horns, often adorned with precious stones or rich enamel.

HAARLEM.

In the North of Holland (Fig. 43) the head-dresses worn by the women are very rich and complicated. The hair is cut short,

Fig. 43. — Head-dress of the Women of North Holland.

and covered with an under-cap of white satin, trimmed with

Fig. 44. — Dutch Head-dress.

black embroidery. Over this cap is worn a pad, which supports a broad circular band, having plates of metal attached to it, and adorned in front with the usual antennæ. Servants wear these ornaments made of silver; richer persons have them in gold.

In addition to these, there is fixed in the hair, at the top of the head, what is called the forehead hair-pin. The married women wear the larger end of it on the right, the unmarried girls on the left. We may also add that rich citizens' wives cover the whole with a bonnet trimmed with flowers (Fig. 44) brought from Paris or London, and the effect is as droll as can be imagined.

The journey from Haarlem to Amsterdam is not a long one. We can see at intervals the gulf of Y. The railroad passes through a district full of country-houses of the most cheerful aspect, but built with little variety. We soon enter a Grecian building, — the terminus. The courtyard adjoining is filled with omnibuses gilded and painted in gaudy colors. We pass under a gateway, a kind of triumphal arch with Corinthian columns, and we are in Amsterdam.

AMSTERDAM.

THE HOUSES. — THE NIEUWE-KERK. — THE OUDE-KERK. — THE WESTER-KERK. — THE KATOLIK-KERK. — THE CRYSTAL PALACE. — THE AMSTEL-HOTEL. — THE MONTALBANS-TOREN.

"AMONG 500,000 men living in Amsterdam, there is not one who is idle or poor, not one fop, nor one who is insolent." - VOLTAIRE.

"Amsterdam is built on herring-bones." — DUTCH PROVERB, seventeenth century.

INNUMERABLE canals covered with vessels; a port dug in mud; a yellow sea which wears away its slimy shores; a soil reclaimed from the water by an incessant struggle; a calm, laborious population; enormous ships going and returning in the midst of a mass of uniform, dismal houses, always closed; large, low, stunted public buildings, without any decided outline; no cries, no songs; people who go on their way without any haste; going out and coming back with unalterable placidity; the same identical expression on every countenance; round faces, with a white and red complexion; behind the windows immovable figures, looking as if benumbed. This was what our first walk through the city revealed to us; and yet we have often heard it compared to Venice. Alas! where is the blue lagoon? where the gay songs of the gondoliers, the Square of St. Mark, and the piazza? Where can we find anything to remind us of that active, lively population, content with the sunshine and their free and easy life?

It is morning. The city awakes. Each inhabitant goes to business, leaves his dwelling, carefully closing the door. The children go to school without noise, without any hurry or disturbance. The servants and housewives, armed with large brooms and gigantic sponges, wash, rub, and polish the fronts of the houses, the footpaths, and the bricks which pave the streets.

The houses resemble those which we have already seen; and the details into which we have entered, when speaking of those of Rotterdam, need but little amplification.

Fig. 45. — Houses in one of the Streets of Amsterdam.

Holland produces scarcely any building materials, except mud. But this, dried and burnt, becomes brick, and thus forms the constituent element of every structure.

These bricks are not laid, as in some countries, with studied care, and with varied combinations of form and color. The Dutch mind is opposed to such labor, such an innovation. The bricks are simply piled upon each other; the lintels of the doors and windows are of iron or wood; the bricks follow, without interruption, their regular lines, only stopped at each opening by the wooden framework that surrounds it; and, at last, after one or more stories, they crown the building with a grotesque gable, the top of which is often decorated with a pineapple, a vase, or a vulgar piece of sculpture.

All these houses follow each other in interminable lines. They are all alike; they have no distinct characteristics. They differ from each other in no special and individual aspect, and can only be recognized by some variation in the shape of the gables; so that we have often wondered how the inhabitants of certain streets of Amsterdam and London, where the same uniformity of plan is adopted, can distinguish their houses from those of their neighbors.

In the plan of these houses there is no more variety than in their façades. On the ground-floor is a long passage serving as a vestibule; at the farther end are the stairs; at the side, the dining-room and drawing-room, separated by a movable partition. On the first floor are two bedrooms, each with a dressing-room. If the house is of sufficient importance, there is another floor above arranged in the same manner; and over this, on the upper story, the nursery and the servants' rooms. In the basement there are the kitchen and several important offices, for good cheer is fully appreciated in this humid climate. In the attics are store-rooms, intended to contain all kinds of provisions and articles for domestic use, since cellars are impossible in such a permeable soil. At the top of the gable a pulley is attached to a horizontal piece of wood, by means of which a basket can be raised or lowered with packages, so as to avoid the inconvenience and injury which might be occasioned by carrying them up and down the stairs within.

In some cases, however, the houses built during the last century show greater variety in their façades and evince a certain amount of taste, and are therefore not destitute of interest.

We give, in Figs. 47 and 48, the ground-plans, and in Fig. 46

the elevation, of one of the houses constructed on the Nieuwe-Mark. What is especially worthy of observation in this house is not the general plan adopted in the decoration, but certain special arrangements made by the builder, which manifest a

Fig. 46. — Elevation of a House in the Nieuwe-Mark, Amsterdam.

conscientious endeavor to carry out the proposed plan in all its details, and to leave nothing unforeseen. Thus, we see beneath the cornice placed at the base of the gable openings about seven inches square, intended to receive the ends of poles by which scaffoldings may be supported, when required for the purpose of cleaning the frontage, pointing the bricks, or otherwise repairing the front of the house. These holes are usually closed by a small stone, by a terra-cotta ornament, or simply by the end of the pole, the rest of which is concealed in the attic.

In the business streets the houses are of a different form. The shops occupy the ground-floor; the upper stories, of which there are never more than two or three, serve as store-rooms or lodgings for the tradesmen. The outer door opens directly on the street. The arrangement is almost the same as with us;

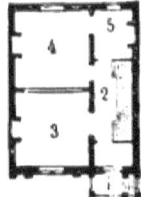   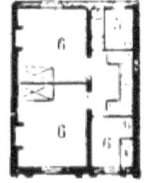

Fig. 47. — Plan of Ground-floor.   Fig. 48. — Plan of First-floor.
(Scale, .078 inch to the yard.)

1. Entry.
2. Hall.
3. Dining-room.
4. Drawing-room.
5. Morning-room.
6. Bedrooms.

with this difference, that the shops are often separated from the public way by an open, covered space, forming a recess in the front wall, and supported on pillars of the height of the ground-floor. This space, forming a kind of porch, facilitates the entrance to the shop, and gives passers-by an opportunity of examining quietly the articles exposed for sale, without interfering with the traffic or blocking up the pavement; but it has this inconvenience, that it darkens the ground-floor (Figs. 49 and 50).

Such of these houses as are used for taverns, breweries, or "*societies*" (nearly the same as our *cafés* or "*cercles*"), generally have the floor sunk below the level of the street, and are divided into two parts, — one for the public, the other reserved for cer-

Fig. 49. — Elevation of a House in the Calver-Straat, Amsterdam.

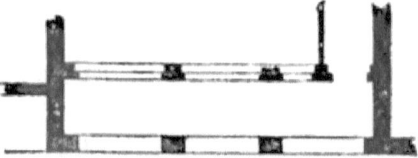

Fig. 50. — Ground-plan of the Frontage.

tain privileged customers.[1] We may see, through the windows,

[1] These *societies*, or places of resort, often bear very pretentious names, such as Prudence, Wisdom, Friendship, and Virtue.

the frequenters of the rooms, sitting apart, immovable in their places, each at his little table, drinking and smoking, without exchanging a word, and without seeming to have a single idea to express.

These rooms, such as they are, correspond exactly with the needs of their inhabitants, and the requirements of their domestic and unsociable life.

Land is so scarce in Amsterdam that fresh buildings cannot be constructed, and it is an almost insurmountable difficulty for a new-comer to establish himself. Each inhabitant lives in his own house, and it is only when he dies without heirs, that any one can hope to procure, not indeed the house which he would prefer, but that which falls vacant. It is true that they are all so much alike, that choice is of no great importance.

When a house falls into ruins it is rebuilt in the former manner, without modifying either the details or the dimensions. This plan, though excellent for preserving the unchanged appearance of the city, is not exactly conducive to the development of an architect's imagination. Yet an opportunity presented itself, and was quickly seized by one of our brethren, to whom was intrusted the construction of some houses to be erected in a spot recently reclaimed from the sea.[1]

These modern houses are of an entirely different character from those which we have already described, and show an incontestable progress; for, besides the talent which their constructor has manifested, he must have displayed considerable energy, and have had great influence over his fellow-countrymen, to induce them to adopt the new ideas and plans which he desired to carry out.

We give two types of these dwellings. First, a group of houses erected in a sort of enclosure, and surrounded by a garden; and then another kind of buildings, with narrow fronts more conformable to Dutch tradition, with an area before and a garden behind.

[1] M. Cuypers, architect at Amsterdam, Councillor of the Government for Historical Public Buildings.

The first type (Figs. 51 and 52) comprises three dwelling-houses united, yet each distinct in itself. On the ground-floor

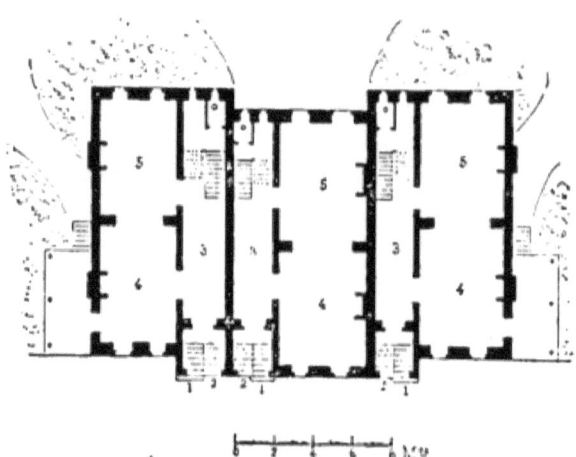

Fig. 51. — Plan of Ground-floor.

Fig. 52. — Plan of First Floor.

1. Principal entrance.
2. Kitchen entrance.
3. Passage.
4. Drawing-room.
5. Dining-room.
6. Bedrooms.

of each of them are two sitting-rooms, one behind the other; in the basement are the kitchens, and on the first floor the bedrooms; in front is a porch sheltering the doorsteps, and forming a balcony above. These balconies are open, — an arrangement

Fig. 53. — Geometrical Elevation.
(Scale, .151 inch to the yard.)

which a Dutchman would certainly not have permitted in a street where there are many passers-by, or on a frequented canal, but which he has tolerated in the midst of an enclosed space. We are, however, assured that a young lady would never come and lean on the rails of this balcony.

Without further reference to this prudery, which loses much of its importance since the house is intended for foreigners, we must, however, admit that, in a climate as damp as that of Amsterdam, an enclosed balcony is preferable to one open to the winds.

The details are well carried out. The bricks, the constituent materials, are employed in various combinations. Glazed tiles,

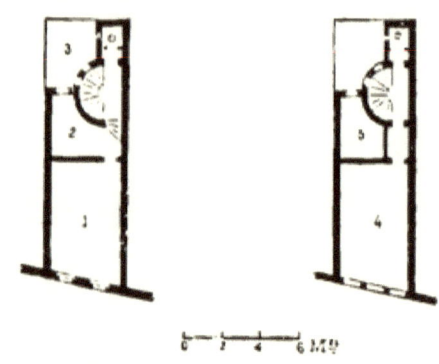

House of Business at Amsterdam.

Fig. 54.—Basement.　　　Fig. 55.—Ground-floor.

1. Kitchen.
2. Wash-house.
3. Courtyard.

4. Shop.
5. Back-shop.

painted of different colors, placed in the gables, enliven the general aspect (Fig. 53), and produce a pleasing effect, especially when contrasted with the neighboring buildings.

The second example possesses less originality. It is too narrow, like the houses of this country, with an area in front, two rooms, one behind the other, on the ground-floor, with a garden behind, and then two bedrooms on the next floor (Figs. 54 and 55).

The façades (Fig. 56) show well-defined outlines and original combinations. The well-staircase, constructed in the inner part of the house, is unusual in Amsterdam. The plan is carefully reasoned out, and the materials are well employed, considering their nature.

It must, however, be remarked how conscientiously the archi-

Fig. 56. — Geometrical Elevation.

(Scale, about 1/5 inch to the yard.)

tect has preserved, in the buildings which he has erected, everything which appeared to him excellent and useful in those which preceded him, at the same time that he used new materials in new forms. For this reason he did not hesitate to have large gables in front, and to utilize the valuable attic floor by means of a large opening and a common pulley. He did not conceal the holes intended to receive the scaffold-poles for repairs, while he contrived to make them subservient to the decoration of the façades. But, though a thoughtful and sensible inventor, he would not, through the desire of novelty, substitute Italian terraces for pointed roofs, and stucco or imitative stone for the excellent bricks which he had at his disposal; but he remained true to the old traditions while he endeavored to bring them to perfection.

Indeed, a work progresses, an art is perfected, only by gradual advances, by taking time to draw conclusions slowly from study and thought, and by never taking one step forward until the preceding one has been accepted. Sudden transformations, hasty and rapid changes which take into account neither received ideas, nor the respect due to the productions of our predecessors, excite party hatred, cause mistrust and fear, and usually end in a revolution, and then in the reaction which is, unfortunately, almost always the fatal result.

But to return to the dwelling-houses of Holland, and to conclude our description of them; it would be interesting to study the habitations constructed by the German, as compared with those of the Latin, races, in order to ascertain by what means each of these races, so opposite in their tastes, and differing so much in their requirements, have been able, wherever they have established themselves, to construct dwellings adapted to their wants, their manner of living, as well as the nature of the climate and the materials which they had at their disposal. We have hitherto been able to touch but slightly on this subject, the further development of which would have too long detained us; but we shall have occasion to return to it, and to complete our remarks by means of examples collected from other countries.

The public buildings of Amsterdam are not numerous; but

they are not without interest, more especially since they allow us to make useful comparisons with our own.

The square called the *Dam*[1] is the centre of the activity, the business, and the life of all the city. The most crowded and frequented streets terminate there, and the most important buildings of Amsterdam have been erected round it, — the Exchange, the Royal Palace, and the Nieuwe-Kerk.

We may notice, *en passant*, the conscientious care with which the Dutch guide-books state how many piles the foundations of the public buildings have required, and the evident pride with which they name certain numbers, as if the interest inspired by an edifice were in direct ratio to the quantity of piles driven in to support its walls.

The Exchange (whose foundations required 34,000 piles!) is a kind of Grecian temple, massive, square, and heavy, of sad and sombre aspect, the construction of which dates from the year 1845.

The Royal Palace, erected in the seventeenth century to serve as a town-hall, is sustained by only 14,000 piles! This building is regarded as the finest in Holland. It is well situated, and produces a good effect. Its architect, whose name is known, — Jacob van Campen, — was imbued with Italian ideas; but he was still a Dutchman. His methodical, regular disposition exercised an influence over the result of his studies of the buildings of another country, constructed during another age. The general plan adopted is cold and monotonous. The symmetry of this immense façade of 110 yards in length is fatiguing both to the sight and the mind. There is nothing to attract or arrest the eye, as it follows the long lines of architecture scarcely broken by the insufficient projections of the extreme wings and of the main central building. Fortunately, however, the profile of the campanile slightly relieves the regularity of the lines of the roof.

---

[1] The word *Dam* means dike. Amstel-dam — whence comes Amsterdam — signifies the dike of the Amstel, on which the city is built.

The basement is so low that it is scarcely noticed. Two high stories, each having a large and small window of the same character, the one placed above the other, alone attract the attention, but are unpleasing on account of the repetition of the same proportions, the same orders, and the same details. There is a still greater fault. There is no projection in the main front of the

Fig. 57. — External View of the Royal Palace at Amsterdam.

building to distinguish the entrance. One cannot understand how those seven low, half-hidden doors can give access to such an immense palace (Fig. 57).[1]

The interior contains many fine rooms, most of them very highly decorated, and some filled with valuable works of art.

[1] The advocates of symbolic architecture imagine that there is an allusion in these seven doors to the seven united provinces.

They are well adapted for receptions and public ceremonies. The great staircase reminds us of the grandeur and the proportions of those of the Genoese palaces. That which is most striking in these saloons is the furniture. A Frenchman recognizes there, even in the most minute details, that of the period of the Empire. In fact, when in former times France gave kings to Europe, she one day placed Louis Napoleon on the throne of Holland, and, by way of doing things thoroughly, she sent all his furniture with him. This has remained intact. The chairs have crossed legs, the bedsteads are ornamented with sphinx-heads, the carpets and hangings represent the exploits of Homer's heroes; the coverings of the chairs and sofas came from Lyons and Beauvais, the porcelain from Sèvres.

In spite of its dimensions and its splendor, this palace, without gardens and with no courtyards except those connected with the domestic offices, cannot be a pleasant dwelling-place; and we can easily understand that the King of Holland prefers to live in the royal palace, or the "House in the Wood," at the Hague.

Holland can scarcely be said to have existed at the time when the public buildings of the Roman epoch were constructed in France. Thus edifices erected at the commencement of the Middle Ages are rare, and those that we meet with scarcely date so far back as the fourteenth or fifteenth century. Their types were all found in Rhenish architecture, or in that of the Ile-de-France; but the application which has been made of these forms and these recollections admits of much discussion. The feeling of due proportion and delicacy of taste are wanting, and they have not always made a happy choice of models. Sometimes, and even more generally, the model has been imperfectly imitated, or subjected to a kind of *adaptation*, so that the original idea is no longer to be found, scarcely even to be remotely recognized; and it requires excessive complaisance, even in a Dutch archæologist, to admit that a certain church resembles Notre Dame de Paris or the Cathedral of Amiens.

Nevertheless, such as they are, and precisely on account of what they are, and of the differences which distinguish them from ours, the ecclesiastical buildings of Holland cannot be passed over without notice by an architect.

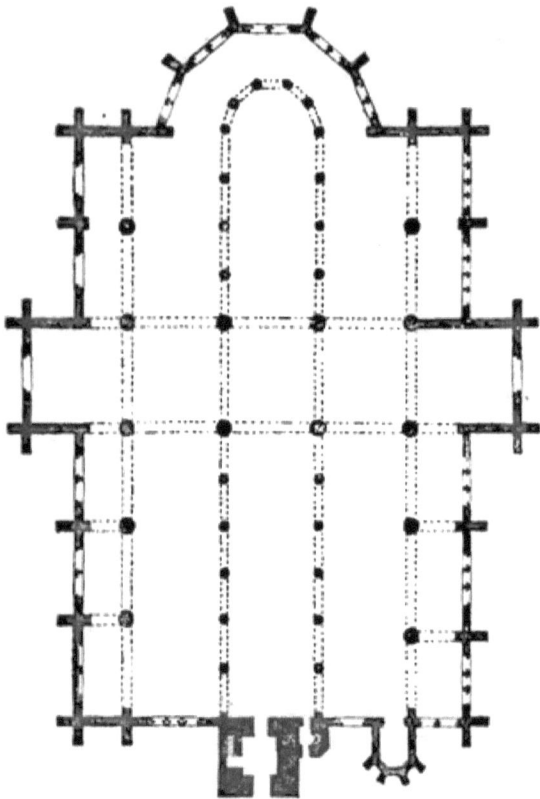

Fig. 58. — Ground-plan of the Oude-Kerk at Amsterdam.
(Scale, .039 inch to the yard.)

When speaking of St. Laurence at Rotterdam and St. Bavon at Haarlem, we have already described the timber roofs which cover most of the churches of the Netherlands. Their architects have thus been able to utilize materials formerly very abundant

AMSTERDAM. 103

in their country, and at the same time to avoid placing too heavy a weight on the very compressible soil on which they erected their structures.

We saw at Rotterdam a remarkable example of these wooden

Fig. 59. — View of the Interior of the Oude-Kerk.

roofs; that which we examined at the Oude-Kerk of Amsterdam is still more interesting.

This church was founded in the fourteenth century, but the greater part of the structure dates from the fifteenth. Its ground-plan (Fig. 58) is composed of a nave and a choir, both surrounded by a very wide side aisle on which open chapels, originally belonging to certain families, who occupied them during religious ceremonies. At the time of its transformation into a Protestant church there were very rich ornaments, valuable works of art, and as many as thirty-three gorgeous altars. All

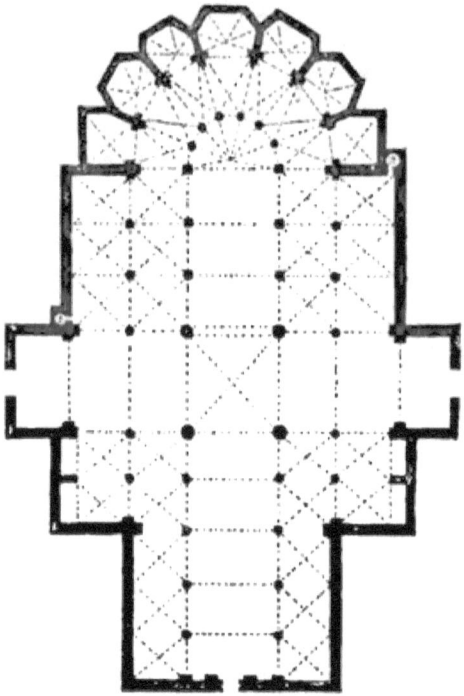

Fig. 60. — Ground-plan of the Nieuwe-Kerk at Amsterdam.

(Scale, .039 inch to the yard.)

these treasures have since disappeared. The walls are bare, poor, and sombre in appearance.

Fig. 59 shows the general arrangement of the timber roof covering the principal nave. This vault is composed of cross-springers as well as wall ribs and diagonal ribs, which have the disadvantage of presenting outlines similar to those which would

Fig. 61.—Section of Aisle.
(Scale, about 1/5 inch to the yard.)

have been given to them if they had been constructed of stone. These arches are connected by cross-beams which render them rigid, and on which rest the planks forming the vault; the diagonal and wall ribs rest on a small corbel, while the transverse ribs spring from a slender column, the base of which rests on a tie-beam placed above the arches of the side aisles. These tie-beams, which break the distance between the ground and the spring of the vault, were, no doubt, intended to maintain the side walls in a perpendicular position, and also served as inter-

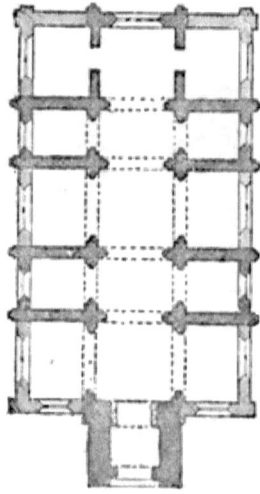

Fig. 62. — Ground-plan of the Wester-Kerk at Amsterdam.
(Scale, .039 inch to the yard.)

nal supports and buttresses, rendered necessary by the nature of the soil. The shaft of the columns is surmounted merely by a heading without sculptured capitals, the mouldings are meagre, the proportion of the arches is disagreeable. The arcades, which are above the arches of the side aisles, are of inlaid work, — a kind of decoration which has a very bad effect.

Another church at Amsterdam, equally worthy of notice, is the Nieuwe-Kerk (the new church), a name to which it has about as great a title as our Pont Neuf, for it dates from the beginning of the fifteenth century. Its ground-plan is superior in grandeur and proportion to that of the Oude-Kerk; it is also

Fig. 63.— View of the Wester-Kerk at Amsterdam.

more compact and correct, if we may use the expression; a rather narrow aisle surrounds the nave. Several chapels erected on the right side of the transept must, by their arrangements, have greatly contributed to the splendor of Roman Catholic ceremonies. The choir is surrounded by aisles and radiating chapels, that of the east end rising above the others. The Nieuwe-Kerk was twice injured by fire. The present vaulted

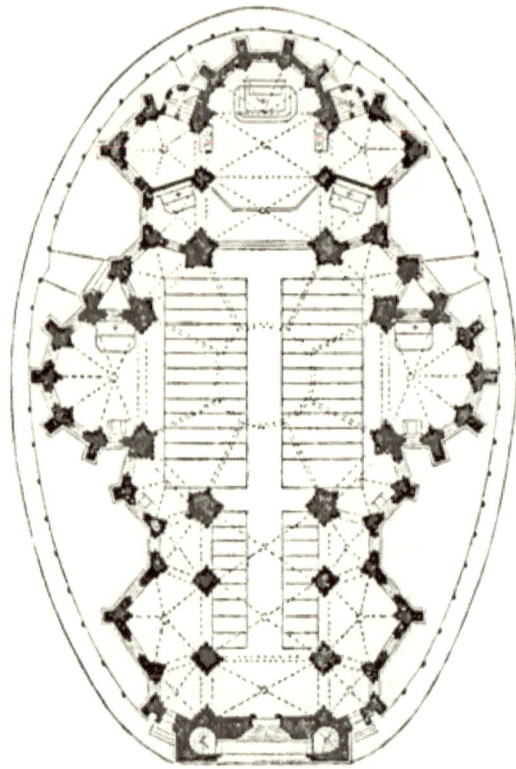

Fig. 64. — Ground-plan of the Church of the Sacred Heart at Amsterdam.
(Scale, .078 inch to the yard.)

roof cannot be earlier than the seventeenth century; it is constructed in the same manner as those which we have already described, but the plan is not so good, and it is not so well executed or so original as that of the Oude-Kerk.

The section (Fig. 61) gives a general idea of the interior of the

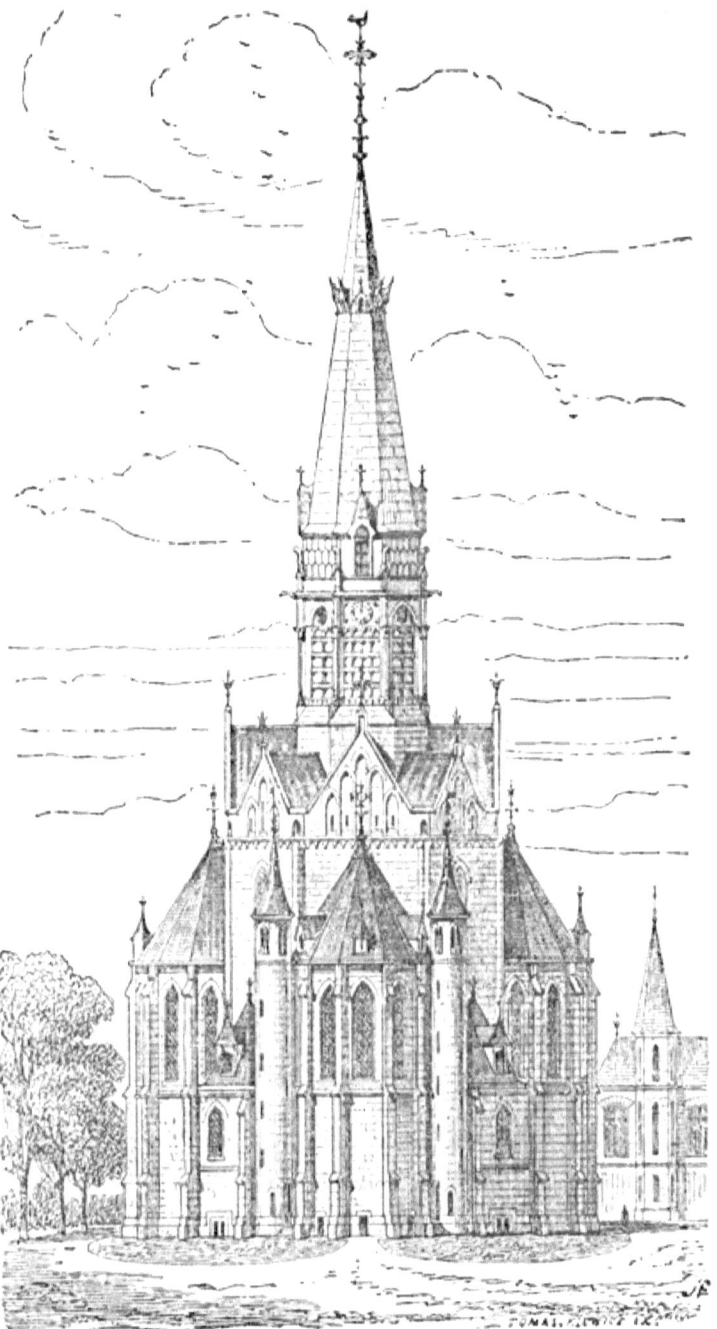

Fig. 65.

building; its proportions are not pleasing, the points of support are meagre, the outlines and the mullions of the windows are slender and bare. We find at the entrance of the choir another bronze screen of elaborate workmanship, but somewhat heavy and clumsy. The two sides of the transept are connected by a gallery. On the walls of the church and on the pavement there are a great number of gravestones and funeral monuments, one of the most noted of which is that of Admiral Ruyter, with the celebrated but not very modest inscription, *Immensi tremor Oceani.*

Amsterdam also possesses many types of churches of that

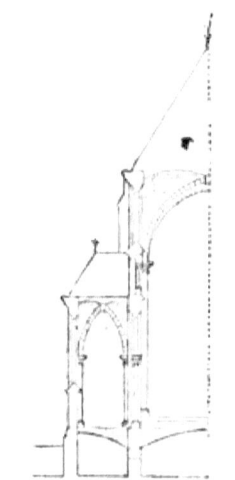

Fig. 66. — Transverse Section.
(Scale, .078 inch to the yard.)

style which we have denominated Jesuit architecture. One of the most complete of these is the Wester-Kerk (the west church). The ground-plan, which we give in Fig. 62, and the elevation (Fig. 63), will enable the reader to form an opinion of the Dutch churches of that period. We will only add that this building was constructed in 1610, and that from its steeple, which is 328 feet in height, there is a beautiful view all around, of the town, the Gulf of Y, and the Zuyder-zee. The Roman

Catholics of Holland, wishing to supply the place of the churches of which they were dispossessed during the sixteenth century, are now erecting a new one, dedicated to the Sacred Heart. The work is not yet completely finished, but we can already perceive what it will be.

The ground-plan (Fig. 64) shows much originality; the nave is wide and short, with chapels forming the side aisles, and it terminates in an immense transept capable of containing more than fifteen hundred persons, all of whom can, without difficulty, witness, from their seats, the ceremonies which are celebrated at one of the three principal altars, or at one of the four secondary ones. Four entrances of equal size allow the congregation to assemble rapidly, and to disperse without inconvenience; the unusual forms of the ground-plan are well adjusted to each other; and, besides this, they all have a reason, and indicate study though but little research.[1] The façades have an irregular outline; that of the apse (Fig. 65) gives an idea of the general appearance of the building, and of the effect produced. This edifice, which would be remarkable in any country in which it had been built, is still more so in one where monotony is so much in favor, and where the same forms are incessantly repeated and reproduced. It is therefore no slight cause for astonishment to see, in the midst of the neighboring structures, what variety Monsieur Cuypers — an artist who has seen so much, and so well understood what he has seen — has introduced into his work. The outlines of the upper part are in good proportion; the difference in the height of the gable-walls corresponds with their lower dimensions; the spire stands well upon its base, and tapers gradually to its extremity.

The vaulted roofs being built of hollow bricks, are consequently very light, and are directly supported by buttresses or arches placed under the lower roofs. Fig. 66 shows the height of the columns bearing the arches of the side aisles, and that of the vaults, as well as the general system of the construction. A

[1] The architect is M. Cuypers.

lantern, which occupies the centre of the steeple, enlarges and lengthens the cupola of the transept.

We give in Fig. 67 the details of the spire from its base. It is, from the very bottom, built on an octagonal plan. Four of the trusses which support its triangular sides rest on the ridges

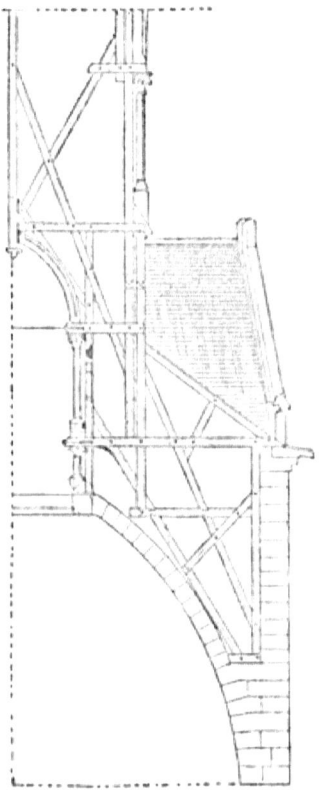

Fig. 67. — Details of the Timbers of the Spire.
(Scale, .157 inch to the yard.)

of the gables of the transept; the four others in the gutters which separate these gables; lower trusses, resting directly on the piers and formed of braces bound together by diagonal ties, sustain the principal trusses, the higher ones forming a fresh octagonal plane reduced to the dimensions of the base of the pyramidal spire. The angles where the faces of this spire meet are constructed of double beams, and are therefore completely rigid; long struts, which take their bearing on the central timbers, the main support of the principal structure, keep these beams in a vertical position; secondary braces also connect the higher part of these faces with the same central timbers; besides those braces which secure the connection of the trusses with each other, other ties, connected in the form of a St. Andrew's cross with the rigid uprights, serve to bind together the several sides of the spire. The eight angles of the spire, therefore, take their bearing on fixed points, free and independent, but yet firmly connected with each other, so that every torsion movement (the ordinary cause of the fall of spires built of timber) that might be exerted on one of the sides would be equally divided among the rest, which would thus be able to resist it.

Tenons and mortises are not used, but are replaced by braces and ties. The wood-work, far from being weakened on this account, preserves, on the contrary, a considerable resisting power. Iron is used only for bolts, and not for cross-bars or tie-rods, etc., which deprive the structure of the necessary elasticity. The scantling of the timbers diminishes in proportion to the height at which they are placed; the weight of the upper part is thus lessened, and it is better supported by the stronger portions below.

As to the external appearance, and to the profile of the roof, the architect knew that objects which are sharply defined against the sky may be easily made to lose or gain in relative importance. He has made use of this acquired experience, and all his attention has been given to the outline of the massive parts, so as to lead the eye upwards from the base to the summit of the spire, without allowing it to rest on any disproportion which might injure the general effect.

The large town-chimes are placed in the Mutz-Toren; at midnight, when the clock has struck twelve, a brilliant peal suddenly breaks forth; at first there is heard the loud whir of revolving wheels, and then come the modulated notes, the deep sounds of the bass united with the shriller tones of the lighter bells, and all the notes in full harmony melt into a cascade of shrill, deep, and mellow sounds. The profound silence of the sleeping city is for a moment disturbed; each bell plays its part, unites its melody with that of its neighbor, and disappears in the concord. It is a brilliant harmony of sharp, clear, metallic sounds, which spread far and wide, recalling an old national air, calling up happy and joyous recollections, at which the half-awakened sleeper smiles; and then the concert ceases as suddenly as it began, while the last vibrations only linger for a moment in the air.

The Crystal Palace is built of iron and glass. It is intended for the same purpose as our "Palace of Industry," but without having so heavy an appearance. The materials employed, the mode of construction, the simplicity of its plan, or rather the absence of decorations, give it the appearance of an immense hall.

The ground-plan (Fig. 68) consists of a nave and double aisles, and of a transept surmounted, at the point of intersection, with an oblong cupola. The means of access are numerous and convenient; principal entrances placed at the extremities, and supplementary doors opening at the sides, allow the crowd to pass rapidly. And then there is an excellent arrangement, too seldom employed in our public buildings, that carriages enter under a covered and enclosed approach, while visitors on foot go in through a special and separate entrance, without being exposed to inconvenience from the horses, or interfered with by the great number of equipages. The stairs which lead to the upper galleries are not of sufficient importance, and the deal employed in their construction gives the idea that the present stairs are only provisional.

The façades of this palace are more varied in outline than the usual Dutch public buildings, and their profile breaks somewhat the surrounding uniformity (Fig. 69).

The section (Fig. 70) shows the plan of the construction; the

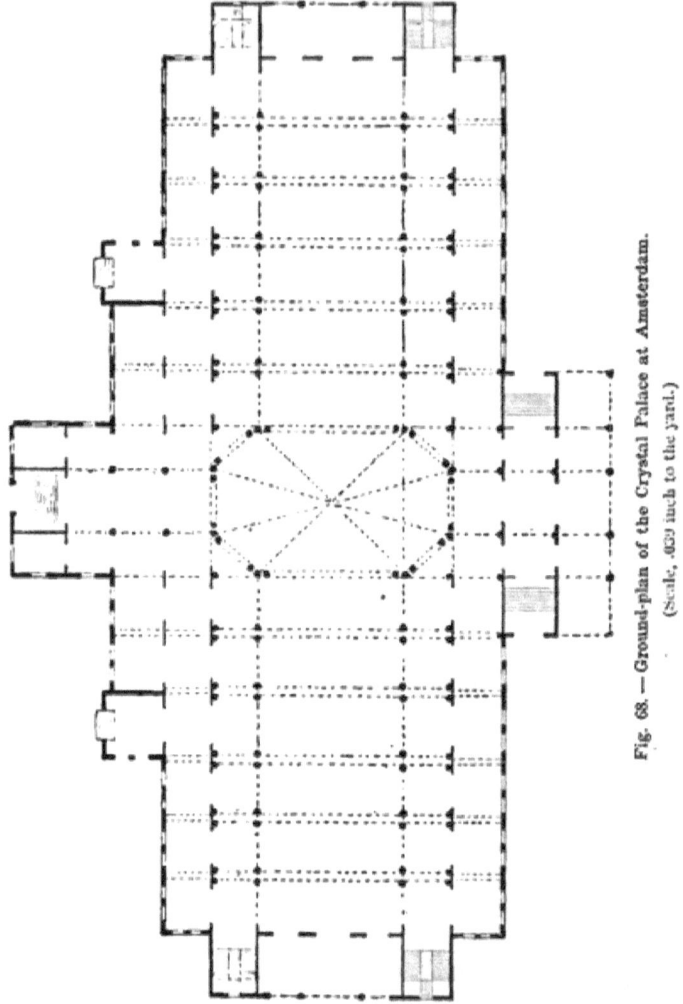

Fig. 68.—Ground-plan of the Crystal Palace at Amsterdam. (Scale, .009 inch to the yard.)

large semicircular arches of the nave spring from a series of cast-iron columns connected in pairs; these are bound together by arches, on which are placed small secondary supports.

AMSTERDAM. 117

The roof is of glass, the walls are of brick, but of no consid-

Fig. 69.—View of Exterior of Crystal Palace.

erable thickness, which causes the air in the interior of the building to be very much affected by variations of temperature.

There is another circumstance connected with this which we might advantageously imitate; the erection of this vast edifice is due to private enterprise. The idea of the building originated with an individual unconnected with the government, Dr. Sarphati, and the engineer and architect, M. Outshoorn.

The Amstel Hotel, also constructed by Outshoorn, is a private

Fig. 70. — View of the Interior.

undertaking, not less worthy of notice than the Crystal Palace; and since so many large hotels for travellers are being built at the present day, it may be useful to enter into some details respecting that at Amsterdam.

It differs from the large hotels at Paris, Marseilles, Nice, Vienna, Geneva, and elsewhere, in this respect. Instead of having a central courtyard, serving as a vestibule, into which carriages enter, and around which are the travellers' apartments and the servants' offices, it has a covered and enclosed porch for the entrance of carriages and the reception of luggage; and beyond this a large hall, on which the various rooms open, and where the stairs are placed; while the travellers' apartments,

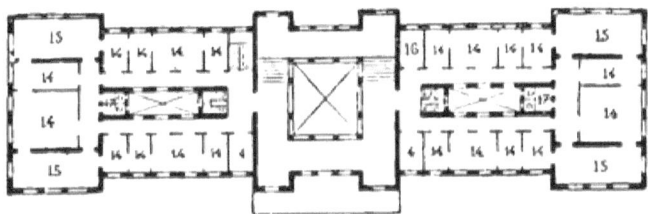

Fig. 71.—Amstel Hotel. Ground-floor.

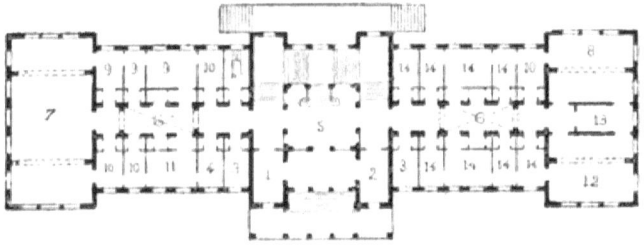

Fig. 72. First Floor.
(Scale, .039 inch to the yard.)

1. Porter's lodge.
2. Lift.
3. Office.
4. Servants' rooms.
5. Large vestibule.
6. Hall.
7. Dining-room, table d'hôte.
8. Breakfast-room.
9. Refreshment-rooms.
10. Store-room.
11. Reading-room.
12. Coffee-room.
13. Directors' room.
14. Bedrooms.
15. Drawing-rooms.
16. Bath-rooms.
17. Water-closets.

out of the way of all noise and disturbance, are arranged to the right and left, with wide and convenient modes of access, connected with halls and galleries which give air and light to every part.

The plan of the ground-floor (Fig. 71) and that of the first

Fig. 73.—General View of the Amstel Hotel and of its Approaches.

floor (Fig. 72) show the general arrangement. The hotel contains, in all, one hundred and twenty-four bedrooms, ten of which have a sitting-room attached; a lift renders it unnecessary to carry luggage and packages up the stairs; and all the bedrooms are supplied with water and gas, and are warmed by heating apparatus, and provided with means of ventilation.

Air is collected and compressed in a reservoir constructed in the underground-floor; pipes, such as are used for gas, distribute it to the various apartments; it can be made to flow in by the simple pressure of a button. The air, as it leaves the reservoir, passes through a jet of finely divided vapor, which gives to it, when necessary, the required hygrometrical condition.[1]

The façades of the hotel possess little originality, and resemble most of our modern buildings (Fig. 73).

The construction of the Amstel Hotel comprised three distinct operations: the first consisted in the embankment of the land reclaimed from the Amstel; the second, the establishment of the foundations on piles, a work commenced in 1864 and finished in June, 1865; the third, in the buildings above ground, which, undertaken in February, 1866, were completely finished in July, 1867; the hotel was ready for occupation on the 15th of that month.

These works cost 600,000 florins (50,400 *l*.), about 25 *l*. for each square yard covered, not including the substructures.

These details are interesting; they show the process of the construction of great public works in Holland, and the different phases through which they pass; and by comparing dates we find that, after a necessary delay, in order that the works should be thoroughly studied and arranged, sufficient activity was displayed to bring it to a rapid completion.

The bridges that we constantly met with in order to cross the innumerable canals by which the city is intersected have a gangway movable in the whole or in part, so as to allow vessels to pass; the contrivance which raises or lowers this drawbridge is continually in action, and works with extreme facility, in conse-

---

[1] A similar arrangement is found in several public establishments in France.

quence of the arrangement adopted (Fig. 74). On the axis of the central piles rise two vertical supports, on the top of which are placed two horizontal beams, corresponding in weight and dimensions with the lower transverse portions of the gangway. These two parts, thus disposed, keep themselves mutually in a state of rest; but if an accidental cause, a difference of weight, however slight it may be, breaks the equilibrium, it begins to swing, the lower branches raise without effort the gangway of

Fig. 74.—A Movable Bridge at Amsterdam.

the bridge, and allow it to fall again gently as soon as the additional weight is removed.

The markets of Amsterdam are not, in all respects, so well arranged as ours. The new market is dark and badly ventilated; its ground-plan, a square each of whose sides measures nearly a hundred feet, required a covering of a special kind. The roof is divided into two sloping portions,—the external skirt from which the water passes into the gutters and the eaves, and thence into the public street; and that which inclines inwardly, concentric with the former, and having the form of a funnel, from which the water descends into a large opening in the central pier, which is placed in the middle of the building to support the beams of the timber-work. This combination has the twofold advantage of lessening the height, which would have been necessary for the roof of a building one hundred feet square, and of avoiding the intermediate gutters between two sloping skirts, which are an incessant cause of leakage, and consequent repairs.

Fig. 75.—Offices of Inspector of Weights and Measures, Amsterdam.

On the fish-market square, *Visch-markt*, we noticed a massive building of extraordinary appearance, with many projections. It is not now applied to any especial purpose, but was constructed in the fourteenth century to contain the standard weights and measures, from which it still derives its name (Fig. 75).

In the centre of another square, the *Boter-markt*, stands the statue of Rembrandt. The sculptor, a Belgian, has represented him in a standing position; he has given him a haughty, proud, and stern look. This statue, however, is not without merit, though it does not well correspond to the idea that one forms of Rembrandt, a good citizen of Amsterdam, a rich and eager collector of objects of *vertu*.

The inscription on the pedestal is full of grandeur in its conciseness, consisting only of two words: "To Rembrandt."

The ancient fortifications of the city are no longer in existence. We still find, however, three of the towers which flanked the ramparts; the Montalbans-Toren is one of these, and formed part of the system of defence constructed at the close of the fifteenth century. At present it is devoted to no particular purpose (Fig. 76).

Amsterdam is defended from the sea by dikes, two immense arms which extend to the right and left; the dike on the right encloses the docks and the basin for the large ships which make the voyage to Oceania. There were serious difficulties in constructing these docks, the walls of which are of considerable height, since they were intended to receive ships in order to take in or unload their cargoes. In fact, to raise isolated walls to the height of from 50 to 65 feet, unsupported by any timbers, with the foundations laid in a yielding and compressible soil, was no easy undertaking. The system employed consisted in the establishment of very firm supports, consolidated by innumerable piles, to sustain the weight of the superstructure; then these foundations were connected together by arches, and the interval which separated them was filled in with comparatively light masonry, not throwing any great weight upon the foundations, and independent of the principal structure, of which it forms no part, and from which it might be detached, even without modifying the general system or even weakening it.

On this account, if any subsidence were to take place in the parts thus filled, the solidity of the foundations of the arches would not be compromised; and if, on the contrary, one of these were to give way, it would be an isolated accident, the consequences of which would probably be but local and circumscribed. In addition to this, it was a great advantage to practical and economical people that this circumstance enabled them to secure the necessary stability for the foundations, by con-

Fig. 76 — The Montalbans-Toren, Amsterdam.

fining to these points alone the labor of consolidating the soil, instead of extending it all round the circumference of the walls. This system, indeed, is only the application of the principle which was carried out in the construction of our large cathedrals of the Middle Ages.

The artistic riches of Amsterdam are its museums, in which are deposited the masterpieces of the Dutch school.

A Frenchman, more witty than wise, wrote, a short time since, during his visit to Amsterdam: "Pay no attention to people who advise you to go and see the curiosities of Holland, for there are none; the museums are few and but indifferent; there are two Rembrandts and one Potter; this is all that is worth seeing; and my guide informs me that the 'Bull' of the latter and the 'Night Watch' of the former are much criticised and depreciated."

This traveller is not to be trusted. He was, no doubt, exasperated by the ridiculous pretensions of the Dutch, who do not hesitate to prefer Rembrandt's "Night Watch" to the "Transfiguration" of Raphael. On the contrary, the museums of Holland, especially that of Amsterdam, will well repay the traveller for frequent visits.

This museum is located in an ancient private house. The pictures are placed in ordinary rooms, which are lighted from the sides; the ceilings are so low that the larger paintings nearly reach the floor, so that, in order to see them, you must stand so as almost to touch those on the opposite side.

It is unworthy of an enlightened people to show such want of respect both to the productions of genius and to the public who come to admire them. But considerations of this kind have but little influence on the Dutch, and they are readily provided with a reply to every remonstrance on this subject: "We are satisfied with things as they are, and if others do not approve of them they may stay at home." This manner of practising hospitality, and of estimating social relations, is not exactly conformable to our ideas, and we give a very different reception to those who think fit to visit us. But the traveller must learn to overcome his angry feelings, for when once he has entered the Amsterdam museum he will quickly forget his first impression.

This museum is the most important in Holland. It is there that we should study this school of painting, the last which arose in the history of art, the only one born on German soil, and whose works show such an incontestable originality.

These artists are wanting in imagination; they do not rise into the ideal world, but remain on the earth; they do not create, but are content with copying; but how carefully they perform this task! With what scrupulous minuteness do they not reproduce even the slightest details of the design of a drapery, its bright colors, or the disposition of its folds! with what care they represent the mouldings of a vase, every hair in a furred robe, the bricks of a house, and even the disproportion of the human body! how accurately they depict the grotesque features and the heavy, broad shoulders of their fellow-citizens! Their entire aim is the glorification of real life, the only one which they can comprehend. They neither understand nor wish to see anything except the quiet repose of a citizen's home, the comfort and conveniences of an apartment kept carefully closed, the sensual satisfaction afforded by a hearty meal. The gayety which they depict is heavy, dense, and trivial; it is that of a tavern, or of a monotonous and regular life. They do not bring before our notice the efforts of man to attain to happiness, but the enjoyment which he derives from the satisfaction of his senses.

Whenever they leave this habitual track, and this general rule of their compositions, their idea is not clearly expressed or rendered evident. The two principal paintings in the museum at Amsterdam, Rembrandt's "Night Watch" and Vander Helst's "Civic Banquet," are proofs of our assertion. The latter represents a citizen scene, national guards seated at table, and all the heads are portraits; the former is a work of imagination, and the subject of it is not, even up to the present time, clearly determined.

But it is the difference of origin alone which forms the distinction between these two works. Both have an astonishing truthfulness and depth of coloring; each personage is depicted with his peculiar character and temperament, expressed not only in his features, but by his precise and sober gestures. As to the details, they are studied with a carefulness and a finish, the value of which can be appreciated only by close examination.

The principal merit which is displayed in these works — a merit perhaps superior to truth of expression, and the exactitude of the scenes represented — is the knowledge and delicacy of coloring displayed by these masters.

In order thoroughly to understand this side of the question, we must know the country in which the Dutch school of painting took its rise, and thus take into account the influence which it has exercised on the artists and their productions.

The deepest impression that can be made on the mind of a painter is that which is produced by the natural objects in the midst of which he is placed. In a varied and rugged country the artist notices especially and almost exclusively the outlines; the mountains are clearly defined against the sky in noble and grand forms. In Sicily and Tuscany, for instance, every object stands out in bold and definite relief against the background formed by the pure and clear sky; in flat countries, on the contrary, the contours disappear, all forms are softened down. In the Netherlands the lines are indistinct, the horizon is sombre and cold; color must come to the aid of drawing, which is of itself insufficient to give effect to form, relief, and outline. It is for this reason that, when making a comparison between the Venetian and Dutch schools, it has been said that, in these two countries, nature has made man a colorist; but Venice had its sun to gild its landscapes, and Holland has nothing but mist, which leaves hers pale and cold. The fair locks of the patrician ladies of Venice do not resemble the yellow hair of the wives of the burgesses of Amsterdam.

Drawing may indeed represent a landscape among the mountains of Provence or Spain, may show the dry and dull aspect of the soil, all the tints of which disappear under the bright light of the south; but in a flat and moist country like Holland, the sky, hidden during a great part of the year, loses all its importance; we see it only as an opaque veil, and terrestrial

objects, consequently, acquire an importance which there is
nothing to counterbalance. These must, therefore, be brought
prominently forward, and thrown into relief. The artist must
represent these glistening muddy streams, changing color every
moment, passing from the most delicate gray tones to those of
moistened soot. He must show the red or yellow fronts of the
houses, or the cattle dotted here and there over meadows always
verdant; objects with but little variety, constantly bathed in
vapor, and standing out against a level and monotonous horizon.

To arrive at such a complex result, it was necessary to unite
with a knowledge of all the niceties and resources of color that
calm, placid, and studious temperament peculiar to the Dutch,
— a gift indispensable in order to bring to a successful issue the
long and patient study necessary to conduct to the end which
has been so happily attained.

We may add to these observations on the Dutch school of art,
that it was the breath of liberty to which it owed its rise, and
that when the Netherlands lost their independence they saw the
last of their great artists pass away.

We are now near the time of the Kermess, the great annual
fair of September. As soon as the gas is lighted Amsterdam
changes its aspect; there is bustle and noise instead of calm and
silence; the whole population begin to prepare for the enjoyment which is about to take place, and present a curious sight.
The principal streets are filled with an impatient crowd, rude in
their movements, and with whom it is unpleasant to come in
contact. In the public squares, booths are erected for the supply of eatables and liquor, and for the sale of articles of every
kind, especially such as are brought from Paris. There are
crowds of servants arm-in-arm with soldiers, all in a state of
inordinate gayety, singing, as they pass, songs which excite
shouts of laughter,— shrill, prolonged cries which fatigue the
ear. But this gayety is coarse, low, and noisy; the animal feelings are unrestrained; they show themselves openly, without
bounds or disguise. The people enjoy to repletion during a

whole week the pleasures from which they have abstained for all the rest of the year; expenses, usually so economically regulated, become, for the time, excessive; calm and quiet are banished from the houses; the Dutchman leaves his home and lives out of doors; though, during the rest of the year, he shows his excessive love for economy, retirement, and silence, yet now, during the Kermess, he spends his money, goes out, and shouts. These trivial demonstrations, this coarse enjoyment, has in it nothing attractive; far from this, it inspires one with a feeling of utter repulsion.

What a contrast with the popular *fêtes* of Paris or Rome! There a display of fireworks, a van full of maskers, a band in the open air, are enough to please every one; the crowd will remain for hours to see a sky-rocket or to hear a song. And how thoroughly they fill up the intervals, while away the time with a rattling fire of personal jokes, an uninterrupted series of witticisms and jests which pass from one individual to another and from group to group! The listeners are the judges of this tournament of fun; their shouts of laughter encourage the merry orators, and loud "bravos" await the happy repartee which procures for its author the difficult achievement of having the last word.

In Holland, these witty contests, these battles of the tongue, are unknown; they do nothing but eat, drink, shout, and fight in an indescribable manner.

Holland has the reputation of pure morals, but it does not deserve this credit at the Kermess. As to other times, after having witnessed certain scenes in the solitary paths of the Wood at the Hague, or in the Calver Straat and other unmentionable quarters of Amsterdam, we may well ask whether this pretended simplicity is anything but the most entire corruption.

NORTH HOLLAND.

"SOME of the details of this singular country would lead us to suspect that a scene had been got up to mystify the traveller." — NIM.

AMSTERDAM is the starting-point for several excursions, the most interesting of which is that through North Holland, a large peninsula united to the continent by a narrow neck of land.

The northern canal cuts through this isthmus, and unites the North Sea with the gulf of Y, and allows ships of considerable burden to proceed, at all seasons, to the port of Amsterdam, without undergoing the delays peculiar to the canal of Holland, or fearing the sand-banks and shallows of the Zuyder-zee.

We pass over the gulf of Y (which froze so conveniently in 1794 as to allow the French cavalry to board the fleet of the Netherlands), and when once we are on the other side we look back at the panorama of the city which we have just left, — a mass of red houses scarcely rising above the water, four or five steeples, gray and yellow blocks of buildings, a slimy and glistening sea, and, if it is warm weather, the aroma of the port and the canals of Amsterdam brought over by the wind. There is nothing here, whatever may be said, to remind one, even remotely, of Venice as seen from Lido.

Nearly in the midst of the gulf, small wooden huts, built on piles, standing by themselves in the midst of the waters, on a kind of dike, are the pleasure-houses of the rich merchants of the city. They come in boats to pass their Sundays in these prisons, and make themselves happy in eating, drinking, and smoking, without the fear of noise or any visit from an intruder.

There are two principal points of attraction for the traveller in North Holland. One is the fantastic village of Broeck, whose fastidious and ridiculous cleanliness is known to all; and the other is the *cottage* at Zaandam, inhabited by Peter the Great when he came to Holland in 1696 to study ship-building.

We passed by these two points, which have become rather hackneyed, and preferred to continue our journey as far as Enkuisen.

It would give the reader no information were we to state that the country is flat; indeed, it would be incorrect and insufficient, for we ought rather to call it hollow. The shores of the sea are slightly elevated by means of dikes; the rest of the country is depressed, and exactly resembles a basin. The canal of Holland, which reaches from Amsterdam to the extremity of the Helder, passes to the left. The road crosses the polders, with their meadows, cattle, and windmills, which are everywhere the same. But in the midst of this monotony, which strikes us more and more forcibly in the country, we see more decidedly the strange and grotesque aspect of the works of man.

The country is very rich. We perceive this by the number of cattle, as well as of houses, and more strikingly by the costume of the inhabitants, especially of the women, whose heads are enclosed in a kind of helmet similar to those which we have already described; but with this difference, that, instead of being made of copper or silver, they are of gold, decorated with valuable stones and *blinkers* of excellent workmanship. The women have an exaggerated reputation for beauty; yet they possess a peculiar charm, owing to the delicacy of their skin, the brightness of their complexion, and the whiteness of their teeth. Their hair, as far as they allow it to be seen, is of a dull, fair hue. Their features are coarse, their gait is heavy, and entirely destitute of elegance or grace.

The farms and houses inhabited by the peasants correspond but little with the idea which that word awakens in us. Instead of heaps of manure, cattle wandering at liberty, crowded farmyards, rooms badly kept and in disorder, and the untidy inhabitants of our houses in the country, the Dutch farms have courtyards well sanded, enclosures in good condition, houses neat and well kept; within doors, rooms of an unheard-of, excessive, inconceivable cleanliness. In one of these the mistress is at work, surrounded by her maids. Their dress is coquettish and even elegant. The stable, which has a direct communication with this kind of parlor, has a floor perfectly irreproachable,

Fig. 77. — Reception-room in a Farm-house in North Holland.

clean, and free from stains. The milk-pans and utensils of every sort shine and glitter with a brightness continually renewed. The bedrooms, on the same floor with the rest of the dwelling-house, contain large beds enclosed in alcoves, which form a kind of cupboard. There are nests of shelves covered with delft ware of surprising value. In the common room we find, hanging on the walls, maps, mathematical instruments, a lactometer, a barometer, a level, a levelling-staff, or carpenter's tools. On a book-shelf are arranged books and newspapers. There are two kitchens, — one for the summer, with a north aspect; the other for winter use, sheltered from cold winds, — and,

Fig. 78. — View of the Exterior of a Farm-house in North Holland.

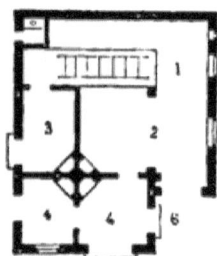

Fig. 79. — Ground-plan of a Farm-house.
(Scale, .039 inch to the yard.)

1. Stable.
2. Cart-shed.
3. Kitchen.

4. Bedrooms.
5. Usual entrance.
6. Special entrance.

to crown all, a room for grand occasions, cleaned every week with the most scrupulous care. This apartment (Fig. 77) is intended for no special purpose, but in it are kept the rich family ornaments, and the *layette* for the new-born child. It is there that the bride puts on her marriage-dress. The coffin of the dead parent is placed there. The door of this room, called the "golden door," opens on the road, but is always kept closed except on great days of mourning or rejoicing,— a baptism, a marriage, or a burial.

We were present at a ceremony of the latter kind. The relations and friends filled the room, surrounding the coffin, the lid of which was partly raised, so as to show the face of the dead. The minister and the schoolmaster were chanting a hymn, in the midst of cries and sobs which seemed to form part of the ceremony. Then the *golden door* was opened, the bier was placed upon a car, and the widow solemnly seated herself on the remains of her late husband to convey him to the cemetery.

Figs. 78 and 79 represent the house of a respectable peasant. It contains a kitchen, a sitting-room, and bedchamber. Behind, and forming a part of the same building, are the barn and a house for six cows. A small gable surmounts the sitting-room, and shows the importance which is attributed to it. The four chimneys unite in a single opening,— a large shaft with a chimney-pot at the top.

Figs. 80 and 81 represent a farm of greater importance. The stable is capable of containing eighteen cows. The dwelling contains two kitchens. That for summer use is isolated, and has wide openings; that used in winter is placed in the centre of the building, with two large closets to contain beds, and is in direct communication with the stable, which is perfectly neat and clean. On the other side of the building are the parlor, the master's bedroom, and the special room with its private door. Beyond the stable are the piggery, and the dairy with the cheese heaped up in the corner, reminding one of cannon-balls in an arsenal; the large roof contains granaries for the storage of corn and fodder.

These two farm-houses are constructed of wood and bricks. The wall of the basement floor is a brick and a half in thickness. The upper walls are of only a single brick; but their

Fig. 80.—View of a large Farm-house.

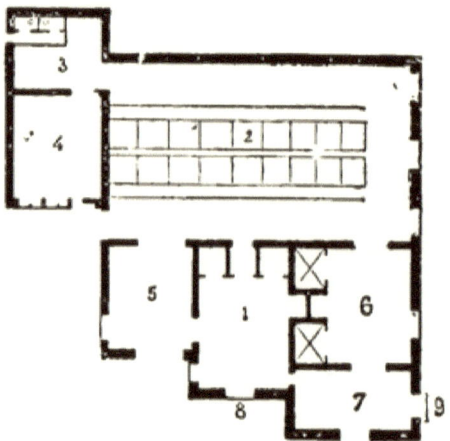

Fig. 81—Ground-plan.
(Scale, .088 inch to the yard.)

1. Winter-kitchen.
2. Stable.
3. Piggery.
4. Summer-kitchen.
5. Sitting-room.
6. Bedroom.
7. Special room.
8. Ordinary entrance.
9. Special entrance.

outer surface is covered with a wainscoting of planks, an arrangement which causes the interior to be perfectly healthy and free from all damp.

The larger farm-house is covered with tiles, the smaller one with rushes from the isle of Marken,—that remarkable little island near the coasts of the Zuyder-zee, the buildings of which resemble those of a colony of beavers. These two houses are most carefully constructed. Among the noticeable details we may mention wooden gutters for the roof, supported by small brackets, discharging arches over the lintels, and projecting ridge-tiles, to prevent water penetrating where the shafts of the chimney pass through the roof.

These buildings, which we have taken as a type among the many of a similar kind that we have met with, are in a perfect state of repair, owing to the constant care bestowed on them by the proprietor. One would suppose that they had been built but yesterday; and yet they date from the beginning of the seventeenth century. There are few countries where buildings so simply and economically constructed, and of materials so little durable, have lasted to the present time, except in ruins, or without having undergone such modifications as have completely altered the original form.

As we continue our journey we find the same strange character showing itself still more and more in the habitations and in the manners of the people. This affords some relief amidst the monotony of the landscape which never varies. In certain parts all the houses are built in the middle of a square piece of land, surrounded by a wide ditch full of water. When one of the inhabitants wishes to go out, he throws over the ditch a movable bridge, formed of a plank, which he kicks back again when he has passed. No risk here of being annoyed by troublesome visitors or prying passers-by! The little gardens in certain small towns are still more curious. We find there rustic bridges, Japanese temples, Gothic chapels, and ancient ruins in close proximity. We even see summer-houses in which are stuffed figures forming groups not easy for the uninitiated to understand. Then, under trees cut out of zinc, there is a piece of water on which black and white swans and tame ducks try to reach cakes which, like themselves, are made of zinc; while red fishes, painted on cement to imitate sand, seem to be swimming in a stream of which we cannot say "susurrans inter lapillos," for it is formed of a certain number of panes of glass. These are but playthings for grown-up children.

Sometimes we see a rich farmer driving at full trot along the road, which is paved with bricks, in order to avoid both mud and dust. His yellow or red cab, the body of which is ornamented with paintings and carving, is mounted on high wheels which pass rapidly over the ground, and is drawn by a black stallion. These equipages are the boast of their owners. The horses are remarkably fine animals, with black coat, and a tail which reaches the ground. We see in Paris their degenerate descendants performing the dismal duty of drawing funeral cars.

In the sixteenth century Enkuisen sent 140 boats to the fishery, and had 20 men-of-war to protect them. At this period it had a port and dockyard for building ships, and its walls enclosed streets with large and luxurious habitations; now the harbor is choked with sand, the dockyards are closed, the edifices destroyed. The grass grows on the remains of the ruined buildings, and Enkuisen has but 500 inhabitants. The sight of this great dilapidation and ruin does not produce such an impression as might be expected. The houses are empty, but they are always clean, and the bricks and stones which fall from the front are carefully heaped together before each house. Time itself has introduced order and method, while it has created such a solitude and desolation.

That which still remains of the church will scarcely give an idea of what it formerly was. It is now a bare chapel, cold, sombre, plastered from top to bottom, and paved with large black slabs. Its rood-loft, of the sixteenth century, is covered with carvings which show a curious mixture of Christian subjects and mythological allusions. We find also some timberwork and a pulpit of the same epoch, which are curious specimens of the Renaissance beyond the Rhine. We will not speak of their form and details; but the execution is remarkable, and shows a patience and manual skill which we can only regret to see employed on subjects of such doubtful interest.

Among the buildings that yet remain, those which are in the best condition are the artisans' houses of the seventeenth century; they are still, as when they were first erected, inhabited by a single family. Their arrangement is very simple: a large room looking on the street, one of smaller dimensions behind, and at the back a courtyard and a little garden; on the upper floor are shops or work-rooms for the inhabitant, if he carries on his trade in his own dwelling-house.

These houses are wholly of brick (Figs. 82 and 83), with the exception of a few parts constructed of wood, and two or three pieces of stone. They are well built, and remain in good repair in the midst of the desolation around them. Their external appearance, characterized by lofty gables of stair-like form, reminds one rather of Flemish gables than the Dutch ones covered with grotesque ornaments; as to the internal parts, like all those that we have already seen, they are replete with everything conducive to the comforts and conveniences of life, and are kept with a scrupulous neatness and care unknown among ourselves.

A little above Enkuisen the Zuyder-zee grows narrower, and the land projects on each side, nearly closing the entrance of this great gulf. The industrious and persevering genius of the Dutch has conceived the idea of draining the Zuyder-zee and converting it into polder. All that would be necessary, says an official report, is to construct a dike from Medemblik, a cape at no great distance from Enkuisen, as far as Stavoren on the opposite shore, that is to say, in Friesland. This dike would be rather more than 31 miles in length, with a variable but insignificant depth; the portion of sea to be drained would yield a surface of 494,228 acres. Engineers are now studying the means of carrying out this plan; bankers are raising capital. The undertaking will perhaps be long before it is completely carried out; but the scheme is feasible, and it is no less certain that, if commenced, it will be successful.

The wind has blown a gale since yesterday, so that, instead of returning to Amsterdam, we started for the Helder to see the effect of the great waves upon the dikes which protect the coast.

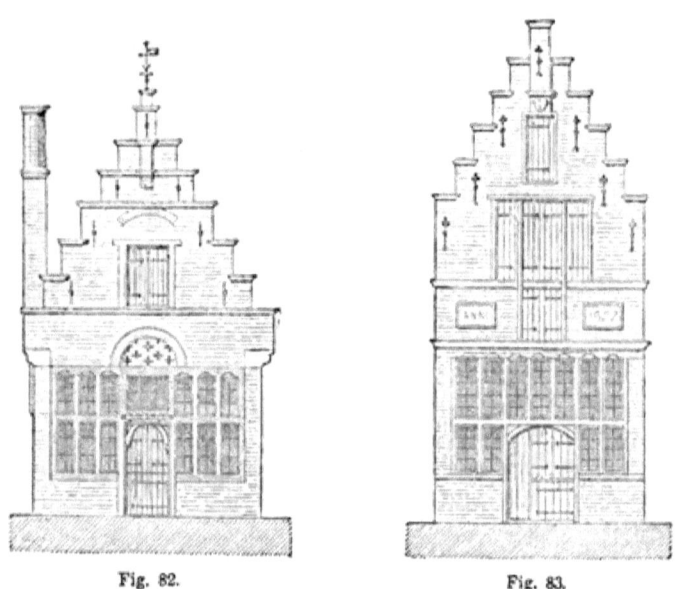

Fig. 82. Fig. 83.

Elevations of Artisans' Houses at Enkuisen.

(Scale of about 1/8 inch to the yard.)

It is a magnificent spectacle. The wind is due north, and there is no land between Holland and the Pole to break the force of the rollers; they are of monstrous size, and their frightful mass dashes incessantly on the granite walls which arrest their course. Not a sail is in sight; the sky is dark and gloomy. It is very cold; the terrible uproar of the sea overpowers every other sound in the heavens or on land. As the night comes on, every one departs. The engineers and those under their command alone remain at their post, ready at the first signal to rush to the threatened point; for upon a breach depends perhaps the existence of the country, since a storm like this might sweep away all North Holland at once.

The dikes, against which the sea spends its force in fruitless efforts, are constructed almost entirely of Norwegian granite; they are about 5 miles long, with an average height of 262 feet, 46 of which rise above the water, and the slope of the masonry is 40 degrees. The upper part serves as a promenade and a public drive.

UTRECHT.

"UTRECHT is, by its University, the seat of Protestant orthodoxy." — ESQUIROS.

FROM Amsterdam to Utrecht there is no change in the usual monotony of the country. We pass, for a short distance, through a large meadow planted with trees, whose trunks are decorated with alternate bands of black and white paint, of equal breadth. The stakes to which animals are tied, the milk-pails, and the wooden shoes of the peasants have all received the same kind of ornament. The road over which we pass is paved with bricks, so as to form black and white stripes. This frightful repetition of the same things and the same colors, a repetition for which no motive can be assigned, troubles the mind and irritates the reason; it is the last and most complete expression of this strange mania by which a whole people is so entirely possessed.

Utrecht is dull and solitary. It is a religious city where old sects are still preserved, the remembrance of which is almost entirely effaced and lost elsewhere. The austerity of Calvinism prevails there without mitigation. A silence peculiar to the cloisters reigns in the streets bordered with houses, which are low, narrow, hermetically closed, without any mirrors suspended at the windows, without anything which can allow those within even to guess at that which is passing without. No carriages, no pedestrians; here and there may be seen a Jansenist, with an anxious look, exchanging, as he passes, a glance of contempt with an orthodox Lutheran; some fair Puritan, with downcast eyes, goes slowly to hear a sermon, and this is all! The greatest

UTRECHT. 143

excitement to be met with is the noise of the little cart drawn by a dog, in which a tradesman is conveying provisions; a female servant, in a violet dress, — for such is the uniform, — her arms bare as far as the shoulders, shows herself at the area, makes her purchases almost without a word, and hastily withdraws; then all returns to the usual quietude, undisturbed even by the sound of footsteps, for even this is dulled by the moss with which the brick pavements of the streets are covered.

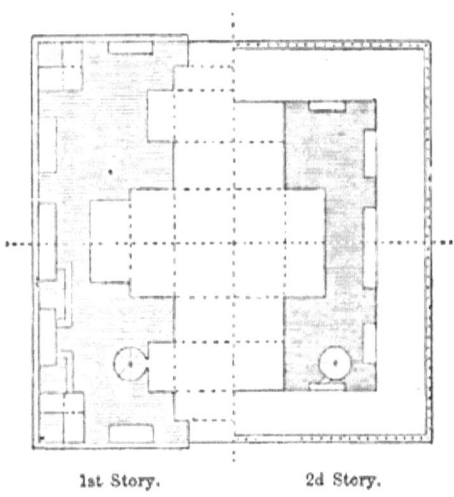

1st Story.   2d Story.

Fig. 84. — Plan of the First and Second Stories of the Tower of the Cathedral at Utrecht.

(Scale, $\frac{1}{10}$ inch to the yard.)

Yet, notwithstanding this sadness and solitude, Utrecht does not fill us with *ennui*. These striking characteristics, so rarely now to be met with, have left upon us an impression on which we love to dwell. We especially remember a very small house, shaded by large trees, by the side of a canal covered with duckweed, — a house where one would love to study quietly. Another, the door of which we ventured to push open, showed us an old man sitting in a large room filled with flowers, singing psalms with his two daughters by his side, who were quietly working on a piece of tapestry, while their mother was preparing dinner.

How can all these people live, and what is their home existence like? It is not easy to ascertain it; and perhaps, if our curiosity were satisfied, it would end in deception, by placing before us individuals filled with the convictions of a former age, and whose ideas do not extend farther than a limited horizon, beyond which, as far as they are concerned, there is nothing.

But Utrecht contains the most remarkable Dutch edifice of the Middle Ages; it is the Dom-Kerk, which has preserved its Catholic name of cathedral.

Built in the thirteenth century, on the ruins of a primitive church, it contains nothing at present except the transept, the choir with its chapels, and the tower formerly placed at the entrance. This tower is now separated from the rest of the structure by the whole space once occupied by the nave, the very vestiges of which have disappeared.

The choir and the transept have been recently restored in a remarkable manner, but the necessary works did not affect the main fabric; we see no traces of important alterations; the details only of certain parts needed reparation. The restorers respected not only the form and disposition of the ancient parts, but also the arrangement and the nature of the materials.

The tower (Domtoren) is the most remarkable part of the building; it rises from a ground-plan 62 feet square, and is about 393 feet in height. This is occupied by two high stories, the upper one being narrower than the lower, and the former is surmounted by a campanile, a sort of open lantern, the lightness of which contrasts with the lower part of the building, which is massive and heavy. The spire which should crown the whole no longer exists.

The difference of width between the two stories is compensated by the excessive dimensions given to the lower walls, which, as they retreat, always leave sufficient space to take the bearing of the upper walls.

This is the plan on which many steeples were erected in France during the Middle Ages (Limoges, St. Leonard, etc.); but the tower of Utrecht, which resembles that of Limoges by being separated from the rest of the church by the space formerly occupied by the nave, was constructed with less science and research. The Dutch architect employed nothing but bricks; it was, therefore, difficult for him to depend on slight

Fig. 86.—Canal at Utrecht.

and but few points of support for the structure; besides this, it would have been imprudent to throw the weight of so considerable a mass on piles of masonry of small dimensions, since the soil in which the foundations were to be laid was of an inferior quality. It was necessary, on the contrary, to divide, as he has done, the weight of the whole work over the largest possible surface, in order to avoid the subsidence or flaws so much to be feared under these circumstances.

The plan of the two stories (Fig. 84) shows the whole system of construction. Intermediate masses of masonry have been constructed to consolidate the original work, which render it difficult to ascertain it with certainty. Fig. 85 gives an idea of the general aspect of this tower, by far the most interesting of all those which we have seen in Holland.

Fig. 87.

The Oude Gracht (old canal), which crosses the city in its greatest length, has by its side quays with two terraces. The lower one, which scarcely rises above the level of the canal, is bordered by arches, which afford shelter to fishermen, sailors, and all those whose business is carried on by water. The extrados of these vaults — which, by the way, are very unhealthy — is converted into promenades, along which are erected buildings of a rich and comfortable appearance, each always inhabited by a single family (Fig. 86).

Utrecht was our last stage in Holland. Beyond this city the nature of the country begins to change. There are no longer those interminable meadows which we have never ceased to traverse since we left Dordrecht. We see ploughed fields, with here and there a copse; a kind of hill diversifies the horizon, and then, towards evening, the last windmill is lost in the mist (Fig. 87).

FINE ARTS.—MANNERS.—CUSTOMS.

BEFORE we reach the frontier of Germany, let us rapidly sum up our impressions of what we have seen in Holland.

Holland has no architecture of its own. Its public buildings and its arts have no peculiar style; its school of painting alone has cast a bright splendor on the seventeenth century. From this period the Dutch seem to have renounced the fine arts, in order to give themselves exclusively to commerce, to trade, and all those professions adapted to ameliorate the physical condition of mankind.

In fact, Holland produces nothing of importance to the literary world,—a subject which does not at present occupy our attention. Statistics prove that though this is the country where the most printing is done, it is, on the contrary, that in which the fewest books are written. Publishers issue nothing but theological works, and more especially translations of foreign productions.

Modern Dutch painters do not challenge notice, and this modesty is not a proof of great artistic excellence.

Dutch architects also produce nothing new; for in all that we have seen and brought before the attention of the reader, nothing indicates an original school, which has a style of its own, and is not a souvenir of the buildings of another country. Some few houses only have a special character,—an arrangement peculiar to themselves.

Upon what does this state of things depend, and how can we explain it? It will be necessary, for this purpose, to enter into some details; and as the nature, the customs, and the tastes of men are always indicated by the dwellings which they rear, and the public buildings which they originate, let us inquire what are the disposition, the habits, and the tastes of the Dutch.

And, first of all, the country. The soil is damp, because of its situation below the level of the sea; then it is watered by three great rivers, the Scheldt, the Meuse, and the Rhine; it is intersected by numerous canals, and in certain parts water stagnates on the surface of the soil. The inhabitants must therefore keep up an incessant struggle to enable the land to defend itself against the water, — a conflict in which the very life of the people is at stake. The climate, saturated with vapor, relaxes a man's nerves, does not excite his passions, but rather tends to calm them; and the precautions necessary for his defence render him persevering, patient, and laborious.

Now let us examine the individual himself. The Dutch race is a branch of the Germanic stock, with fair complexion, blue eyes, and light hair; they are jocosely said to have turnip-juice in their veins. The Hollanders are tall, well formed, but without elegance; carved, as it were, with the axe. Their features are bony; they have a heavy and dull look, with no resemblance whatever to *Grecian statuary*.

They receive impressions from without but slowly; their intelligence is neither active nor alert; they are wanting in what is called quickness of apprehension (*esprit*); if you ask them for information or direction, the answer is slow in coming; you notice a painful effort which is shown in the face, — an evident difficulty in finding a suitable reply. A dealer in cigars threw himself into a perspiration one day in explaining to me, very insufficiently, the value of the national coinage. The Dutch are not very refined in their pleasures; during the Kermess the people give way to low debauchery. They are indifferent to the gratification of vanity or glory; their calm, unimpressionable disposition deters them from ambition. They know how to be content; and when they have attained the end proposed, we see them give up business, while yet young, to enjoy a repose which will allow them to live, for a long time, on the fruit of their labors.

The Dutch are domesticated, economical, rather unsociable. When together they are good listeners; they will remain immovable for several hours; they are not dazzled by frivolous appearances, but wish to go thoroughly into a question. It is on this account that their banking-houses are so prosperous and so firmly established. They shut themselves up in their homes, living a family life, devoted to a certain routine of religious observances, and never seem to dream of anything beyond this limited horizon.

Public assemblies are very rare; social meetings are almost unknown. At Scheveningen, the most frequented seaside town in the North, we may see mothers at work, surrounded by their children, and forming each a separate clan, without uniting in groups and coteries, as among ourselves; they have even invented, for this purpose, a kind of hut or watch-box, which, under the pretence of sheltering them from the wind and the sun, serves to isolate and conceal them from each other; and in these the women work for hours together, without speaking or even stirring. The love of gain, and the desire of promoting their worldly interests, occupy all the powers of their minds, and divert them from the search after intellectual or metaphysical enjoyments.

Religious questions, in which they are so intolerant, disturb and trouble them. They have established neutral schools, reasonably hoping that children of various religions, subjected to the same rules and the same instructions, will, when they have grown up, be more ready to make concessions, and be more tolerant towards each other.

Their calmness and tenacity of purpose easily turn to obstinacy. One evening at Amsterdam, in the Dam Square, an omnibus contained one passenger too many. They were going to a kind of promenade concert which closed at ten o'clock. It was already eight; the conductor refused to start, the passenger to get out. The conveyance drove once, twice, three times round the square, and then returned to the starting-point. A crowd gathered round; there were no shouts, no angry words; they discussed seriously the rights of the passengers and the duty of the conductor. At ten o'clock the coachman took out his horses and went home to bed; the passengers also left the vehicle and returned home; they had lost their evening's amusement, but they had not yielded the disputed point. It is worthy of notice that the police had no occasion to interfere, and that no one had even thought of them.

The family is, with them, the object of a truly religious worship. Ill-conducted households are very rare. The birth of a child is announced to the public by a small cushion suspended outside the house, and the sight of this imposes on those who pass by certain notice and attention.

The tastes of the Dutchman are all directed to the satisfaction of some material wants. The most strongly developed of these is the love of good cheer, for he has an excellent appetite. Next to peace of mind and repose, which he loves above all things, he enjoys the happiness of a comfortable, neat home, a quiet hearth, exempt from storms. He excels in such works as demand great patience, attention, and perseverance. It is among the Dutch that we meet with the best diamond-cutters,— a profession at which a workman must be occupied for months together in cutting and polishing a small precious stone of insignificant dimensions.

The Dutch feel no desire to talk or to sing. It is only during the Kermess that we hear for a few days in the streets the songs which are so frequent in our Southern towns. Dealers who sell their wares in the streets do not attract purchasers by their cries; they pass silently along, always at the *same hour*, before the houses of their customers.

Their love of cleanliness has become a mania, and the seemingly incredible exaggerations which we hear of this quality are only simple truth.

The desire of gain has induced them to conquer their love of repose. Hardy mariners, skilful merchants, they have profited in a remarkable manner by their intercourse with Japan; squeezing the inhabitants dry, buying for a trifle that which they sell in Europe for gold, and, until lately, they were the only people of the Old World who had a factory in Japan.

Their servants are not, like ours, lodged in the upper story of the house. They are few in number, have apartments near their masters, and are in constant communication with the mistress, who is not satisfied with merely superintending and directing them in the cares of the household, but she assists with her own hands in domestic affairs.

Charity is entirely dependent on private enterprise, and yet there is no country in Europe which possesses so great a number of establishments for the relief of human misery. They make some display of this very natural feeling, and the odd uniforms in which they dress the paupers in their almshouses must at all times lessen the dignity of the unfortunate recipients and the modesty of their benefactors.

They are generally rich, sometimes very rich, and pay exorbitant taxes. It is requisite, in order to become an elector, to pay in land-tax alone, nearly 150 florins, about 12 $l.$ 12 $s.$

They do not like discussion, and are good listeners, as we have already said; therefore the representative and parliamentary régime suits them admirably, and their political organization is carried on in a manner which may excite our envy. It is not the same with religious questions; and, while they agree on political matters, they can never come to an understanding on religious dogmas, which are the source of constant and interminable discussions, in which they almost lose their temper.

It is easy, from what has been said, to understand why the architecture of Holland is such as we have found it. Except a few churches of the Middle Ages, bequeathed to them by the Roman Catholic religion, the Dutch have no ecclesiastical buildings worthy of the name, because they are divided into so many sects that a small space is sufficient to conduct the worship of each.

They have no theatres because they are not fond of meeting in public; and in literature, as well as in painting, they care only for the representation of the ordinary actions of their daily life, — subjects, as we may believe, but little adapted to excite the genius or imagination of foreign poets or musicians.

We have already seen that they themselves neglect literary productions.

They have no splendid buildings for their museums, since they do not value external appearance, and are insensible to that which speaks merely to the eye. They consider the riches of a museum to consist only in the works of art which it possesses, and not in the building which contains them.

For the same reason they dispense with elegant buildings for their town halls and courts of justice, as well as for the dwellings of their princes and high functionaries; since they despise everything which has for its aim outward appearance, — that which merely pleases the eye, without having any useful and remunerative purpose; this causes them to neglect the decoration and ornamental arrangement of their towns.

On the other hand, they have schools, hospitals, asylums for the poor, dikes, harbors, roads, canals, and railways; works in which practical ideas prevail rather than the imagination, and where we find, combined with an outward form almost always unpleasant and of doubtful taste, a skilful carrying out of the proposed plan, and a logical, clever adaptation of the means necessary to attain the desired end.

They have especially dwelling-houses very well suited to their character, their tastes, and their wants. These are small, sombre, detached, all alike, perfectly neat within and without, divided into a limited number of rooms of considerable size, with a small garden, where they cultivate the flowers which they love so well. This affords the Dutchman the most complete satisfaction of his desires and aspirations. He is there alone and at peace, shut in, with no neighbors, no prying looks, no noise. These houses are as well adapted to their inhabitants as the inhabitants themselves seem made for them.

Such dwellings as these would be utterly unsuitable for us who are so fond of variety and novelty, who change our habitations ten times in the course of our lives, modifying our abode according to our situation at the time, our present resources, or the increase of our family. If the Hollander grows rich, he improves the interior arrangements of his house, but without changing his residence; if his family increase (never beyond a certain number), the children are crowded together, and leave their home while young to seek their fortune elsewhere, — in Java or the Indies, — but the idea of the removal of the household would never occur to them. There are no apartments to let at Amsterdam, Rotterdam, or the other large towns, and a house is never rebuilt till it falls down.[1] The system of tracing out new streets by expropriation is entirely unknown.

The plan of building detached houses inhabited by a single family has not yet been adopted by us, and it is probable that it will be long before we imitate it. The excessive value of land in large towns is doubtless one of the reasons of this, but not the only motive; since in London, where land is as expensive as at Paris, each person has his own house. The true cause of this habit depends upon our natural disposition and our origin. We are of Latin race, and we like to make a show. Everything which is brilliant and splendid pleases and attracts us. We are fond of beautiful stuffs, of bright colors, of palaces, and all that can throw an illusion over our life and the social position we occupy. We should never be contented to inhabit a house built of bricks, mean in appearance, with contracted windows, low doors, and narrow passages and staircases. We require large vestibules, a hall with a wide *porte-cochère*, a grand staircase, an ornamental façade, and all those external signs which

---

[1] They have, however, lately endeavored to build, in Amsterdam, a quarter where new-comers may be able to take refuge.

would give a stranger an idea of our fortune and position in the world. We can only satisfy desires of this kind at great expense, and a private individual cannot procure the enjoyment of them from his own resources; therefore several unite their funds and inhabit a large house, with such conditions of outward appearance as please them best, the expenses of which are less since they are divided among a greater number.[1]

A private house includes in France not only the expense of the first establishment, the price of the land and of construction, but the additional outlay for decoration, repairs, servants, porter, gardener, and other expenditure of the same kind; which, as we have seen, the economical Dutchman is singularly able either to restrain within due bounds, or to avoid altogether.

We will not here discuss the question whether we are right or wrong, — whether we are the madmen, and the Dutch are wise. We merely state facts, show the conditions under which we live, the details of our social life which distinguish us from the Hollanders; and we will conclude by saying that the Dutch houses, so well adapted to their inhabitants, would be as little appreciated by us, as our spacious habitations, in which several families live side by side, would be suited to their tastes.

[1] It is understood that we here speak of only the middle ranks both in France and Holland. The higher or lower classes are not affected by these considerations.

GERMANY.

HANOVER.—HAMBURG.—THE DUCHIES.

FROM UTRECHT TO HANOVER.

THE COUNTRY, THE JOURNEY, AND THE TRAVELLERS.

IT was with a heart-rending feeling that we approached the frontiers of Germany. We thought with sadness of all the harm that had been done to us by those who had come from that country. The image of our disasters, of the terrible misfortunes of which we had been victims, recurred to our mind, with the remembrance of all the painful details and the mournful scenes which had accompanied them; but an interest which can easily be understood urged us onward. We wished to see in their homes, to study in their own country, those Germans who know us so well, and whom we know so imperfectly and so little. We had already visited Germany, but before 1870; and since that time both the people and the country appeared to us in a new light and under another aspect. In order thoroughly to attain our end, we ought perhaps to have gone to Prussia; but our courage had failed us, and we had, on the contrary, chosen for the scene of our new journey those provinces of this great empire which were the least Prussian, and had been the most recently annexed.

At Oldenzaal the Dutch custom-house officers, dressed in white and red, bade us adieu. Those who received us at Bentheim had the rough speech and the appearance of soldiers. The railway-station is fortified; the employés wear the military costume; they are armed, and you would imagine that you were entering a fortress. Germany, from the very first, appeared to us under that aspect which is the basis of its character, — that of military government carried to the last extreme; society, as a whole, organized like an immense regiment, in which each member, from the highest to the lowest, is but a *number*.

Custom-house officials do not in any country assume attractive forms, but nowhere are they so disagreeable as in Germany. Rude and imperious, they thrust everywhere their villanously dirty hands, indulging occasionally in coarse jests, repeated with the accompaniment of rude shouts of laughter. They take an immense time in performing their duties, and confiscate every doubtful article with a zeal that reminds one of the former custom-house officers of the Italian principalities.

But everything comes to an end in this lower world, even a visit from German officials; and at last they allowed us to return to our carriage and continue our journey.

The railway from Rheine to Minden — a point where it joins the line from Hanover to Cologne — is a new route, still but little known, and which appears picturesque to a traveller arriving from Holland. He sees cultivated land, high hills covered with woods, cottages painted with cobalt blue or vermilion, carts passing with the last loads of the year's harvest; all around are numbers of young men and girls, strong, vigorous, and well proportioned. Near Osnabrück, the centre of important iron-mines, we saw an immense assemblage of workmen, — a sort of meeting preparatory to a strike. In the country, at the entrance of the towns, and at the gates of the stations, are large direction-posts covered with notices, showing the name of the province, that of the commune, the number of the regiment, of the battalion, and of the landwehr company, of which the adjoining country forms a part. This is one of the elements of the district organization which renders it so easy to concentrate rapidly mobilized troops, since each soldier belonging to them knows beforehand the place of meeting. At the more important stations — that is to say, almost every hour — there is a long stoppage. The train is emptied, the travellers rush out into the refreshment-rooms, take by storm mountains of rolls filled with ham or cheese, which they wash down with large glasses of ale drunk off at a draught, and then return supplied with sufficient provisions to last until they reach the next station.

The passengers are unoccupied during the journey. They do not read, converse but little, and hum occasionally some patriotic airs. Their only amusement, when they cease to eat, is to smoke enormous pipes. Sometimes they smoke at the same time a cigar and a pipe, taking alternate whiffs at each.

Contrary to what takes place among us, who have a smoking compartment, they have one for those who do not smoke. The men appear rough, brusque, unpolished. They thrust aside without pity the women and children who come in their way, in order to get first into the carriages and secure the best places. The jokes which pass among them if they are successful, and the gestures by which they are accompanied, are rude and foolish; but these excite loud and boisterous laughter, the repetition of which is annoying and fatiguing. Happily the carriages are comfortable, and each compartment is, as a rule, far from full. There are four classes; the first exactly resembles our *coupés*. As to the fourth, it is no better than our cattle-vans. The seats in the second-class carriages, placed opposite to each other, can be drawn nearer at night, and form an excellent bed. The express trains usually have carriages of all four classes.

The station at Minden looks like a veritable fortress, with an external rampart protected by forts. The railway here enters the valley of the Weser,—a very strong line, and well defended. All the railway-stations have the appearance of fortifications (Fig. 88). They are built of brick, with watch-towers, machicolations, and loopholes. One would imagine them to be great playthings, if the Germans were fond of play. It is most reasonable to suppose that our prudent neighbors have desired to provide against the possibility of an attack in the northwest, and to arrange that in case of defeat they might be able to fall back and re-form under the shelter of a second line resting on the sea, and extending along the course of the Weser.

The views and landscapes which succeed each other are varied and interesting; but they are wanting in animation and cheerfulness, in that joyful festival air which gives such a charm to the countries of the South, where you constantly hear the shouts

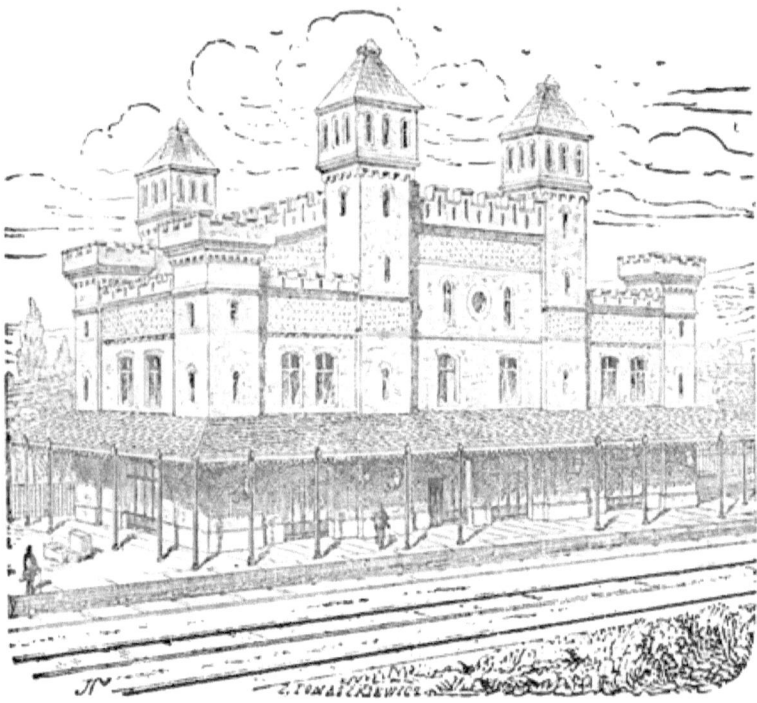

Fig. 88.—Railway-station in Germany.

and lively songs in which the people of France, Spain, and Italy take such delight.

The buildings, which lie on each side of the road, bear no resemblance to those which we have hitherto seen. Their form and arrangement are infinitely varied; the exteriors differ greatly, and the picturesque is developed freely on the façades.

The materials employed are brick and the white stone of the country. These bricks are used in every possible combination. They have also special forms of them, which are adapted for use in a manner unknown among ourselves, and which produce unusual forms of great originality. Their colors are as varied as their shape. Sometimes the angle of a brick is removed; several bricks, thus broken, being placed by the side of each other, produce an effect like the teeth of a saw. Four bricks, with the angles thus taken off, joined together, leave a small dark opening which throws the courses into relief. Occasionally, bricks alternately red and white are laid edgeways, so as to show the narrowest face, and are surmounted by black bricks cut to an angle of 45°, presenting the appearance of a kind of arcade, etc. The joints of bricks are also often filled with a cement, the color of which contrasts with them, and forms a fresh design. The sills of the windows, the chimney-pots, and the spaces above the doors, being carefully studied and more richly decorated than the rest of the building, present salient points which attract attention.

All the buildings, whether great or small, are formed on the model of French architecture of the Middle Ages, adapted to modern requirements with a remarkable skill and a care which are the result of long and patient study. We do not move for a moment from the window of our carriage, being anxious to lose nothing of what is passing before our eyes. As we approach Hanover, where the Gothic style has so remarkably flourished during our own times, we begin to believe that the marvels that have been promised to us will not prove illusory, and will not prepare for us, as is usually the case under similar circumstances, a bitter deception.

We reach the station. The public crowd on the platform, for they have free access to receive the friends who are arriving, and to bid adieu to those who are going. The waiting-rooms of all classes have refreshment-rooms, which you can enter or quit as you please. There are long sofas by the side of the walls, with tables before them, on which to place parcels,—advantages reserved in our *equal* republic for the passengers of the first class only. The offices are open to the platform; immense maps cover the walls. The foreigner, if he finds any difficulty in making himself understood, can point out the place whither he wishes to go. By looking at these maps during the long hours he has to wait, even an ignorant man would at last receive into his mind certain configurations, certain traces which are thus unconsciously imprinted on his memory, and which may recur to his recollection at a time when he may need them. Announcements in English, French, and German show the traveller the direction in which the trains pass. While he has to watch over his own personal safety, it is not easy for him to ascertain which way he should go, while trains passing in different directions are crossing each other. Happily an attendant came to our assistance, and almost immediately we found our way into the city.

The impression made by our first walk through the streets of Hanover is still present to our mind. Night was coming on, and the large buildings and houses on each side of the wide streets through which we passed assumed a fantastic aspect, which carried us back to another epoch, and made us dream of other ages; so that the morrow, which was to transform the illusion into reality, seemed very slow in coming.

HANOVER.

I.

GENERAL APPEARANCE. — NEW STREETS. — THE OLD TOWN. — THE RATHAÜS. — THE MARKT-KIRCHE. — THE RESIDENZ-SCHLOSS. — THE OPERA-HOUSE. — THE GYMNASIUM. — THE SYNAGOGUE. — THE SCHOOLS.

THERE is no European city which has been remodelled during the present era, according to a decided and well-determined style of architecture, and in which the public buildings stand in due relation to the private dwellings, where we do not find Gothic churches by the side of Grecian palaces, placed in the midst of houses of the Renaissance. Munich contains, in the works carried on by King Louis, only copies of buildings of every age, of all countries, and every style of architecture, without any connection between them; it is a museum of copies. St. Petersburg, Vienna, Geneva, and many other towns, have lately done nothing but reproduce Parisian buildings, which are not very remarkable for their homogeneity, or the expression of a unique idea or a dominant principle.

Hanover, for some reason which we can neither ascertain nor understand, has given birth to a school of learned architects who have pursued their studies at home and abroad, more especially in France, as we may say without an affectation of false modesty. The works of this school are already numerous and important. We can recognize and follow step by step, in the modern structures in Hanover, the manner in which they first felt their way, the progress attained by slow degrees, and their influence in the former kingdom of Hanover, afterwards extended to many cities in the German Empire.

The first step in these attempts was the study of the old buildings, — types that remained of the architecture of a former age and of another country, transplanted to this foreign soil. This architecture, which, properly speaking, does not belong to Germany, was inspired by Rhenish buildings, and the examples of our old French architecture of the Middle Ages.

The Germans, who have schools of literature and music of their own, have none of painting or of architecture. They have no national architecture; and we see this great German race borrowing from the Latins, the Slaves, and the Saxons, who are on their frontiers, the form and construction which are to be seen in their private and public edifices.

For this reason we cannot discover in Germany a gradual development of artistic facts, a relation between the various buildings, or that regular gradation which they display everywhere else. The transitions are sudden; or, rather, there is no transition between the various periods and the different styles. They received the Gothic in its completeness, they applied it without effort or study; all at once, without passing through our Renaissance, they advanced from Gothic to Rococo, — and what Rococo it is! When we built Versailles, they constructed their palaces at Berlin and Vienna. They have never originated anything, and have always copied; but we cannot but acknowledge one merit which they possess: that they have known well how to choose their models.

The same thing which the Germans did in the Middle Ages and at the period of the Renaissance they know how to do in the nineteenth century. After having taken as their examples the Roman and Gothic buildings of the Rhine and the Ile-de-France; after having endeavored, without any result, to comprehend our Renaissance, and having transformed it in a manner so well known, the Germans have, at the present day, entered on the path which archæological studies and labors had begun to open in France thirty years ago; and since then they have made such rapid advances in the career they had traced out for themselves, that sometimes, as at Hanover, they have excelled us.

We knew what to expect at Hanover. Drawings, photographs, descriptions, had prepared us beforehand to see Gothic architecture[1] valued there more than among ourselves; but our expectations were exceeded, and—a thing which seldom occurs—we found works better planned and more numerous than we anticipated.

The new city is intersected by magnificent avenues, the principal of which — Schiller-strasse, George-strasse, and Eisenbahn-strasse — are nearly 100 feet in width. These roads are, in their whole extent, bordered by modern buildings, almost always in the most original and varied style. Not one of these houses resembles the adjoining one; each has its own peculiar form, its distinctive aspect. The proportions are not always agreeable; the details show somewhat of pretension and research, but the entire effect is pleasing; it excites and retains the attention.

We lingered long over our first walk. We were never tired of gazing at the façades of public buildings, or of private houses of brick or of stone, on which were to be seen bold projections formed by loggias, covered balconies, veritable *moucharabys* surmounted by extraordinary gables. We glance cautiously through an open window, at some drawing-room on the ground-floor, some half-hidden interior, thus preparing in our own mind a plan for a visit and examination which promise such attractive studies, so fertile in information and satisfaction of every kind.

It is not so easy as may at first be thought to find one's way in the midst of buildings so varied, but between which there is such a family likeness, that some time is required to arrange and classify them thoroughly. Nevertheless, we were not long

---

[1] We employ the word Gothic to describe the architecture derived from the recollections of the Middle Ages in France, because we have no other which we can use.

in conquering this difficulty. A little observation alone sufficed, and it soon became easy to ascertain our bearings.

We soon begin to make certain classifications and remarks, the result of which serves to show how much care and study have been devoted by the authorities of Hanover to the task of constructing the new quarters of the city. Nothing has been left to caprice or chance; and yet it is easy to see that the greatest liberty of action has been allowed to the skill and the individual tastes of the architects to whom was intrusted the duty of carrying out the plan.

One of the most important questions to be solved in a new city, when once the general outline is adopted and the plan laid down,[1] is the study of the angles formed by the meeting of two streets. In certain towns—as at Turin, for example, which is the perfect image of a draught-board—no particular arrangement is necessary. In Paris we see the houses at important angles, such as those which are at two cross-roads, distinguished from the rest by a special combination. Unfortunately, all the houses constructed under these conditions resemble each other so strongly, that it is not always easy to recognize them a second time.

At Hanover the houses at the corners of a cross-road, or those fronting a square, are treated differently, according to the form of the site on which they are built, and the effect of perspective which they are intended to produce. When the disposition of the public road leaves a large vacant space before the building, the façade of such a house is treated otherwise than if it were built in a narrow road; and as, in spite of the width of the streets, the buildings which form them are relatively low, the system of ventilation is excellent. On a public promenade or before a square the look-out is skilfully arranged, so as to allow the inhabitants within the house to enjoy the prospect without.

---

[1] In order to discuss the plan of Hanover, it would be necessary to have a knowledge of the local topography, which we do not possess, and we must therefore consider this plan a good one until the contrary is proved.

HANOVER. 171

The windows have then a special form: they are wider and descend lower, and bay-windows are thrown out to enable persons to see what passes on every side.

A few sketches will illustrate what we have already said, and what is to follow.

Fig. 89. — A Corner-house in Hanover.

Fig. 89 represents the front of a house, by Mons. Oppler, architect, built at the corner of two streets, forming an acute angle with each other; the angular point is occupied by a bay-window of picturesque appearance; the two retreating fronts are much varied in their outlines, with very decided projections; their principal lines being also broken up by buttresses and gables, as well as by many recessed and prominent portions, the whole, from a front view, would have a heavy appearance, but seen sideways it is foreshortened, and a lighter effect is produced by the contrast of light and shade which soften down the details.

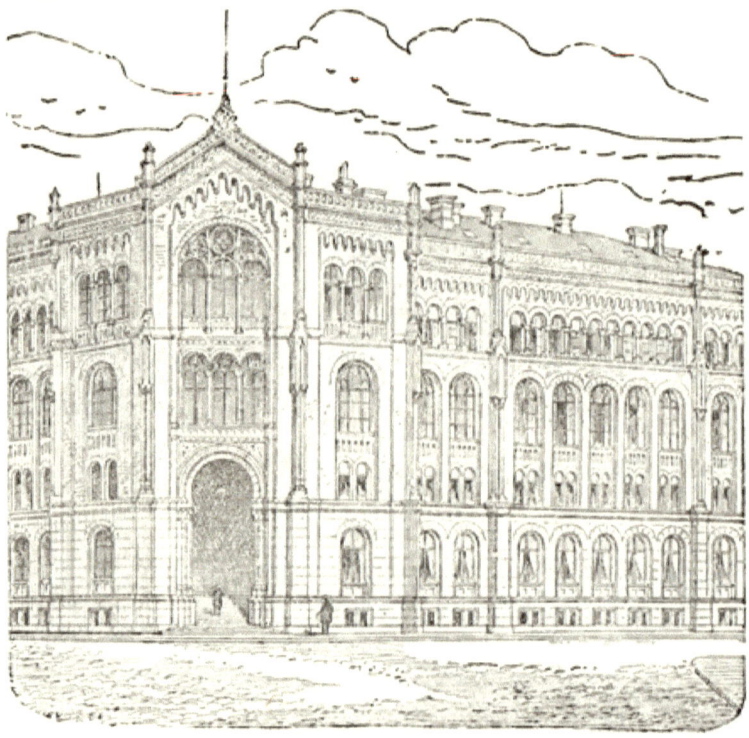

Fig. 90. — House in Hanover.

At an obtuse angle, on the contrary, as in Fig. 90, the façades are thrown forward, and may be taken in at a single glance; there would be, in such a case, some fear of the monotony resulting from a long line of similar openings; in order to obviate this inconvenience, the façade is unequally divided, and the principal part projects beyond the wings. The lower lines extend regularly along the building, passing over the projecting portions, and thus producing a good effect; while in the wings

Fig. 91. — View of a House in a Square.

there are the divisions with their projections. The stories vary in height, according to their importance and the part which they are intended to play; and in the thickness of the walls there are recessed balconies, surmounted by large arches, which extend over the windows on two floors. The whole is very subdued, and does not aim at effect so much as the preceding example, where the attention is arrested by each separate point; while here, on the contrary, the mass of the work was of sufficient importance to make it necessary to divide it, so as to allow the spectator easily to take in the whole effect from one extremity to the other, and, by means of breaks and intervals skilfully interposed, to diminish the extent on which the eye would have to rest.

A building erected in a square (Fig. 91), by Mons. Oppler, the architect, resembles in many respects the preceding structure; but with this difference, that the principal projection is more prominent, and assumes the proportions of an important decoration. The wings are relatively sacrificed to it, and throw into relief the middle of the building, which is treated in a more elaborate style, and differs from the rest both in form and the nature of materials. It is evident that a square, surrounded by buildings with such outlines as these, looks brighter and more cheerful than if the houses were uniform in appearance and height. It may indeed be replied, that the latter plan — adopted, for example, in our Place Vendôme and Place Royale, etc. — gives to them, according to academic conventionalities, a grander and more monumental aspect.

When a house is to be erected at a corner formed by the intersection of two or more cross-streets of secondary importance, the plan adopted is less rich, but the result obtained is always original, picturesque, and remarkably varied. We see that the architect has endeavored to produce a good effect with regard to perspective, and an outline which is striking at a distance.

Figs. 92 and 93 represent a small corner-house: it is distinguishable at a distance, and cannot be confounded with the neighboring houses; the angle, being cut off, is superseded by a plane surface supported by a small column, rising to the level of the ceiling of the first floor, and sustaining the balconies of

Fig. 92.—Corner-house in Hanover.

the upper stories; and the whole arrangement carries out an ingenious idea, the conception of which is analogous with those to which we have already alluded, the principal aim being to attract attention to one special point, throwing into the background the other portions of the frontage, which are to some extent sacrificed.

These examples are only intended by us to explain the principal combinations adopted in the façades of Hanover. As to the use which the builder has made of the materials employed, and the arrangement of the ground-plan, these are questions which will occur hereafter, when we come to examine the interior of these dwelling-houses.

We will merely remark here that the houses to which we have just alluded are built, some entirely of bricks, and others of white stone and brick; that these bricks are of various colors,

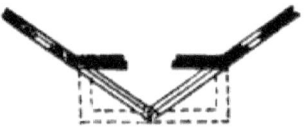

Fig. 93.—Ground-plan.

yellow, red, or black; that their form varies, as we have already shown; and that, according to the manner in which they are employed, they are well adapted to imbricated work of every kind, thus giving to the façades an appearance entirely new to us. We also feel assured that the inhabitants must find in the interior of their dwellings an enjoyment as great as the exterior produces on the passer-by. We can easily imagine what a charm must be added to an apartment by a bay-window filled with flowers, well exposed to the sun, with an extensive view, which diffuses animation and cheerfulness over the whole room.

We may also remark that these are not peculiarly luxurious houses or sumptuous mansions, but lodging-houses, intended to be used by several lodgers; the ground-floor containing shops, and the upper stories the ordinary apartments.

The new streets of Hanover are usually quiet, and the crowd is not great. They possess an importance not in keeping with the rest of the city; they seem to have been built on too grand a scale. It is true that when Ernest Augustus undertook the embellishment and enlargement of the city, Hanover was the capital of the kingdom, the seat of government, and the residence of the Court, and that no one could foresee that some day Prussia, taking possession of this little State, would constitute it a province of the German Empire.

Hanover is an ancient city; it possessed considerable importance even in the twelfth century. In 1553 it accepted the Reformation, and increased rapidly after the year 1763, when George III. caused the surrounding fortifications to be demolished. In 1801 the kingdom lost its autonomy, became first a Prussian province, then a French department, and was reconstituted in 1817, to become once more a German province in 1866.

The old city has preserved the characteristics of the Middle Ages. The streets are dull, narrow, dark, and in many places there are still wooden houses with gigantic gables, the height of which extends to five stories.

These houses (Fig. 94) are of various periods; some as old as the fourteenth or even the thirteenth century. These are the most ancient: the different stories project one over the other, supported by small wooden corbels; the intervals between the cross-beams are filled in with earth or brick. Other houses, more numerous, date only from the sixteenth and seventeenth centuries. They show many details of the architecture of the Netherlands united with those of the style called by the Germans the *German Renaissance*, and which is, in fact, only a species of Rococo, ugly in form and disagreeable in its proportions. This kind of architecture has for its distinctive characteristic swollen balustrades and columns, pinnacles wider at the top than at the base, and also (but this is an advantage) projecting loggias, a kind of bay-window extending down several stories, a modified form of which we have already found and noticed in the modern buildings of this city.

The Germans are eminently a conservative people; this is one of the fundamental qualities of their character. No Euro-

Fig. 94.—House with ancient Gables in a Street in Hanover.

pean nation—for the Dutch are decidedly of German origin—has taken more care to preserve the public buildings and works

of art which it possesses. We do not meet in Germany with
those zealous authorities who demolish an edifice in order to
collect portions of it in a museum. On the contrary, the council
of a town or commune will, on all occasions, take every precaution most lovingly to protect the ruins which they possess, and

Fig. 95. — The Rathaüs, Hanover.

adorn them so as to render them more pleasing, restoring them
as far as possible, and always preserving them. The smallest
public building is brought under our notice, the most modest
gallery of paintings exhibited so as to attract attention and to
acquire celebrity. If there is any remarkable work of art in an

unimportant town, public notice is given of it, and as soon as the traveller leaves his railway-carriage he is made aware of what there is to excite his curiosity, and by what means it may be gratified. We ought, indeed, in some cases, to distrust the enthusiasm which has its source in so good a motive, but which too often ends in deception.

Disappointments of this kind await the traveller who expects to find in the Rathaüs or the Markt-Kirche, at Hanover, buildings worthy of his attention.

The Rathaüs (town hall), Fig. 95, is a large building detached on three sides, of grotesque appearance, and dwarfed by an enormous roof. The first floor is irregularly pierced by windows of various dimensions; the upper cornice is no longer in its original form; dormer windows, of late construction, occupy the places of gables like those in the principal front, and change the original proportions of the roof.

The gables at the end of the building, which are very pointed, are composed of five rows of square brick pillars, which present to the view, not one of their flat sides, but an angle; the intervals are filled with masonry work in very thin bricks, so as to allow the angles of the pillars to project boldly from the front; between each of these pillars there is a narrow opening. This remarkable feature, almost entirely detached from the mass of the building, gives a striking but not very attractive appearance to the whole. On the ground-floor, and covering the outside steps, there is a porch with a square balcony, built at a much later period than that of the rest of the Rathaüs, in the architectural style of that German Renaissance of which we have so often spoken. This does not produce a pleasing effect, either in its entirety or its details.

In the whole of this building the proportions are very defective. The openings and the solid parts are badly arranged; the projections are too pronounced, the outline is therefore hard and exaggerated, and our French taste does not readily accept the excessive means employed under the gray sky of the North to produce the effect which the warm light of the Southern sun gives so readily elsewhere. As to details, they are but few; those which we find are reminiscences of other models, and often badly placed.

Near the Rathaüs stands a modern building which serves as a butchers' market, the details of which are somewhat interesting, since they evince care in the plan on which it has been erected. The hooks on which the animals are hung, the stalls of the dealers, the beams of the wooden ceiling, the decoration of the walls, have not the usual commonplace forms and colors; but the whole plan has been well traced and reasoned out, and all is truly Gothic.

On the market square stands the Church of St. George, the only ancient ecclesiastical edifice in Hanover which is interesting (Figs. 96 and 97), and in which we find the union of the two distinctive characters of the churches of the Middle Ages in Westphalia, the vaults of the side aisles raised to the same height as that of the nave, and the columns without sculptured capitals. The interior contains painted glass windows of Middle-Age workmanship, which, although they do not equal those of our fine French cathedrals, are, in some parts, admirable both in color and design. They have been recently restored with much care and good taste. These Germans can neither destroy nor create, but still they know how to preserve most admirably; while to demolish, or to replace an old thing by a new one, is opposed to their nature. There was, in a corner of this church, a plumber occupied in repairing the narrow leads of a glass window which had just been taken down. He proceeded leisurely with his work, making his repairs with great care, measuring slowly on a rule pieces of lead an inch and a half in length; and he took delight in this monotonous and tedious occupation. A French workman would soon have cast aside all these morsels; his master would have preferred that he should use "new stuff"; but the Germans are patient and thrifty; they bear, without any inconvenience, the monotonous labor imposed upon them.

Being economical, they never go to any useless expense. It never comes into their minds to employ a new thing when the old one can be utilized.[1]

A guard-house with Doric columns, which reminds us of the old barriers in Paris, indicates from a distance the Residens-Schloss (the royal residence). We passed before a line of soldiers. In a corner there was a little, low, and narrow door, and,

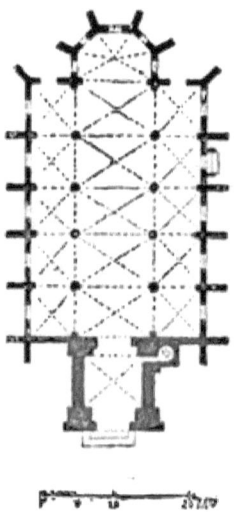

Fig. 96. — Ground-plan of St. George's Church, Hanover.

after many formalities required by a disobliging porter, we were left to the care of a guide, who went with us across a dismal and solitary court. There was no noise, no other movement than that of the monotonous and regular steps of the sentinels; one would think that it was a prison rather than a palace. The pavements are damp, and grass grows among the chinks; it seems as if life and animation had disappeared forever from the

[1] The Germans carry the principles of conservatism to such an extent, that they have not yet removed from the uniform of their soldiers the three buttons which Frederick the Great caused to be sewn on the sleeves of his grenadiers, to prevent their making use of them instead of pocket-handkerchiefs.

place. Its masters are gone, and the latest resident, blind and in exile, is spending his life with his daughter sadly and far from his country.

Fig. 97. — View of the Church of St. George and its Surroundings at Hanover.

Our guide was able to read our name and that of our country inscribed in the register. After having led us through the porch, he began his description in French, very good French; and, noticing our astonished looks, he said, with an expression that cannot be described, "I am from Metz." There was a profound sadness in his voice, and this short phrase showed in its utterance such great grief, — it was so eloquent in its brevity, — that we dared not ask him, though we could easily guess, what were the circumstances which had thus driven him from his country. We held out our hands, and wrung his in silence. What a sad similarity between the destinies of the King and this simple citizen, two beings placed at so great a distance from each other in the social scale, and on whom the same hand had inflicted the same misfortune! The one driven from France, deprived of his cottage, finds an asylum in Hanover; the other, deposed from his kingdom, driven from Hanover, takes refuge in France.

The royal palace is a princely residence, furnished luxuriously. The façades have no distinguishing characters, but we were struck with the interior; first with the floor, and then with the decoration of one of the apartments, and this neither the largest nor the most elegant.

The floors, constructed of wood of various kinds, are covered with inlaid work, forming arabesques and geometrical designs, sometimes even representing bunches of flowers or human figures. This marqueterie, executed with as much care as in minute articles of Parisian workmanship, shows a finish and perfection not easily attained, both as regards composition and execution. We must, however, add, that in some parts the more difficult scroll patterns are traced by means of colored cement let into the wood, thus allowing the artist to obtain effects more agreeable and more uniform than those that could be produced by inlaid wood alone; but these artifices are too rare to diminish the merit of the whole work. The room, the decoration of which struck us most, is of moderate dimensions, and we have forgotten its precise destination. The walls are painted with trellis-work, between the irregular lozenges of which are interlaced vine-branches and flowers; the ground is of a milky-white tint, and through the intersections pass garlands of flowers and leaves; the tones of color are but slightly varied, — red, yellow, green, blue, all clear and fresh. The drawing is exquisite, and with a truly astonishing richness of imagination on the part of the artist, notwithstanding so great a number of objects of the same nature and the same kind, not one resembles another; each has its special form by which it is distinguished, — its physiognomy, if we may so call it. These paintings have not the usual error of ordinary decorations in imitating conventional lights and shadows, — a deception which is modified by the time of day, and the effect of which is not the same in the daytime as by candle-light. The subjects are painted without the help of light and shade, and the effect is produced only by the contour of the forms and the purity of design.

The royal palace contains several other apartments remarkable for many reasons, but which unfortunately resemble those of all possible palaces. One of these, the *Silber Kammer*, formerly contained about twenty tons' weight of silver plate, which may now perhaps be seen at Berlin. Another, a kind of long gallery, in imitation of the "Galerie des Glaces" at Versailles, looks out on the valley of the Leine, and gives a distant prospect of smiling meadows, a sweet and animated landscape, varied with copses on the hills, at the foot of which are situated the dwellings of Montbrillant and Herrenhausen. In this room there are several pictures remarkable for many reasons, and among others the portrait of Duke George Louis, before which the courtiers used to bow every Sunday when this prince had quitted Hanover in 1714 to occupy the throne of England under the title of George I.

As we returned into the new town, we perceived at the end of a large square, ornamented with plantations of trees, a vast edifice, which at first sight seemed larger than it really is. This is the new opera-house, opened in 1854. We know not why this building, a specimen of Italian architecture, has been erected in the midst of this new Gothic city, and we were not able to ascertain the reason; but the opera-house at Hanover, such as it is, deserves a visit (Figs. 98 and 99). The carriage entrance is a covered space under a porch wide enough to allow two carriages to pass each other without inconvenience; visitors on foot enter by two side doors, which are reserved for them, and they thus escape any danger from the horses or the wheels; afterwards those who come either on foot or in carriages meet in the vestibule in front of the ticket-office. To the right and left, two

Fig. 98.—The Opera-house, Hanover.

winding staircases, the steps of which are more than six feet wide, lead to the floor containing the first tier of boxes; secondary staircases lead to the second, third, and fourth tiers.

Each tier contains twenty-two boxes, and, besides, there are the stage boxes, and the grand royal box, which, as in the Italian theatres, occupies the centre of the house and the height of two tiers. The King had also a private stage box allotted to him; he reached it by a special staircase leading from an inner courtyard, where the escort and the carriages were stationed. The "foyer" is on the first floor. It opens on a terrace, which, during summer evenings, forms an agreeable promenade for the spectators. To this foyer is attached an immense refreshment-stall, — an indispensable accessory to all places of public resort in Germany.

The interior of a theatre, seen by daylight, and between the hours of representation or rehearsal, has always a fantastic, strange, disquieting look. The body of the house, plunged in silence and obscurity, seems sombre, dark, and frightful; there is nothing there but emptiness and solitude. A human figure wandering in the midst of this darkness reminds one of a ghost. The stage, only lighted by a few attic windows in the roof, which give but a pale and dull light, assumes grotesque, incomprehensible proportions; the decorations, seen out of the proper point of view, show strange outlines without any intelligible signification; the side wings, brought close to each other against all the rules of perspective, look like a shapeless, incongruous, and falsely colored assemblage of palaces, churches, ruins, houses, gardens, and forests. The mind cannot take in the meaning of this mass of objects: the ropes, pulleys, ladders, the accessories and decorations piled up everywhere, heaped together without order or symmetry, or strangely hung one over the other, seem as if in an inextricable confusion, in which it appears as if it would be impossible to find at the time of representation anything necessary for use at the proper moment. Sometimes a sudden noise, without any apparent cause, is heard in the roof; it resounds, awakening the echoes of the vast space, and makes us shudder involuntarily. A beam cracks, — the acoustic effect gives us an idea that the whole building is about to fall. A cat utters a loud mew, and it seems as if all the fantastic animals which people the cardboard menagerie start at once into life and motion. The imagination is strongly and strangely moved by the scene. We were in this excited state, when suddenly, from the royal box, came a full, youthful, vibrating voice,— that of a woman; an Italian voice, whose accents filled the whole house. She was singing that grand *morceau* from the first act of the Traviata:

"Tutta sola perduta in questo deserto."

Poor girl! She had left her bright sunshine, her cheerful and gay fellow-countrymen so easily pleased, for this gloomy and cold sky, these heavy dull people, who come and listen to her as they digest their *sauer-kraut*. But what a pleasure it was to us to hear instead of rude German accents the soft and winning intonations of the sweet language of Italy!

Then silence returned, more entire and deep than before. This song had in a moment transported us far away, calling up such a crowd of recollections as the slightest incident is able sometimes to evoke, and over which perhaps it is well not to linger.

Let us return to our visit to the opera-house. Besides the theatre, properly so called, there is a concert-room containing 430 square yards. The principal entrance is through the foyer. Being lighted by windows on both sides, this hall serves also for meetings in the daytime. The opposite wing contains the rehearsal-room, three rooms for the practice of the ballet-corps, and of the musicians and dramatic artists, with rooms open to the air in order to isolate them from the rest of the building and to avoid noise; and then, at the back of the stage, the various offices and accessory rooms, the wardrobe, and the dressing and retiring rooms for the actors.

This building, as we have said, is entirely detached, and placed at the highest part of a large open space. This position gives it importance, and it appears higher and more elegant than it really is.

Its façades (Fig. 98) have, on the whole, a grand appearance. The details are wanting in originality, but are very simple and kept under due restraint. The proportion of the various stories, and their dimensions when compared with the main body of the building, as seen from without, are too uniform. There is also another more serious defect. This building — the idea of which has been derived from an architectural style belonging to another country, under a climate less rigorous than that of the north — has the great disadvantage of having roofs formed

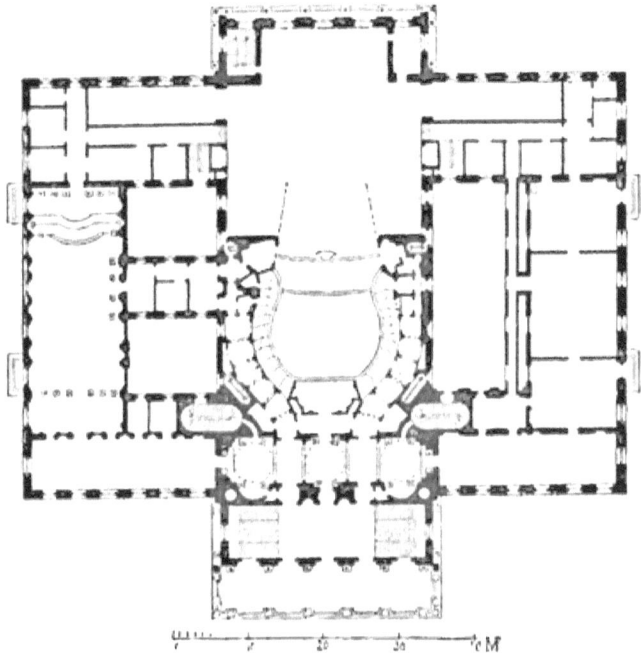

Fig. 99. — Ground-plan of Opera-house, Hanover.

into terraces — a deplorable condition in a damp country under a dull and cold sky; and, although it is only twenty years old, it already shows traces of deterioration, which will only be aggravated by time.

We noticed on our way home a curious structure, which presents a striking contrast to the opera-house. This is the Gymnasium, built by Messrs. Schulz and Havers, architects.

The principal portion of the building fronts the public road (Fig. 100); it includes one story above the ground-floor, which, being dwarfed and low, gives the upper part greater importance. The ornamental portion, placed over the entrance-door, is some-

Fig. 100.—The Gymnasium, Hanover.

what complicated, but is ingeniously arranged. There are many details in which the German taste has endeavored to represent, after its manner, Gothic ideas. The effect produced is original, since it shows so plainly its origin and the transition from the heavy, harsh forms of Teutonic Gothic to the new proportions;

not, indeed, invented by the Germans, but so well adapted and applied by them. There is, however, a redundancy of ornament and a want of simplicity in the whole conception; thus the

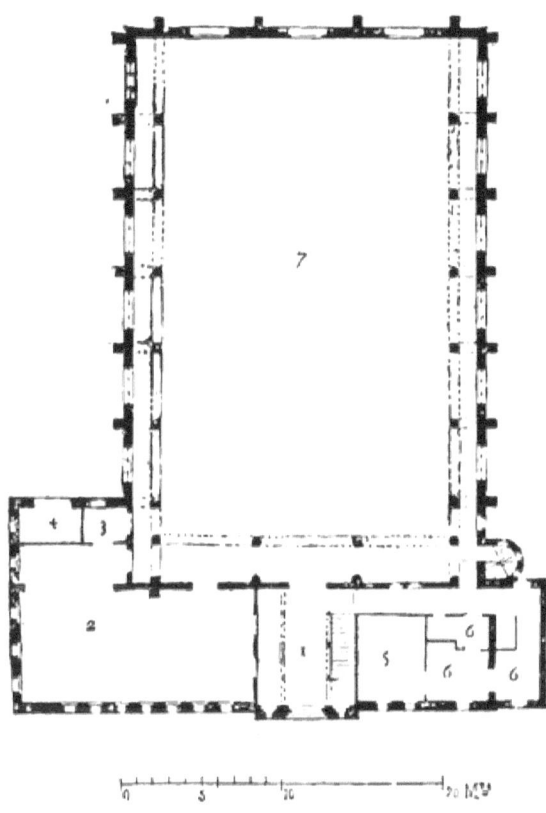

Fig. 101.—Ground-plan of Gymnasium at Hanover.

1. Hall.
2. Men's dressing-room.
3. Washing-room.
4. Room for apparatus.
5. Office.
6. Attendants' rooms.
7. Gymnasium.

principal projection does not correspond well with the side portions, so that instead of a homogeneous whole we have two distinct things having no relation to each other.

The ground-plan (Fig. 101) is anything but academical. In the principal building we find on the ground-floor a vestibule, a kind of English hall, enclosing on the left the staircase, the dressing and washing rooms for men; on the right the office and the apartments for the attendant, with a sitting-room for the professors. On the first floor (Fig. 102) there is a separate gymnasium for the exercises of women and sick persons under special treatment, and opposite to this is the women's dressing-room. One of the apartments also serves as a dancing-room. In the building at the back of the first floor is placed the large

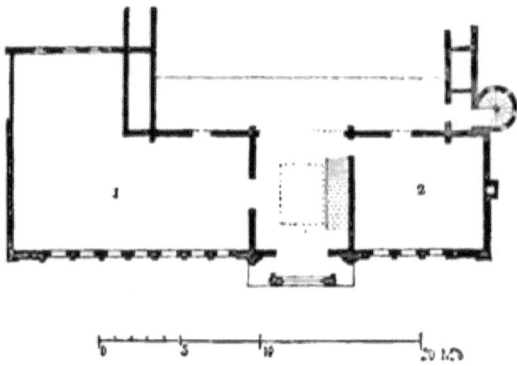

Fig. 102.—Plan of the First Floor, Gymnasium, Hanover.

1. Gymnasium for women. | 2. Women's dressing-room.

hall for gymnastic exercises (106 feet in length, by 72 in breadth). It is divided into eight compartments, each about 13 feet wide, with the exception of the last two, which are only about 6 feet 6 inches, and on which rests a gallery, approached by a staircase from the ground-floor. This hall is covered by a unique roof, the timber-work of which is as curious as we have ever seen (Fig. 103).

From isolated stone pillars, only 9 feet 10 inches high, spring arches which separate the nave from the side aisles. These very narrow side portions, being only 4 feet 3 inches in breadth, have a cylindrical vault turned over them, while a lower arch connects the isolated pillar with the outside wall, which is only about 1 foot 8 inches in thickness, but is supported by buttresses. The construction, up to this point, is precisely similar to that adopted in certain French churches of the Middle Ages; for instance, La Souterraine, in the department of Creuse. But, beyond the nave, the resemblance between these buildings disappears; for, instead of a stone roof like that which covers the

Fig. 103.—Section and View of Roof of Gymnasium.

French building, an uncovered timber roof, of a special construction, has been erected over the German edifice.

The top of the pillars is about 9 feet 10 inches above the ground, as we have already said, while the height of the ridge-piece is 54 feet, and the distance of the opposite pillars from each other is 59 feet. The erection of a timber roof of these dimensions, without any intermediate support, presented great difficulties, which the Hanoverian architects have surmounted in a most intelligent manner. On the top of the walls they have placed a hammer-beam, supported by a brace, which forms a right-angled triangle with the wall and the under part of the beam. Above this hammer-beam the same triangle is repeated by a vertical bearer supporting the principal rafter; the brace of the lower triangle, prolonged so as to meet the king-post, forms with the principal rafter a system which the triangles, firmly braced together, render rigid and unyielding. Above the lower hammer-beam a boarded vault has been constructed on an arch occupying the space between the principal and secondary rafters, so as to render the interior of the building less affected by cold and heat. This vault, the upper part of which is, unfortunately, rather dark, serves, by its form and importance, as an ornament to this large hall. As to the thrust exerted on the walls by the timber-work and the very heavy roof which it supports, it is perfectly resisted by the pillars connected with the walls and the counterforts, the construction of which we have before explained.

The masonry is in stone and brick, the wood-work in deal; and neither the vault nor the roof has shown the slightest indications of giving way.

It may be said that it would have been easy, by employing iron, to have attained this end without having to overcome so many difficulties. Our answer is, first, that the employment of iron would have been much more expensive, and also, that it would not have been possible to erect roofs of the size required, so as to afford the same protection from heat and cold as those which have been adopted; thus a zinc roof under similar conditions does not avail unless complemented by an inner layer of wood. A glass roof would have been too hot in summer and too cold in winter; and would, besides, have been obscured by snow at the very time when the light afforded by it would have been most needed. A tiled roof would have required iron supports of enormous dimensions, and consequently very costly; and, indeed, when we see what results have been attained, we may surely concede to the Hanoverian architects the right to build as they think fit, and to prefer the timber, which they have ready to their hands, to iron, which must have been procured at great cost.

While we are speaking of buildings departing from ordinary rules, we may also mention a church now being erected in Ægidien-stadt (Figs. 104 and 105). We see there the same isolated pillars, the narrow aisle, forming a kind of internal buttresses which we have already noticed at the Gymnasium; so there is no necessity to allude again to them. We will only call attention to the method adopted for the roof of the nave, and which consists in long tie-beams, supported by two rows of braces of unequal length, from which annular vaults spring. This combination is ingenious, but the effect is heavy. The dimensions which are necessarily given to the timbers dwarf the lower parts. It is a kind of compromise between some churches in the Netherlands and certain of our modern ones, in which barrel vaults have recently been constructed. Still, while accepting ideas of this nature, it is evidently an advantage, with regard both to the appearance, the construction, and the durability, to substitute, as we have done, stone arches for the wooden tie-beams from which the vaults spring.

The most important modern ecclesiastical building in Hanover is the new synagogue, the architect of which is Mons. Oppler.

The synagogue was anciently the place where the Jews met to pray, to read and expound the sacred Scriptures. This custom has not been changed; and the Hebrew worship, after the lapse of three thousand years, requires no modification of the arrangement according to which the temple of Solomon was built. It seems, therefore, at first sight, that the plan of this temple ought to have been adopted for all synagogues in every country; but, though the creed and mode of worship have not been altered, the requirements of different climates are not the same. It was necessary to unite the modern necessities of the West with the conditions required by a religion which originated in the East, and to plan an edifice which by its form, its

Fig. 104.—Interior of a Church in Ægidien-stadt, Hanover.

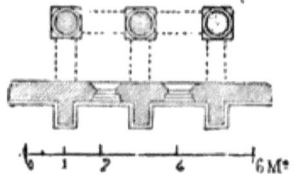

Fig. 105.—Ground-plan of the same.

character, and the system of its construction, is adapted to present circumstances, and, at the same time, in accordance with the traditions which it must recall, and the fundamental principles which it must transmit. Synagogues, like all other buildings, vary, therefore, in form as much as in architectural disposition.

The ground-plan of the Hanover synagogue (Fig. 106) is conformable to conventional notions. It assumes the form of a rectangle, but the greater width to the right and left of the nave would, unfortunately, recall the idea of the cross, were it not that this transept is so disposed as to present, with the prolongation of the nave and the choir, a vast central division, which, correctly speaking, forms in itself the main portion of the building, divided from the aisles by arches springing from isolated pillars.

Before the entrance, which is at the west end, is a porch, to which open the staircases leading to the galleries; the vaulted roof of this porch is supported by twelve columns, intended to represent the twelve tribes of Israel. Beyond the nave or *holy place*, is the sanctuary or *holy of holies*, placed at the east end. In the central part a large cupola rises higher than any other part of the building, and symbolizes the idea of the unity of God.

Near the sanctuary there are two vestries, to the right and left; and at the entrance are two other rooms. In the large space on the ground-floor are raised seats reserved for men, and on the first floor those allotted to women. Within the choir are the stalls of the grand rabbi, of the members of consistory, and of the administrative commission. In front are the pulpit, the seven-branched candlestick, and the traditional lamp; in the apse, the ark or chest, a souvenir of the ark of the covenant, in which the Jews keep the five books of the law of Moses, written by hand on vellum, and rolled up in the ancient manner.

We may notice among the architectural details of the interior

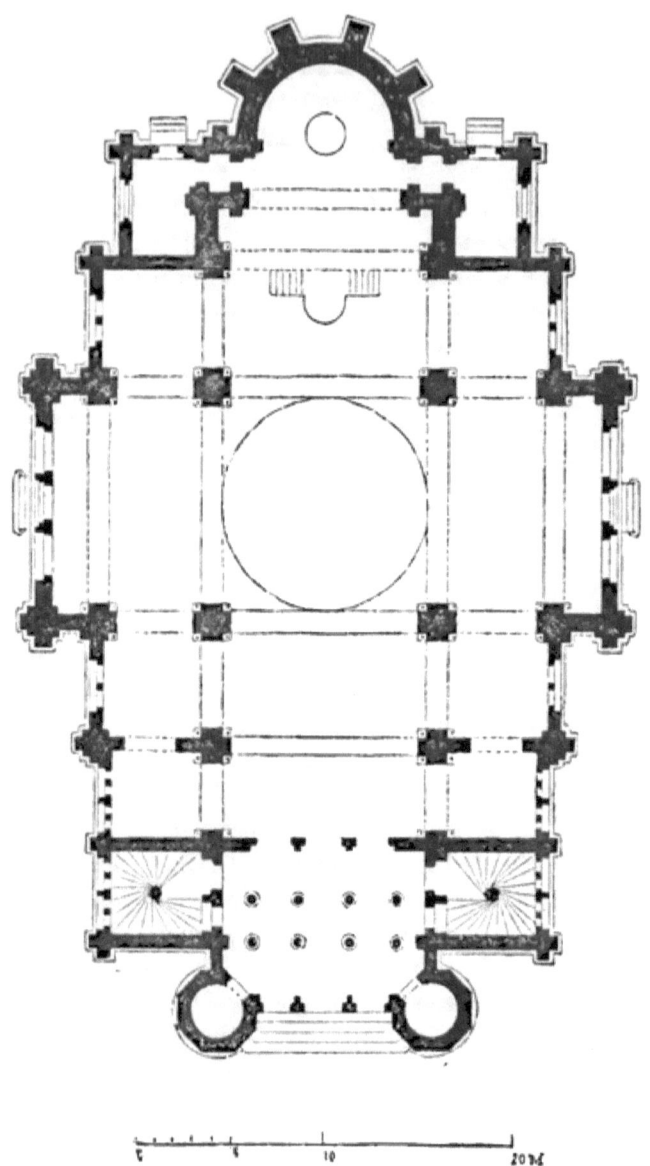

Fig. 106.—Ground-plan of Synagogue, Hanover.

(Fig. 107) the large arches of the nave, which occupy its whole height, from the ground to the roof, without being cut by lower arches intended to support the galleries. These remind one of the ancient churches in Westphalia, in which the aisles were always as high as the nave. The galleries are sustained on pillars and consoles of wrought-iron, and seem to be independent of the structure, so that they might be removed without making any other change in the disposition of the building. This is, perhaps, a fault, but, on the other hand, the plan adopted is novel; it increases the elevation of the vaults, since no combination of details interferes with their height. The cupola is supported on four squinches, formed of retreating arches successively lessening as they recede. The rest of the building is covered with groined vaults with projecting ribs. The whole has a comfortable and rich appearance, which will be still more augmented by the decorative parts, which are far from being finished at the present time.

The principal arrangements of the ground-plan and the interior are evident in the façades (Fig. 108). We can easily recognize, as we examine them, the large central hall, mentioned before, surmounted by a cupola, and defined by four projecting pillars. We may remark that the vaults of the nave might, perhaps, be dark at the upper part (for they receive only borrowed light from the windows of the aisles), were it not that, on account of the comparatively little length of the ground-plan, the building will be lighted by the large windows at the extremities of the transept.

This synagogue is built of freestone, as well as bricks, wood, and iron. This is one of the few buildings in Hanover in which we have noticed the employment of iron. Its use has been so well understood, and it has here been employed in forms and combinations so appropriate to its nature and to the part which it plays in the construction, that it is evident that its unfrequent application is not owing to Hanoverian architects not knowing how to employ it with effect. It rather depends on the influ-

Fig. 107. — Transverse Section of the Synagogue, Hanover.

ence of wise economical views which cause timber to be preferred to iron, since the former is still abundant in the country and comparatively cheap.

Fig. 108. — Synagogue at Hanover.

The Gymnasium and the synagogue are two such interesting

buildings that they certainly deserve the detailed descriptions which we have given of them. The architects who planned them have had the merit, rare among our German brethren, of not borrowing and appropriating to themselves the results of the studies of others. These public buildings constitute, each in its kind, works of great personal ability, including, as we see, many diverse elements; but these reminiscences are wisely co-ordinated, and placed in perfect agreement with each other, and produce, on the whole, a combination much to be admired.

We enter a primary school, where we find the playground small, the class-rooms insufficient, the ceilings too low, the children too crowded together, the school furniture unsuitable. One master presides over and teaches more than a hundred scholars at once. The light is not good; the building, originally a private house, has been transformed into a school, and this transformation has not been judiciously effected. We pay a visit to a second school. This is not so badly arranged and kept as the preceding, but still it is far below what we meet with in the modern schools of France and England. It was very warm there, and the odor produced by the assemblage of so many children was intolerable. We asked the master what means he had at his disposal for ventilating the school-room. It was necessary to repeat the question several times, and, then his countenance suddenly lighted up; he understood, and rushing to one of the windows, threw it wide open with a triumphant air.

The Polytechnic School is an establishment which nearly corresponds to our large lyceums, or rather to the Rollin and Chaptal colleges in Paris. The class-rooms are small but well ventilated, and the pupils have a respectable appearance. Not being desirous of showing our nationality as Frenchmen, we asked one of the elder lads a question in English. He replied in very good French that they did not learn English, but French only, as this language alone is obligatory. He was a boy of about fifteen years of age, and he expressed himself easily and without embarrassment. We doubt whether many of the pupils of our *lycées* could make themselves so well understood in German. The uniform consists of a minute white cap with a wide red band round it. Many of the children wear spectacles; we might almost say that those who do not are in the minority. Short sight, indeed, is an infirmity which is distressingly on the increase in Germany, and is generally attributed to the defective manner in which the rooms are lighted, and to the insufficient plans adopted for the construction and arrangement of the primary schools.[1]

Hanover possesses one of the six military schools of Germany. We shall only notice them in order to show what kind of instruction is given to the fourth division, which includes a knowledge of every document connected with the armies of foreign governments. These documents, modified every day, keep the students perfectly acquainted with the armaments, the position of the various *corps d'armée* and the strength of each regiment, the places where they are stationed, the names of the officers who command them, the cannon with which they are provided, and the war material in the arsenals of Europe. It was the exact knowledge of all these details which we attributed to the spy system, not being able to explain it otherwise during the war of 1870.

The students, during their last year, undergo frequent examinations on these subjects. They are expected, in answer to the questions proposed to them, to give, for instance, the numbers of the regiments forming such or such a *corps d'armée* in a foreign country, the military stations, the local resources, the importance and the nature of the productions of every commune, the names of the generals of brigade and of division, with the particulars of the service which they have seen. The camps, fortresses, and arsenals are the subjects of similar study and of the same careful investigation. A German officer ought also to know thoroughly the network of railways throughout Europe,

---

[1] See "Constructions et installation des écoles primaires," par Félix Narjoux, architecte. 1 vol. in 8vo. Librairie Morel, 13 Rue Bonaparte, Paris.

the manner in which they are worked, the points of bifurcation of the lines, and the quantity of rolling stock belonging to the companies. The bridges over the larger and smaller rivers are indicated on special maps, with an estimate of the weight which they are calculated to bear. The width and depth of rivers and canals are exactly quoted and learned by heart. Nothing is neglected, so that during a campaign there should be no obstacle whatever due to ignorance or irresolution, so as to delay the advance of troops.

The pupils, both of primary and secondary schools, engage with eagerness in gymnastic exercises. The importance given to the buildings of the Gymnasium (Figs. 100, 101, 102, and 103) shows what interest the Germans attach to such games as develop the body and give it the strength necessary to maintain a just balance between the physical and mental powers.

We have no intention of instituting a thorough comparison between the secondary schools of France and Germany; but still we will notice the most important points of difference between the two systems. Germany has established the tutorial system so much in favor in England, by substituting for large boarding-schools, smaller ones for eight or ten pupils, limited establishments kept by professors of colleges. The professors receive these boys into their own families, accompany them to school, hear their lessons, watch over their conduct, and take the place of their absent parents. There are no regular and obligatory hours of study; the children work whenever they please; provided that their duties are performed at a given moment, the master requires them to give no account of their time. Instead of junior masters, there are monitors chosen by the pupils, and taken from themselves. The classes, instead of lasting two hours each, are only three quarters of an hour or an hour in duration, and are always separated by a period of recreation.

If the higher German studies lose themselves in the mazes of metaphysics, and a sort of poetical dreaminess full of minute details respecting the analysis of the sentiments, the secondary teaching for younger lads is, on the contrary, eminently practical; and young pupils are well grounded in geography, history, mathematics, the natural sciences, singing, drawing, and one or two living languages, taught by means of *long conversations* between the professors and the pupils. Primary instruction, when the somewhat slow intelligence of a German child is able to follow it, is rather advanced. The pupils have greater knowledge of singing, arithmetic, and geography than the children of the lower classes in our country.

The last observation that we shall make on this subject is, that during several visits paid to Germany, we have always been struck — long before 1870 — with the great number of maps which cover the walls of the railway-stations, taverns, and restaurants; in fact, of every place of public resort. There were among them many maps of France, and we still find them there. They are, we must say, excellent substitutes for the pictures, in such bad taste, unfortunately so much in favor among ourselves and elsewhere.

This use of maps appeared to us so advantageous, that when we were requested, soon after one of these visits, to draw up a plan for a school-house, we proposed to paint maps on the walls of the class-rooms and playground. This proposition was received by the local administration with much laughter at our expense. The same result followed our suggestions in Paris with respect to the construction of workshops for a large number of men. We then suggested that maps, tools, models for calculation, writing, design, or the usual requirements of the business, should be painted on the walls. "That would distract the attention of my workmen," replied the master.

HANOVER.

II.

THE HOUSES, THEIR FURNITURE, AND THEIR INHABITANTS.

BEFORE speaking of the houses of Hanover, let us notice their inhabitants and the general aspect of the city. Though it is still early, the streets wear already an animated appearance; housekeepers are going to market in their red or blue bonnets; the mistress of the house does not consider it beneath her dignity to go herself to make her purchases, accompanied by servants who, with their arms bare as far as their shoulders, carry in their large baskets an enormous load of provisions of all kinds, and are prodigal of their smiles to the helmeted soldiers whom they pass. Groups of persons are frequently seen. Those who compose them remain indefinitely rooted to the same spot, and yet their conversation does not seem very animating or interesting. Two men meet; they stop and smoke by the side of each other their long porcelain pipes; they exchange but few sentences, but are contented with uttering now and then a word which appears to be very significant, for it is sufficient to give fresh *life* to the interview and to prolong the time of their stay. There are not many vehicles drawn by horses, but a great number of hand-barrows, in which a single man is able to take a considerable load. Clerks go to their offices with that weary look, that indefinable expression of ennui, which, in every country, is given to their features by the monotonous and regular life that they lead. We see regiments of soldiers drawn up in line; the men are strong and robust; their natural powers are developed, their physical force is very great, but there is but little intelligence shown in their eyes or their brows. The discipline appears to be excessive, and is maintained with exemplary severity. If an officer passes, the soldiers stop and salute; if it is a superior officer, not only the common soldiers, but the officers whom he meets, draw up, salute him, and continue on their way with the regularity and precision of an automaton when the spring which moves it has been touched.

At meal-times — and they frequently recur — the restaurants are filled immediately the former guests have left. Enormous dishes full of meat, prepared with but little delicacy, are placed before customers who are always hungry and eat greedily, scarcely stopping for a moment to empty large glasses of beer, which they drain at a single draught. Between meals, they frequently take rolls filled with ham, cheese, or cold beef, and wash them down with beer or brandy. The men lay down their pipes only when they are eating, and resume them immediately after they have finished. One may easily understand that their manners have but little refinement and politeness. The time which is not given to business is often passed at the tavern. The women sometimes exchange visits in the afternoon; these little social meetings are called *Mittwochnachmittagcaffegesell-schaft!* They then partake of slices of bread-and-butter and cups of *café au lait;* these slices and cups are of considerable size, and nevertheless the former rapidly disappear, and the latter are frequently refilled.

When one of the guests, seated at the door of a tavern, makes a joke, he smiles blandly, his countenance expands with simple and dull enjoyment; the jest passes from one table to another; each one repeats it to his neighbor, even repeats it to himself that he may thoroughly understand it; at last they begin to laugh, and their mirth increases in intensity, so that there is no end of it; a quarter of an hour afterwards it still continues. They dwell upon a single word or a gesture which they think worthy of attention, and ponder it in their minds, heavily engrossed by it. In one of the grand taverns near the railway-station a stout officer had just taken his breakfast. The meal which he had swallowed would frighten the reader; but having at last finished with a salad-bowl full of herrings and potatoes, and a soup-plate of *café au lait*, he felt satisfied; then, rising from table, adjusting his spectacles and buckling on his belt, our hero began to sing with a thundering voice and an accent impossible to describe, *Mein Herr Malporough s'en va-t'-en guerre!* The applause which he obtained was prodigious. Every person present repeated the words, passed them on to their neighbors, told them to the new-comers, and then came shouts of laughter and stamping of feet. An hour afterwards the excitement had not calmed down, for it only ceased to begin afresh. The famous phrase was repeated and commented on in a hundred ways with evident satisfaction and admiration, and certainly provided sufficient intellectual employment for the whole of the day.

The vanity of these people is unbounded;[1] you notice it in every word and gesture. These *parvenus* of victory have endured our supremacy and our influence in all European questions for many years, and they are now determined to have their revenge; but they do not understand, as we do, true glory and pride, and they remain inferior to us in greatness and generosity. The splendor of triumph is sufficient for us, but they can understand only the outward and material aspect of conquest. A title of honor is the reward of a French general who returns victorious. German generals, like barbarians, gorged themselves with gold after the war of 1870.

We stop before a cabinet-maker's shop. The men are working conscientiously, steadily, and without spirit, yet still without wasting their time. The one who was nearest to us was

---

[1] On a table in the museum of Sans-Souci at Berlin there is a large book bound in red velvet. On the first page we read, in letters of gold, "The Austrian campaign"; then beneath this, "It occupied Frederick the Great for seven years"; and on the opposite page, "William I. concluded it in seven days."

connecting two oak planks by a groove and tongue joint; every moment he fitted his boards together, tried them, turned them over, and compared them; he took a small piece off the tongue, and then enlarged the groove; then he tried them afresh, endeavoring to drive one into the other with his mallet; then he examined his boards on every side. The work was certainly done firmly and well, but he had occupied twice as much time as a Frenchman would have done; and, after all, it was finished without taste. The veins of the wood were not matched; they crossed each other instead of meeting at the central line, and spreading afterwards so as to form the *aigrette*, so much admired in our cabinet-work, and which would not have been forgotten by a French workman who was skilful and who was fond of his trade.

There are no beggars in the streets, for mendicity is strictly forbidden in Germany, and in some of the northern towns a fine is inflicted on every person convicted of giving alms.

We do not see so many women in the streets in the afternoon as in the morning. They go out but little, and pay but few visits to each other; which accounts for their eagerness to form groups in the streets, and to exchange a few words when they are out and happen to meet.

The men are heavy, dull, stout, gross, but strong and robust; we seem every moment to meet with all the shoeblacks, tailors, and shoemakers that we have seen in France. Benjamin Constant was right when he once said of these people: "The Germans are ponderous in their reasoning, their jokes, their tenderness, their diversions, and their quiet hours, — they seem to think that it would put them out of breath to be cheerful, and that they would be thrown off their guard if they were polite."

Theatrical performances begin and conclude at an early hour. The women go in morning dress; they listen without stirring from their boxes, or paying visits to each other; the men frequently go out to eat, drink, and smoke, and return with great noise, still wearing their overcoats, and affecting in public a deplorable want of decorum and consideration for others. They have not yet, however, adopted the custom of the inhabitants of Breslau, who enter the theatre with muddy boots, and place them on the railing in front of their box, where they form a kind of decoration, which has, at least, the merit of originality.

The inhabitants of Hanover seem to have considerable taste for the theatre; their opera-house is open during eleven months of the year. The *repertoire* is chiefly composed of comic operas, a few ballets, some translations of French pieces, and the works of native authors.

One of the favorite amusements of a certain class of the population is chamber-music, for which German composers have written so many pieces, and by the harmony of which they are able to produce a wonderful effect, even with but few performers.

These people are not rich, and they spend but little, so that their income and profits are small; and the balance-sheet is not always in their favor, since they are often in debt.

The dress of the women is modest, but in bad taste. They are in themselves neither graceful nor elegant; many of them wear glasses, and all of them show in their intercourse with men a strange want of reserve, which is singularly repugnant to our ideas of propriety and decorum. At a *table d'hôte*, before a hundred persons, a woman will kiss her husband; she sits on his knee in a railway-carriage, and sings to him, in a low voice, melodies in that sweet language which we in France consider fit only for horses. If they are merely engaged to each other, he only presses her knees under the table, and sends her kisses from his fingers' ends. It must be remembered that we are here speaking of persons who, by their fortune and position, evidently belong to the higher classes in society. It is said that such free manners show the innocence and simplicity of those who practise them; it seems to us, on the contrary, that they are a proof of a defective education, and of the absence of delicate and elevated feelings.[1]

The middle class possess neither the influence nor the power which they have in France; where, in these later times, they may be said to be absolute masters. In Germany they are in a rudimentary position; they have but few possessions, and are either absorbed into the higher class, or not distinguished from that beneath them. They are of an anxious temperament; their debts occupy their whole attention, and are the sole object of their thoughts. These form an inexhaustible subject of conversation, and the theme of anecdotes, remarks, and stories of all kinds. This impression we received many years ago; for tedious histories of debtors and creditors formed the staple of all the themes and exercises contained in the grammar from which we learnt so imperfectly when we were at college this terrible German language. One of the subjects most frequently treated of in their works of fiction is the rapid acquisition of fortune, not by industry, but by some accidental cause: an unknown rich relative is all at once discovered, or an unexpected inheritance is left by some great nobleman, who forms a just appreciation of their merits.

Their life is simple, and exempt from trouble. Violent passions are rare; all their interest centres in the family, and everything is so arranged in the household as to secure the influence of the father, and to simplify the duties of the mother, who undertakes the education of her children, of whom there are often a great number. The family hearth is never abandoned, except for weighty reasons; when the fortune of the parents permits it, the home contains all the elements necessary to render it agreeable, and is abundantly provided with linen, china, plate, and more especially with flowers.

Gold is very rare in Germany; our French coins have no circulation there; but as soon as a five-franc piece is offered to a

---

[1] In France, eight per cent of the children are said to be born "en-ante naturels"; in Germany the percentage is fourteen.

tradesman, he seizes it, presses it fondly, and looks particularly radiant if he can extort one or two silver groschen as a premium for exchange.

We must, however, make one remark in favor of the Germans. During the whole course of this excursion, made soon after the war, and a second visit paid since, we never in any town heard a single insulting expression relating to our defeat, or recalling

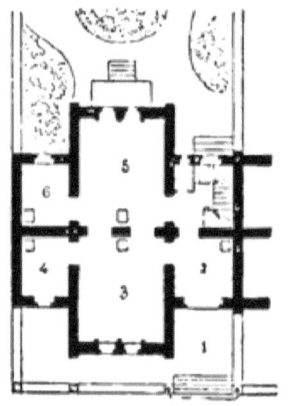

Fig. 109. — Plan of Ground-floor of Private House.   Fig. 110. — Plan of First Floor.

1. Porch.
2. Hall.
3. Drawing-room.
4. Breakfast-room.
5. Dining-room.

6. Library.
7. Bedrooms.
8. Dressing-rooms.
9. Terrace.

(Scale, .008 inch to the yard.)

it in such a manner as to hurt our feelings. A considerable foreign element is to be found in Hanover, principally of English residents. The bonds which unite England with Hanover are of ancient date. They were for a long time under the same sceptre, and the race of their kings, as well as their political interests, have been entirely separated only by the events of the last few years.

This rapid sketch was necessary to give an idea of the manners of the inhabitants whose dwellings we desired to study. The principal points worthy of notice, and on which we wished to dwell are: first, the mediocrity of their resources, their calm and peaceful habits, the love of home, the absence or at least the rarity of social meetings, and, as a consequence of this, the necessity of remaining usually in the bosom of their families. In order, therefore, to minister to these wants, they require cheerful and convenient habitations, containing all those arrangements for comfort which make home life agreeable; and these must be of sufficient size, so that the inhabitants may have plenty of room and everything that they may require.

The house, of which Fig. 109 represents the ground-floor, and Fig. 110 the first story, is a semi-detached double house, being intended for two families who wish to live side by side and united, yet entirely independent of each other, — a combination frequent in the North, where families and friends love to assemble in the same quarter and the same streets. A dwarf wall, surmounted by a balustrade, is built in front of the public road, and a free space, serving as a terrace-walk before the drawing-rooms, separates the building from the street, and keeps passers-by at a distance.

A covered porch protects the front steps, which rise from the level of the street to the ground-floor. The kitchen and its offices are placed in the basement; on the ground-floor are a drawing and dining room, each having attached to it a secondary apartment. These two rooms, the most important in the house, are comparatively small, but they can be united so as to form but a single room. On the first floor there are two large bed-chambers, with dressing-rooms, and above these the school-room for the children, the nursery bedroom, and two for servants.

This dwelling-house is well adapted to a private family. The rooms are lofty, being thirteen feet in height; the mode of access is easy, while the terrace-walk and the balcony allow the residents to go in and out, and add a charm to the interior of the house.

Fig. 111.—Semi-detached Houses, Hanover.

The architectural forms adopted in the fronts (Fig. 111) are not like those which we are accustomed to see in modern French houses; they rather resemble certain monastic habitations of the

Middle Ages, views of which are given in archæological publications. The proportions are not perfect, but the details have been carefully studied, and show that the architect has endeavored to give to his work a special appearance peculiar to itself.

The mode of construction is in good taste and keeping. Bricks, with a few blocks of stone, form the principal part of the building. These bricks are yellow, red, or black. This variety of color has permitted the introduction of imbricated work, the use of which enlivens the general effect. The dimensions of these

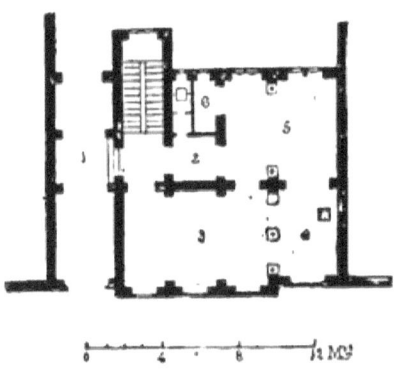

Fig. 112.— Ground-plan of Private House, Hanover.

1. Passage to carriage entrance.
2. Antechamber.
3. Drawing-room.
4. Back drawing-room.
5. Dining-room.
6. Store-room.

bricks are rather different from those employed by us, being about 2.36 inches in thickness, 5½ inches in width, and 9.6 inches in length. The stone is white, and of a good quality.

We may remark, before we proceed further, that two circumstances give to the houses of the North in general, and to those of Hanover especially, a peculiar aspect: on the outside the absence of blinds; and within, that there are no fireplaces.

The custom of standing at the window is not permitted; and so the window-sills do not project beyond the outer wall, but are flush with the inner surface of the frame, and incline outwards to the front. On this slab flowers are placed, and sometimes birds are kept in the intervening space. On the inside a second glazed window-frame forms an enclosure, opening by a small casement, rather larger than our usual panes of glass, which is intended to give fresh air to the apartment.

Stoves are substituted for fireplaces. The heat given by them is more equalized; it is greater, and especially more economical, than that of an open fire; but this plan deprives the room of an ornamental feature, which stands out so prominently, and by which we produce such striking effects. The looking-glasses have no invariable position; they are of small dimensions, and many rooms are entirely without them. Clocks are rare, *even at the present time;* and what we are accustomed to call chimney ornaments are usually placed on a console table fixed to the wall.

The reception-rooms in the interior of these dwelling-houses are not decorated in a manner out of proportion to the fortune of the inhabitants. Stucco-work, imitation marble, plaster ceilings with gold on a blue ground, and cupids in *papier maché*, are not in favor. The construction is simply carried out, and the parts thrown into relief are decorated in a manner, the least merit of which is that it is reasonable and sensible.

Figure 112 represents the ground-plan of a small mansion, the arrangement of which, we must say, is open to criticism.[1] We enter directly from a rather narrow vestibule into a large drawing-room adjoining a smaller one; the door of the diningroom is opposite to that which leads from the passage forming the carriage entrance. The vestibule is too small, and the visitor and the friends who receive him are crowded into too little a space, but the internal decorations of the drawing-rooms amply deserve the praise which we have already given.

The dining-room is separated from the large drawing-room, and that again from the smaller one, by wide openings (Fig.

---

[1] See, for further details, "Habitations modernes en Europe," par MM. Viollet le Duc et Félix Narjoux, architectes. Librairie Morel, 13 Rue Bonaparte, Paris.

113), which can be closed by thick leathern hangings. The framework of these openings tends to lessen the apparent height of the apartments, and in the dining-room supports a partition wall. The whole of this combination is in oak; some parts are decorated and enriched with very brightly colored designs. The walls are hung with printed calico (Fig. 114), covered with foliage patterns of bright colors, and with figures of men and

Fig. 113. — View of Interior.

animals, hunting scenes, in the midst of scrolls of flowers and leaves, the whole being in imitation of tapestry; but the designs are in outline and not relieved by shading.

The ceiling is oak, formed of small bare beams with chamfered edges. The long intermediate panels are painted of a uniform tint, with a few stripes of another color. The pilasters have chamfered edges, and, above the fillet which divides them midway, they are ornamented with designs in trellis-work.

The large stove which warms the drawing-rooms is made of enamelled terra-cotta, the colors of which, however bright they may be, are a poor substitute for the cheerful blaze which the eye looks for in vain during the long winter evenings. Terra-cotta is much used in Germany, and this manufacture has been brought to great perfection in that country. We will not enter

Fig. 114. — Decorative Paintings.

into any further details respecting it, as we shall have to return to this subject when we describe our visit to the porcelain and pottery works at Hamburg.

We give in Fig. 115 the ground-plan, and in Fig. 116 that of the first floor, of a mansion more important than the preceding.

In Paris it would perhaps be considered only a private house, but here it occupies a much higher rank.

Carriages do not enter under a covered way, which is, especially in the North, an unfortunate omission. It is true that a projection of the gable shelters the steps and protects visitors. The front wall is separated from the public way by an area, in which is the kitchen entrance; the servants and tradespeople do not cross the threshold of the principal door, which is covered

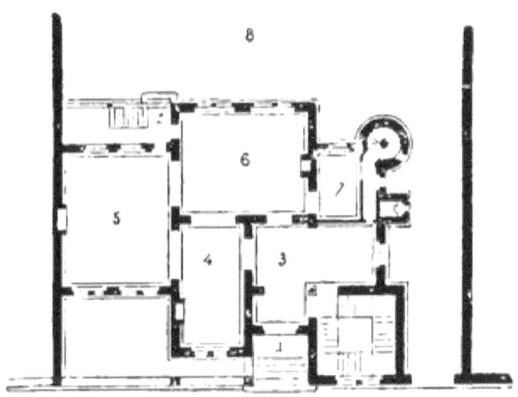

Fig. 115.—Ground-plan of a Mansion, Hanover.

1. Porch.
2. Garden entrance.
3. Hall.
4. Small drawing-room.

5. Drawing-room.
6. Dining-room.
7. Library.
8. Garden.

(Scale, .098 inch to the yard.)

by a projecting porch. The hall is divided into two unequal parts; the largest of these serves as an anteroom, and is of sufficient size to be used as a cloak-room, and to contain benches for servants while they wait for their masters. An isolated column, which indicates the point of separation of these two portions, as shown in Fig. 117, gives an air of elegance to the hall, and this simple arrangement enables one to understand the construction of the staircase.

By a door on the left hand of the vestibule we enter the smaller drawing-room, and directly opposite is the entrance to the larger one. The dining-room communicates with both of these by wide openings, thus allowing all these apartments to be easily thrown into one suite on reception days.

The kitchen and its dependent offices are connected with the ground-floor by a spiral staircase in a turret, which is approached by a wide passage leading to the closets. We must not forget that the servants in Germany are not entirely sepa-

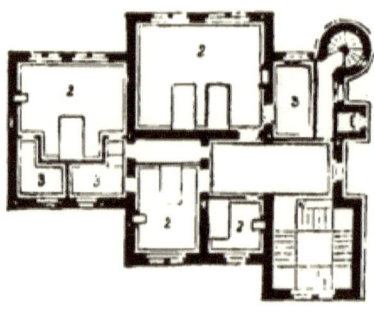

Fig. 116. -- Plan of First Floor.

1. Antechamber.   2. Bedrooms.   3. Dressing-rooms.

rated from their masters, but live more with the family than is the case with us; and the mistress of a house on the other side of the Rhine does not consider it derogatory to go occasionally to superintend the kitchen department.

On the first floor is a large antechamber where the children can play. Then there are very large and lofty bedrooms, each with its dressing-room, fitted with hot and cold water, a large bath and shower-bath, — the latter an English fashion.

We must here notice the manner in which the beds are placed. There is no recess; but the bed stands with one of its shorter sides against the wall, so that it projects into the room and leaves both of its longer sides exposed. This arrangement, when the size of the room will permit, is the most convenient and the most healthful, and is especially useful in cases of sick-

Fig. 117. — Hall, with Staircase.

ness. It is always employed in large state bedrooms in palaces, and was constantly found in those of the Middle Ages. The want of space is the only reason which can induce people to prefer the position now commonly adopted.

The façades (Figs. 118 and 119) resemble those which we

Fig. 118. — External Geometrical Elevation of the Façade of a Private Mansion, Hanover.

Fig. 119.—Country House, Hanover.

have already seen. There is too much variety in them, and they
have not a quiet appearance; but the principal parts of the
structure are well indicated. The spiral staircase (Fig. 119), as
well as the drawing-rooms and vestibules, project externally;
large double windows give light to the principal apartments,
and, contrary to the laws of symmetry, lesser ones open into the
smaller and secondary rooms. Imbricated work plays an important part in the decoration of these façades, to which both
recessed and projecting arches give a varied outline. Terraces
and covered balconies render the interior of the house more
agreeable, and allow sedentary inhabitants frequently to take a
little exercise.

We might multiply examples of these dwellings; but we must
not delay, as we have still to examine at least one public hotel
and one country-house.

The hotel of which the ground-plan is given in Fig. 121, and
the plan of one of the upper stories in Fig. 120, is one of the
second rank. It is not intended for tourists travelling for pleasure, who are accustomed to luxurious dwelling-houses, and to
whom expense is of secondary importance. Those who use it
are either commercial travellers, or persons living in the environs, who come into the town on fair or market days on
business.

Rooms for reading and conversation are therefore unnecessary.
The apartments must be of no greater dimensions than are absolutely necessary. They must be convenient, warm in winter,
and cool in summer. Dressing-rooms and reception-rooms would
be superfluous.

Under the carriage entrance, which is enclosed by three glazed
doors, intended to give sufficient light while they protect persons
from draught as they enter or leave their vehicles, is the lift,
which receives the luggage at once from the roof of the omnibus, thus sparing the servants fatigue, and avoiding the inconveniences of carrying heavy articles up the stairs. By the side
of this lift is the entrance to the hall, and on the left the lodge

HANOVER. 225

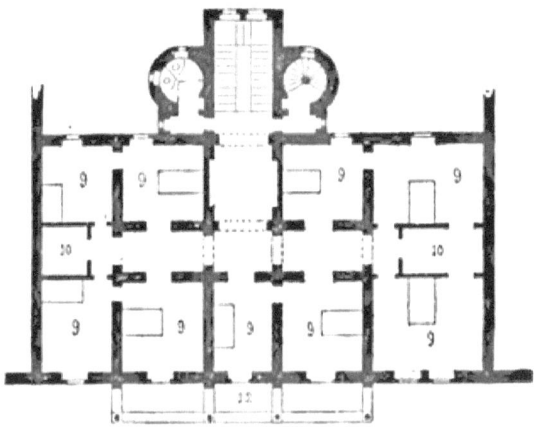

Fig. 120. — Plan of First Floor of Public Hotel, Hanover.

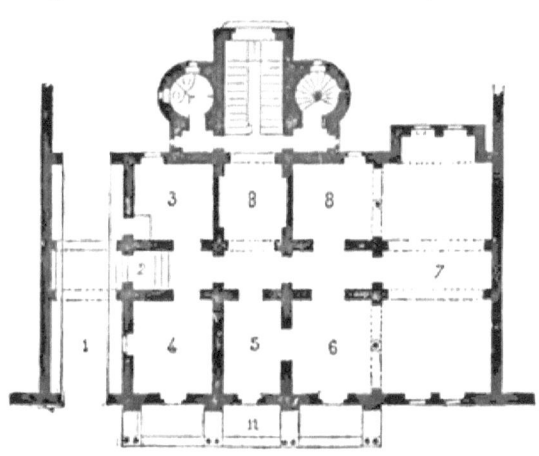

Fig. 121. — Ground-plan.

1. Carriage entrance.
2. Front door.
3. Porter's lodge and lift for luggage.
4. Office.
5. Drawing-room.
6. Breakfast-room.
7. Table d'hôte.
8. Housekeeper's room and store-room.
9. Bedrooms.
10. Dressing-rooms.
11. Balcony on ground-floor.
12. Ditto on first floor.

of the porter, who plays so important a part in the towns of the North, and acts as a special providence to foreign travellers. This porter, who differs entirely from our *concièrges*, always speaks German, French, and English. It is he who gives all the necessary information to travellers, sees that passports are *viséd*, obtains permission for residence when any is necessary, procures cards to visit museums and public buildings, and knows the hours of arrival and departure of trains, diligences, and steamboats.

He sells also French cigars and photographs, keeps samples of articles of local manufacture, procures couriers, settles disputes with the drivers of vehicles, and neglects no means of obtaining from the traveller — whether or no he is willing to bestow them — all kinds of gratuities.

In front of this useful functionary's box is the door of the office, which is divided into two parts; the first serves as a waiting-room for travellers, the second for the money department. After these come four rooms, separate, yet connected with each other, — the smoking-room, where the newspapers can be read; the large dining-room; the breakfast-room (for meals are too frequent, and follow each other too closely, to allow persons who wish to take some slight refreshment to obtain a place at the *table d'hôte* in the large room); and then, facing this smaller room, there is another, of the same form and dimensions, which can be used for private dinners, and in which the dessert is prepared, the meat carved, and the dishes placed when removed from the general tables. These two rooms communicate with the large dining-room (Fig. 122) by means of arches, which can be closed by thick hangings. At the end of the large room there is a recess in which a table can be placed when required, and where persons may sit while waiting for the dinner hour. The office, the coffee-room, and the small dining-room open on a terrace, on which, in summer, tables are placed for those who may feel inclined to look out on the busy streets while they take their meals.

HANOVER.

Fig. 122.—Interior of large Dining-room.

The stairs turn to the right, with a large landing ornamented with flowers; and at the bottom is a hall, the walls of which are covered with maps and notice-boards of all kinds. To the right and left hand are two turrets, one containing two closets, the other the kitchen stairs. On the walls are maps, useful notices in various languages, a table of the comparative value of money in different countries, and a complete list of everything curious and worthy of notice in the town.

There are no fireplaces; but in their stead are large earthenware stoves, which reach from the ground to the ceiling.

The furniture of the bedrooms is simple, but very neat and well kept: a wash-hand stand, a chest of drawers, two chairs, and one of those terrible German beds,—instruments of torture which will never be forgotten by one who has been condemned to them even for a single night.

The rooms are high-pitched, the ground-floor is 15 feet high, the other stories 13 feet and $12\frac{1}{2}$ feet. There are twenty-five bedrooms; and the dining-rooms would be too large for such a limited number of travellers, were it not that, besides those in the house, this establishment accommodates many persons coming from the neighborhood only to take their meals, so that it serves as a restaurant for a great many inhabitants of the town.

The façade resembles those which we have already described, and our sketch (Fig. 123) renders any further notice unnecessary. The building is constructed, as usual, of brick and stone, and the framework of wood, with the exception of the large covered balcony, the supports of which are of cast-iron, and its roof of wrought-iron.

The country-house, the ground-plan of which we give in Fig. 124, is honored with the name of a château. The ground-plan is rather wanting in regularity. The taste and wishes of the proprietor have perhaps influenced the architect, Mons. Oppler, and interfered with his plans, for we have seen many of his works superior to this; yet it is a complete example of a modern country habitation in Germany, and as such is worthy of attention.

The arrangement of the rooms is very peculiar. It corre-

Fig. 123. — View of the Façade.

sponds with wants very different from our own, and on this account loses much of its interest to us. As to the façades (Fig.

125), they have too strong a Teutonic character to please us; there is too great a desire for novelty. One cannot imagine what motive can have induced them to erect those square gables of exaggerated form, with so many arched apertures, through

Fig. 124.—Ground-plan of a Country-house in the Environs of Hanover.

1. Veranda.
2. Antechamber.
3. Dining-room.
4. Store-room.
5. Smoking-room.
6. Parlor.
7. Library.
8. Drawing-rooms.
9. Oratory.

which the outlines of the roof can be seen. But, in spite of these defects, we are struck with the general outline when we do not examine the details, and with the effect produced by the many projecting parts, which indicate externally the distribution of the rooms within.

Fig. 125.

The building is constructed with conscientious care. The proportions are correct, and in accordance with established rules. The height of the stone courses corresponds exactly with an entire number of bricks, without rendering any contrivance necessary in order to obviate a difficulty of this kind, or ever showing a *loup* or wolf[1] in the facings.

Great care in the employment of materials, as well as regularity and scientific knowledge, are usually shown in German buildings, and constitute one of their chief merits; and for this reason we dwell on this important matter, which is too frequently neglected in our modern structures.

All the dwelling-houses which we have described, and which are only examples chosen from among a great number, have excellences and defects in common, on which it was necessary to make some observations. They are adapted to the tastes, the wants, and the social habits of the persons for whom they are intended. They vary according to the position, the profession, and the fortune of their proprietors. We have not been able, in these notes of our travels, to enter into details which would have become tedious, or to give a greater number of examples in support of our observations, since time would have failed us. We could not give sketches of houses adapted to certain professions; one for a physician, for example, with a special antechamber, a consultation-room with two distinct entrances, the whole being separate from the family apartments. We should have liked to describe fully a certain architect's offices, containing a large lofty room, with a gallery midway towards the ceiling serving as a library, and cases filled with architectural models; there are tables for daily work and a retired bay, where one could study of an evening calmly and quietly. At the side is a separate room, intended for the reception of clients and contractors, and there is convenient communication between these offices and the family apartments, the entrance to which is

---

[1] A French workman's phrase, signifying an imperfection in the construction. — Tr.

separate. If we had noticed all these houses we must have sketched half the city of Hanover.

In all these buildings no space is lost. The staircases, which are fully in sight, are easy of ascent, and have wide and low steps turning to the right hand, and the landings are decorated with flowers. The apartments correspond with the importance of the house, and the social or secluded habits of the inhabitants. Thus there is often no drawing-room, it being considered unnecessary for quiet people of moderate fortune; but then the dining-room is very large, and the family live there, thus saving fire and lamps. The same character of economy and foresight is shown in the façades. The front is not covered with a costly coating of plaster, which is expensive to repair; there is no cement facing loaded with very perishable mouldings, and no widely projecting cornices covered with sculptures executed in very bad taste, and with gutters formed of imitation stone, through which the water percolates to the inside of the walls. But, instead of these, there are level fronts made of bricks, so laid that the outline of the materials is clearly displayed, with a cornice, or rather a simple projecting coping, supported on corbels. Above this there is a wide zinc gutter, a complete passage round the roof to facilitate repairs. There is no fear of infiltration to the walls; it is easy to examine the roof, and consequently it is better kept in order. There is economy both in the original construction and in the subsequent attention which it may require.

Yet, in order to carry out the views which prevailed in the construction of these houses, some improvements might perhaps have been made. Thus for persons of moderate fortunes, kitchens placed under ground are inconvenient. It is impossible to have servants on every story at the same time; the frequent journeys up and down the stairs are trying to them, and take up much of their time. The mistress of the house is less able to have its arrangements under her own eye; it entails upon her greater fatigue, and she involuntarily hesitates at going up or

down the stairs, when she would willingly cross a passage.
Whoever is acquainted with a German household and the economical principles which govern it, will understand the importance of this observation. There is another important matter. The principal rooms are large and well ventilated, but necessary conveniences are wanting. The closets are insufficient or too few in number; the modern requirements of a large house expect these to be placed near the principal bedchambers, as well as a bathroom and dressing-room. Germans, it is true, are more easily satisfied than we are. They are more simple in their habits, and are not accustomed to the refinements of our civilization, and to the necessaries which administer to our comfort. So much for the interiors.

On the outside, as we have already said, the façades are too complicated. Both in public edifices and private buildings, they strive after exaggerated and unusual effects. These are, in fact, the expression of the characteristics of the German mind, which imitates, lays a stress upon, and draws attention to delicacy and elegance of language, yet cannot comprehend them. The details are heavy, forced, and pretentious in execution.

It may be said that this is a matter of personal taste, on which it is impossible to give a decided opinion, resting on a firm and incontestable basis. A Frenchman, for instance, could never persuade a German that the latter wants taste, and that his own ideas are preferable. The reasons which each one advances to support his own opinion are the same; they may, with the same success, be used on each side, and therefore it is impossible for either to be convinced.

One of those foolish remarks on this subject, which are constantly repeated in every country, is, "that artistic education should be made to agree with the public taste." This signifies, on the part of the artist, that he ought to impose upon the public his peculiar tastes, which are superior to all others; and, on the part of the public, that the artist should be compelled to produce nothing but that which pleases the said public, who are better judges than any one else of their requirements and desires. We may also remark that French, English, German, Italian artists, and others, all wish to reform the public taste, — that is to say, to impose upon it their own, — and not only do these various tastes differ, but they are destructive of each other. Therefore, although there exists a standard of measure, the metre, to which reference can be made in case of disagreement, no one has yet invented a standard of taste, so that every one persists, and will still persist, in his own, and in the conviction that it is far superior to that of his neighbor.

Now that we have examined the Hanoverian houses with reference to their construction, we must pay attention to their furniture, and internal decoration, in which respect they are well worthy of notice.

In France the interior and exterior of our houses bear little relation to each other, which is explained by the simple reason that, being but rarely the owners of the house in which we live, we cannot modify our furniture at every change of residence. Besides, these discrepancies unfortunately do not shock us. We have no objection to a Renaissance house with furniture and decorations belonging to another period, or to Moorish apartments with Gothic furniture, or that of the age of Louis XV. The exaggerated fondness for knick-knacks at the present time has favored and justified this strange eclecticism. These incongruities are not so readily accepted in England and Germany, for there the style adopted in the façade of a house is usually followed in the interior. In a word, if the fronts of houses that we have seen there are Gothic, the interiors are in the same style, and the furniture has some of the characteristics and remembrances of the Middle Ages, — souvenirs which are shown not so much in forms modified and adapted to the wants which they are intended to satisfy, as in the application of principles which have guided the study and adaptation of these forms.

The people of the North, so skilful in all carpentry-work, are not less so in the manufacture of furniture. They know per-

HANOVER. 235

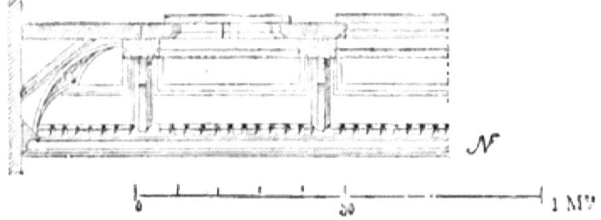

Fig. 126. — Surface and Section of a Panelled Ceiling, Hanover.

fectly well how to give to all kinds of wood those forms which correspond to its nature and the purpose for which it is intended.

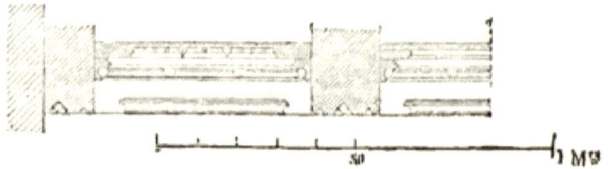

Fig. 127.— Surface and Section of Panelled Ceiling.

Timber is still plentiful in Northern Germany, and it has supplied builders with materials which they have so happily em-

Fig. 128. — Chimney-piece.

ployed in the decorations and furniture of their dwelling-houses. As German masons have respect to the value and nature of the stone which they employ in their buildings, so do their cabinet-makers study the value and nature of wood. They employ it according to its characteristics and qualities, avoiding useless waste and large curved portions which interfere with the grain of the wood; but, on the contrary, they always form combinations with it in the direction of the fibres, and so preserve all its strength. As to the taste shown in the execution of this kind of work, the reader must judge for himself.

Thus, instead of our plaster ceilings,— which conceal the timber and lessen its duration, which are subject to cracks and crevices which cannot be avoided, and require continual attention and expensive repairs,— they have constructed panelled ceilings, of which Figs. 126 and 127 afford two examples. These ceilings seem, at first, to remind one very strongly of those of the Town Hall at Augsburg, and the Presle mansion at Nuremberg. They are not, therefore, interesting in respect of originality, but of very ingenious adaptation.

The ceilings of public buildings of the twelfth and thirteenth centuries consisted only of bare joists resting by each extremity on a wall; or, if the distance was too great, on an intermediate beam. There were few or no openings in the walls to receive them, but corbels inserted in the masonry to support the ends of the beams. The edges were chamfered, the intervals and projecting parts were painted, and sparingly decorated. In the fourteenth and fifteenth centuries these primitive arrangements were transformed and enriched. The beams were placed so as to form panels and compartments ornamented with carving and painting; and at last the decoration assumed the principal feature, being distinct from the timber-work to which it was affixed, and thus ceasing to be an integral part of the structure.

The ceilings represented in Figs. 126 and 127 are, as we have said, copies from fourteenth-century models, and in reality present only the lower face of the boards, thus showing plainly the nature of the construction which they embellish. In the ceiling (Fig. 126) the panelling is attached to the lower surface of the joists; in Fig. 127 it is supported by furring nailed along each principal and cross beam. The carvings are in solid wood, and the ground-work of the panels rests on planks cut so as to give them the necessary projection; our sketches show the plan of construction. Above these large girders are joists of sufficient thickness to support the upper floor, and to fill up, in certain parts, the intervals between the beams. The height of

Fig. 129. — Sofa Table.

the room in which these ceilings are placed is 18 feet, which accounts for the outlines being so bold and the carvings so decided. As to the price of these ceilings, it is somewhat high, the square foot costing 2½ thalers (about 9 s. 4 d.).

The chimney-piece (Fig. 128) stands in a large vaulted hall of octagonal form. It is made of white sandstone and polished serpentine. By means of a combination of colors which cannot be seen in our sketch, the union of stone and marble of different tints gives the colors of the armorial bearings of the proprietor, whose scutcheon is placed over the mantel-piece. The table

(Fig. 129) is intended to stand before a sofa in a drawing-room. The dimensions of its various parts may perhaps appear exaggerated, when compared with those of our modern furniture; but, on the other hand, they increase its firmness and durability. The legs spread out at the end, by means of an oblique arrangement, which gives greater support and steadiness to the upper part. The braces and cross-pieces, which connect the extremities, are rather high, in order to prevent persons placing their

Fig. 130. — Table with Cupboard below.

feet upon them, contact with which injures them so rapidly. This precaution may appear trivial, but it is the mark of a practical and thoughtful mind. This table in walnut wood cost 65 thalers (about 9 *l.* 16 *s.*).

Another table (Fig. 130) may at the same time serve as a cupboard in the lower part. It is made of oak, and copied from an old engraving of the fourteenth century, from Ramerstof. So true it is, that in small things as well as great, the Germans prefer to copy rather than originate.

The "what-not" (Fig. 131) is intended to hold albums or curiosities. It is made of oak; but its supports, which are

Fig. 131.—What-not.

rather heavy, and its prominent carvings, render it unsuitable for a drawing-room. It cost 32 thalers (4 *l.* 16 *s.*).

The bedstead (Fig. 132) is entirely in red deal (pitch-pine), which possesses the great advantage of never being attacked by

HANOVER. 243

Fig. 132.—Fine wood Bedstead.

Fig. 133. — Walnut-wood Cupboard.

vermin.[1] Excepting the angles, which are carved, all the rest

[1] This kind of wood is used in Alsace for a similar purpose and for the same reason.

Fig. 134. — Walnut-wood Bureau.

of the decorations are painted and varnished, for the sake of cleanliness. The price of this bedstead, exclusive of the painting, is 30 thalers, equivalent to 4 *l.* 8 *s.*

246 GERMANY.

Fig. 135. — Bookcase.

The cupboard (Fig. 133) differs from the preceding articles of furniture, and those which follow, in the quiet character of its ornaments. The hinge-plates on the doors are of polished iron, and the wood employed is American walnut.

The bureau (Fig. 134) is an article of furniture of a very complicated construction, and is intended for a lady's use. The wood employed is also American walnut; the metal-work, which is very rich, is polished iron. The scrolls repeat the letter E,

Fig. 136. — Arm-chair.

the owner's initial. The figure placed at the top represents Albert Durer. This bureau is too richly ornamented; there is a want of simplicity, and of that which is highly necessary in every bureau, sufficient room for work. In the midst of the many partitions, drawers, and doors, there is scarcely room to hold a sheet of paper. This bureau cost 160 thalers (24*l.*), which is rather dear.

The bookcase (Fig. 135) has perhaps the same defects, but this is atoned for by an arrangement which allows it to be adapted to the circular form of the room in which it stands, since the two wings can be placed obliquely.

The chairs (Figs. 136, 137, and 138) are in oak or walnut;

Fig. 137.—Chair.

the arm-chairs, without the covers, cost 50 thalers (about 7*l.* 9*s.*). In order to avoid the usual manner of connecting the back of the chair and the hind legs, the designer (Mons. Oppler, the architect) has obtained the necessary inclination for the back by causing the framework to go down to the middle of the hind legs, which are placed at a more oblique angle than those in front.

This idea, which is very simple and ingenious, is also applied to the construction of common chairs, which are thus more steady than ours, the legs of which are united with the back at the level of the seat, and they are more comfortable than those with upright backs. The price of common chairs is 2½ thalers (about 8 s.).

Fig. 139 represents a bracket, intended to be fixed against a wall to support a statuette, or any other work of art which stands out in relief against the background of velvet. A looking-

Fig. 138. — Chair.

glass is often substituted for the velvet, and serves as a reflector for a lamp placed in front of it.

These articles of furniture resemble joiners' rather than cabinet-makers' work. They are really strongly made, and their construction is well planned and executed. The wood is of fine quality, well cut according to the grain, with sharp and well-defined sides and edges. The joints are made with the greatest care, always fastened with wooden pegs, without any parts let into each other or nailed. There is no veneering or gluing. On the contrary, the mouldings and carvings are cut out of the solid wood; but there is often a deficiency of grace and elegance in the workmanship. The general effect is heavy, clumsy, and massive, and, when they do not copy ancient models, there are often defects in the proportions.

Fig. 139. — Bracket.

Having now visited the different public buildings, and seen the exteriors and interiors of the houses of Hanover, there remains nothing, before we go, except to add a few words respecting modern German Gothic.

The Germans, as we have already said, have never had any architecture peculiar to themselves; they take their ideas from the buildings of foreign countries, and copy those of past ages.

The types of Gothic architecture which they possess are far inferior to the magnificent examples of the Middle Ages to be found in France; and they did not dream of reviving this style in Germany till after the appearance of those buildings which were the results of our first archæological studies, which, twenty-five years ago, led us to regard with honor edifices till then considered rude and barbarous. They followed in our steps, profiting by our attempts, our studies, and our faults; translating into their language, without compunction, extracts from our works, in order to apply the results of our researches. And in the same manner as the German who built the cathedral at Cologne knew and imitated those of Amiens, Beauvais, and Troyes, so modern Germans, finding in a neighboring country information, hints, and formulæ ready to their hand, have, with great skill and much success, appropriated to themselves all that could be useful and profitable. But while, amongst ourselves, the architects of the Gothic school limited their works to the restoration of ancient buildings and to the construction of churches, the Germans, on the contrary, went farther, and following out the ideas which they had received, erected ecclesiastical and civil structures, both public and private, said to be Gothic, in which, while they respected the fundamental principles of the logical reasoning which had served as a basis and starting-point, they varied the forms and multiplied their combinations, so as to obtain different results, and to carry out varied plans suited to all the requirements of public and private life.

Their want of imagination in works of art was of service instead of hindrance to them in the laborious task from which they derived such excellent results. Being cold and conscientious reasoners, they did not allow themselves to be carried too far. Not overstepping the bounds of nature, while trusting to their taste and skill, they have hitherto avoided excesses and exaggerations into which others, as the English for instance, have fallen, while following the same path. The Synagogue, the goods station at the railway,[1] the Gymnasium, and most of the houses of Hanover, are illustrations of what we have stated.

As to our influence in the country, it is latent, but incontestable; facts prove it, though not a single German has had the good taste to allow or own it. They copy our architecture and our works of art, they act our plays and perform our musical compositions. They almost all know our language, read our literary and scientific publications, and are eager for articles of Parisian manufacture. Their women ape ours, and think that they resemble them. They have conquered us, and yet the conquered people inspire them with a terror, an envy, and a mean jealousy which they can neither overcome nor conceal; and the phrase "to live like a God in France," has passed into a proverb, which is often on the lips of the people.

If they know us so well, we, on the contrary, know little of them, and that little but imperfectly. On our return from one of our visits to Germany, a friend, an eminent architect, said to us one day, "What induced you to go to that country? there is nothing to be seen there, not a single public building; there are scarcely any railway-stations." We then showed him some of our sketches. He could not contain himself, made a hundred exclamations, and, like a true Frenchman, passing from one extreme to the other, he declared that these people were "very clever, cleverer far than we"; which was as foolish a saying as if any one were to assert that the reflected ray was more bright and luminous than the source from which it emanated.

It is, unfortunately, one of our national characteristics to yield too readily to the excitement and impressions of the moment. Ever since the misfortunes which have befallen us, two trains of thought and feeling have been manifested among us. Some, filled with foolish pride, and unwilling to acknowledge either

---

[1] We twice endeavored to sketch the goods station, but each time we were interrupted and expelled in a manner so essentially German, that we did not think it prudent to make another attempt.

our misfortunes or their cause, consider themselves greater than
before. Others, on the contrary, giving themselves up to an
exaggerated humility, have too low an opinion of themselves,
and think their adversaries in every respect superior. We must
avoid falling into either of these opposite extremes. But, without entering into considerations foreign to the scope of this work,
we can but see that the efforts made by the Germans to copy us
in artistic matters, prove that we have excelled them, and that
they have been our imitators. It is for us so to act that we may
maintain this position.

HAMBURG.

FROM HAARBURG TO HAMBURG. — THE ELBE. — HAMBURG. — THE ALSTER. — THE JUNGFERNSTIEG. — THE OLD TOWN. — THE CONFLAGRATION OF 1842. — THE NEW TOWN. — THE PUBLIC BUILDINGS. — THE HOUSES AND THEIR INHABITANTS.

FROM Hanover to Hamburg the country is flat and unattractive. In the midst of a large sandy plain we notice Zela, whose inhabitants speak, it is said, the purest German, but which does not sound to us on that account sweeter or more melodious. Then we come to Luneburg, with its houses with pointed gables, and its town-hall full of artistic curiosities, the merit of which has been greatly exaggerated. Happily, the country is adorned by the guard-houses and the stations, which are by the side of the line. These small buildings are constructed entirely of brick, with the exception of a few blocks of stone; the platforms are protected by sheds, made entirely of plain wood. Climbing plants cling here and there, mount to the roof, and fall in rich festoons, covered with brilliant flowers. A fountain is playing in one corner, and through the open doors of the waiting-rooms we see large earthenware stoves, which mitigate the cold in winter, and the stalls of the refreshment-rooms covered with provisions and large glasses of sparkling ale. These refreshment-bars play an important part in the stations of German railways, and all are provided with them. They are attacked on the arrival of every train, and the formidable appetite of the people is a constant source of astonishment to the foreign traveller.

We leave the railway at Haarburg, and embark on the Elbe

to follow it as far as Hamburg. This is the most interesting part of the journey. The boat at first descends the southern stream of the Elbe, and then, by a lateral branch, reaches the northern Elbe. From this moment we perceive Hamburg, with its steeples, its buildings rising in the form of an amphitheatre, and the astonishing activity of its immense harbor.

First we reach Altona, formerly the second city of Denmark, but now absorbed into the Empire of Germany. To the right is the large island of Wilhelmburg, across which Marshal Davoust, in 1813, raised a causeway to connect Haarburg with Hamburg by means of a bridge of boats.[1] Boats find some difficulty in making their way in the midst of the enormous quantity of ships with which the river is covered, and among which the large vessels of the Hamburg Company, which put in at Havre on their passage to New York, occupy the first place. Our poor little steamer was obliged to stop every instant, and to back, sometimes almost going about, in order to prevent her bow getting fouled; and at times being scarcely able to proceed. No river in Europe serving as a port to a large city, with the exception of the Thames in London and the Clyde at Glasgow, can give one an idea of this state of confusion, — this incessant and ever-varying bustle.

Large vessels laden with emigrants are just beginning their long voyage, escorted by boats full of friends and relations who wish to bid them farewell; the men may be seen clinging to the nettings and waving their hands, the women weeping and holding their children above their heads to let them have a last look at their native land, which, for the most part, they will never see again. The officers of a man-of-war are going ashore in a twelve-oared cutter. It flies over the water, regardless of all the boats that are in its way. We pass close by a magnificent iron-clad frigate; the sailors are in the rigging, sing-

---

[1] These works have been since destroyed; and until the bridges and the railway, now in course of construction, are finished, they have stationed here steam ferry-boats of sufficient dimensions to receive six carriages of full size.

ing one of those old airs whose monotonous melody is heard in every sea. Fishermen are tacking out to sea, for the season is already advanced, and the lucrative northern fishery will soon commence. Some little coasting vessels, laden till they are ready to sink, are passing up the river made fast to a tug, and seeking a convenient place to unload. We are proceeding very slowly; but the scene which passes before our eyes is so varied, so picturesque, so full of life and color, that we feel that we have no reason to complain. And now we no longer look around us, but forward, and try to make out the large city which stands out so massively against the blue sky. Rising above our heads is a terrace-walk, passing along the crest of an eminence; it is the extreme point of the enclosure formed by a network of canals. The city begins to show itself: first come the high roofs of the public buildings, which rise above the low, narrow, filthy houses which lie along the quays. As we draw nearer, the details begin gradually to appear; the buildings around the harbor are black and dirty, and the inhabitants of these wretched hovels resemble them. The aspect of Hamburg, as seen from the river, is anything but attractive; we would fain turn back to gaze upon the moving vessels with their busy crews, and upon the outline of the city defined against the horizon; but our trip is over. We land, and a drosky conveys us through a labyrinth of miserable streets and filthy canals to the magnificent quays of the Alster, where in our astonishment we ask if we can possibly be in the same city, of which we had a glimpse but a moment before.

Night came on before we had walked round the quays of the lesser Alster, known under the sweet names of "Neue und alte Jungfernstieg." These quays are lined by lofty houses (Fig. 140), five stories high, almost all hotels or large establishments. The shops are in two tiers; those underground, in which live those who keep restaurants and taverns, and dealers in eatables; the ground-floors, raised very high above the level of the street, contain shops of all sorts, brilliantly lighted. Crowds of people come and go, and everything shows the activity of a great city. A number of persons are standing before a large placard illustrated in the English fashion, and which represents two people fighting a duel; above this is a woman dressed in a shroud, and

Fig. 140. — View of the Alster Quay, Hamburg.

laid on a bier. We follow the current, and enter the exhibition of Jenkins Brothers, "citizens of free America." At the moment that we took our seats the stage was occupied by the persons represented in the bills; they were clothed in an odd costume, the one being dressed like a Hungarian, and the other in a sort of pelisse resembling that of a Russian peasant. They clash their sabres against each other with looks as terrible as their blows. After a short time and many attempts, the Hungarian gives his adversary a severe cut through his sleeve; the hand of the Russian, dropping the sword, rolls down to the middle of the stage before the horrified spectators. Blood flows from the wrist in large drops, and stains the floor; the wounded man turns pale, and falls. They rush to him, and carry him off, while the Hungarian, picking up the hand of his opponent, waves it over his head, showing the contracted fingers, the blue nails, and the bleeding wound; it is a hideous sight. The stage remains vacant for a few minutes, till the two antagonists return, show their four hands uninjured, bow to the company, and the curtain falls.

When it rises again, there is nothing on the stage but a box of oblong form and dismal appearance, the sight of which in such a place makes a painful impression. When the spectators have had time to contemplate this sight, and their emotion is sufficiently excited, a man enters, dressed in black with a white neckcloth, armed with a hammer, and with his hand full of nails. He opens the box, which resembles a coffin, turns it all round, strikes it on all sides, and invites those present to examine and see that it is fastened tightly together.

During this preliminary operation a fresh personage, a woman, makes her appearance, dressed in a winding-sheet, which covers her from head to foot, and fits closely to her body. She places herself in the coffin, and her companion carefully nails down the lid; then he spreads over it a black pall, covered with white spots resembling tears, and, having done this, he retires.

We looked on with much astonishment, not understanding the whole proceeding, and unable to guess what was about to happen, when the coffin suddenly begins to tremble, the *dead-alive* struggles, and begs, as well as she can, to be released from her prison. At first there are nothing but dull sounds; then

you hear her heels beating against the sides of the coffin, and
the head moving up and down in despair; the hands endeavor
to tear with their nails the smooth surface of the wood : the
most frightful silence reigns in the hall; you may imagine that
you hear the panting breath of the woman thus struggling between four boards; then cries of fear are heard among the spectators, which are instantly hushed. But the movement of the
coffin becomes more sudden and violent; it rolls about, shaken
by the poor creature supposed to be in such fearful convulsions,
and struggling in her anguish, a prey to terror and fright. We
seem to see her, with her writhing and bleeding limbs, dashing
herself, without a moment's cessation, against the walls that confine her; she loses her senses, she sees nothing, feels nothing
now; there is not sufficient air for her to breathe; her strength
is exhausted, and her cries are stifled. Then the movements
become less rapid; they cease for a while, only to recommence
with greater energy and courage; then all is quiet again; the
dismal box shakes for the last time, and all is over. They throw
the pall over the coffin again, and carry it away not a moment
too soon. What a nightmare it seemed! but the movement
given to the coffin by a person thus enclosed within four planks
of wood, and without space to move and throw about her limbs,
must be a very difficult gymnastic feat.

Fortunately, to revive our spirits a young girl appeared, extremely pretty, but so lightly clad that one knew not whether
she were about to dress, or had just finished undressing. She
was well formed, however, and took no pains to conceal it. She
advanced timidly, with downcast looks and trembling voice;
her beautiful eyes scarcely dared to glance around. This behavior contrasted so strangely with her dress, that we asked ourselves, as in the preceding scenes, what was about to take place.
The heroine crosses the stage, and sings, in French it was said,
and we suppose it was, some lines from the "Belle Hélène."
When this was over, she turned, and found herself confronted
by a person in the fancy costume of an executioner — one half

red, and the other black — who seized her by the nape of the neck. She fell gracefully backwards, and he stabbed her with a poniard in the breast. The blade disappeared; the executioner gave it a slight twist, and drew it out again; the blood flowed, dyeing the white robe of the victim who fell, with her hair dishevelled, her eyes closed, her face, her arms, her breast, and her limbs livid, yet still exhibiting in her fall the remarkable plasticity of her frame.

This trick was less successful than the preceding; it was too evidently seen that the executioner, while twisting his dagger in the wound, fixed on the bosom of his victim an adhesive picture, intended to favor the deception; but how was it possible to produce in a moment such decidedly deathlike hues?

This little performance satisfied us, and we did not care to wait for the conclusion of the exhibition, but hastened to our lodgings for the night. Fatigued with our voyage, and having eaten for supper some fowl and gooseberry jam, lying on a German bed, and lulled to sleep by the remembrance of the scenes which we had just witnessed, it may well be imagined what nightmares embellished our dreams, and how often the foolish saying recurred to our mind till we were inclined to curse it, "a bad night is soon over." We had, however, long before been convinced of the contrary fact, that a good rather than a bad night seems of short duration.

Early the next morning we began to examine the labyrinth of streets which compose the old town. Some of the worst streets of Frankfort, Genoa, Naples, and London may give some idea of those which form the ancient quarters of Hamburg, and of the picturesque appearance of all these houses built of wood, with their tottering gables advancing irregularly one over the other (Fig. 141).

The timbers are sharply defined on the brown ground of the bricks or mud with which the framework of the wall is filled in; they are sometimes relieved with a red band, forming around them a kind of frame. These houses are lofty, for land has always been dear in large cities; they have sometimes four and even six stories. The dates of their construction are exceedingly various, and they have been so often modified and restored that they possess now no other interest than as objects

Fig. 141. — An old Street in Hamburg.

of curiosity, the greatest merit of which is their undoubted antiquity.

These old houses are found everywhere, along the sides of narrow streets and tortuous canals; they all have gables with openings through which the light can be seen, narrow windows, and plastered walls falling to decay. Not one of them resembles its neighbor; each has its peculiar appearance and different character, and one is never tired of examining them. These quarters are often the scene of painful incidents, showing no very high sense of moral obligation, or any very refined taste in those who are connected with them. Brutality, desire of gain, and roughness of manners form the prevailing characteristics.

The maritime population live near the harbor or the canals. Another quarter is almost exclusively occupied by the dwellings of the Jews, who are very numerous at Hamburg, where they carry on profitably many of the favorite callings of their race; but, throughout all the ranks of their social life, the types have remained the same. And on the thresholds of the doors, or through the panes of the windows, may be seen beautiful girls with dark hair, white teeth, and hooked noses, whose profile resembles that attributed by tradition to Rachel or Sarah.

We may easily understand the result of a fire, when it breaks out in these hovels of worm-eaten wood, and what its ravages would be among so many elements so well suited to aid in the work of destruction; and we may imagine what the terrible conflagration of 1842 must have been. "The Great Fire," as it is still called at Hamburg (where this event occupies so important a position that it divides the history of the town into two portions, the one before and the other after this disaster), was almost as terrible as that of which London was the victim in 1666.

It began on Thursday, May 5. There was a report that a fire had broken out in a cigar manufactory in Deichs-Strasse. The devouring element soon assumed such proportions that ordinary means were insufficient to resist it. There had been a month of great drought, and the canals were dry. On the first day twenty-two houses were consumed, and the Church of St. Nicholas fell into the flames with a dreadful crash; and the next day the sun rose over an ocean of fire, throwing far around a shower of ashes and sparks, the violence of which increased every moment. Cannons were employed to clear a space around the burning houses; but through the violence of the flames the wind blew from every quarter, and changed its direction every instant, rendering it excessively difficult to approach the places that were attacked. The cries of the terrified crowd, the heart-rending scenes that occurred in all directions, prevented aid being given with sufficient activity and authority to render it effectual. The metal ran down from the roofs, covering the spectators with a shower of fire. All the inflammable materials had been thrown into the canals, and had there taken fire, and, like a river of flame, carried on all sides fire and death. In every street might be seen vehicles loaded with furniture and valuable effects, mothers rescuing their children; some, who had become mad, throwing themselves headlong into the burning mass. Then, all at once, there arose a fearful cry; the tower of St. Peter's Church began to totter on its foundations; its bells, set in motion by the action of the fire, tinkled for the last time, and the enormous mass was overwhelmed in the immense furnace below. On the same day the Bank, the Old Exchange, and the Town Hall were destroyed.

Assistance came from every quarter. Altona, Lubeck, and Bremen sent provisions, men, and troops. On the 7th a merciful shower of rain fell, which restored courage to those who were employed in the work of extinguishing the flames; and finally, on Sunday, the 8th, the fire may be said to have been got under control.

It had lasted three days and three nights, — had destroyed sixty-one streets and two thousand houses (a fourth part of the city). A hundred persons had perished; twenty thousand were reduced to poverty, and were without shelter. The loss in money was estimated at one hundred millions of marks banco (about 7,520,000 $l.$). Subscription-lists were immediately opened in Europe and America for the assistance of the unfortunate people who were thus left without any resources. The sum obtained amounted to more than 400,000 $l.$; and thus the victims of this frightful disaster were enabled to procure for themselves the indispensable necessaries of life. At Hamburg the inhabitants engaged to raise among themselves a sum of 2,000,000 l. for the rebuilding of the town. All traces of this calamity have now disappeared. New buildings have arisen instead of those quarters that were burnt. These are built of stone, erected along wide, well-planned, and well-ventilated streets; the noisome

Fig. 142.—Flower-girl.

canals are arched over; and Hamburg lays greater claims than ever to be "the finest city in the North of Europe."

When the Exchange is closed, and the day's quotations have been telegraphed to the whole world, the business day is over, and that of pleasure begins. All the mercantile and laboring population of the town repair to the Jungfernstieg, which at this moment exhibits a spectacle of which the Unter den Linden at Berlin and the Prater of Vienna may, to a certain extent,

give some idea. The crush is great under the trees which line
the Alster; cafés established in small tents till rapidly; a number of boys bring, on pewter trays, refreshments contained in
vessels which resemble the birettas worn in our churches. Carriages throng the road; the promenaders, among whom may be
seen the most distinguished of the *demi-monde*, exhibit gaudy
costumes in extravagant and glaring colors. Among the wheels
of the carriages and the groups of promenaders may be everywhere seen flower-girls (Fig. 142) in a singular dress, — a very
short red petticoat with a broad green border, showing a great
deal of a leg with red stockings, and feet which are rendered as
narrow as possible by tight shoes. The body of the dress and
the apron are violet, and the arms are left half bare. In winter
long white skin gloves reach to the elbow and meet the sleeves.
They wear on the head a straw hat which strongly reminds of
the women of the Bay of Tourane in Cochin China. These
young girls, who are not overburdened with modesty, accost
unceremoniously every new-comer; fortunately they express
themselves in German. When they find that their eloquence
is in vain, they stick a rose in your buttonhole, and then demand a few groschen with an importunity which is soon complied with.

Workmen who are enjoying their leisure seat themselves at
tables by the side of the road, smoking and drinking, and from
time to time venturing some rude joke, of more than questionable taste, on some woman who is passing, and who replies in
the same strain, without being disturbed, and without any hesitation. As the evening advances the meal-time arrives. Then
the restaurants are filled; the counters are covered with attractive and choice eatables. The salmon of the Elbe, geese from
Stettin, game stuffed with prunes, roast beef with pears, raw
hams, and smoking pies are displayed on the refreshment-bars
so as to be seen from without. The customer can judge of the
resources of the establishment before he enters. But there is
no exquisite cookery, — none of those choice sauces, the glory

of French *chefs;* but quantity and solidity are substituted for delicacy and skill.

When once they have taken their places the people all eat greedily, with their elbows on the table, without troubling themselves about the glances of strangers, who are very numerous at Hamburg, and who, seated by their side, are astonished to see them satisfying so unreservedly and so grossly their physical wants. They shock, though unconsciously no doubt, all the instincts of elegance and delicacy of people of Latin race. They are stolid, heavy, and impolite. Their women are ignorant of the laws and resources of the toilette; they know neither how to make a bed nor prepare a dinner, and spoil the best things by mixing them in a manner contrary to all the rules of taste and reason; they have no idea of self-restraint, so that they sometimes forget even the respect due to themselves. We have been often told that this arises from artlessness and simplicity. As for German simplicity, where shall we find it? These people are utter *roués;* we have seen them in their unguarded moments, alas! In what does their simplicity consist? In embracing each other ridiculously in public? Or is it because they have more natural children than any other nation in Europe? Or because they hoard the few crowns which they possess, and never give way to any sentiment which will not yield them either advantage or profit?

To-day we entered a school; there were the maps on the walls, and we had no need to examine them to know what country they represented. It was France, with its rivers, railways, and mountains. There were references to printed details of the nature of local productions, and information respecting the means of communication and the obstacles which might present themselves.

Opposite to these was a large map showing the extent of the Empire of Germany, with the Duchies, Hanover, Saxony, Alsace, Lorraine, Bavaria, Baden, Wurtemberg, etc. Looking at such a map, we are at once struck with the idea that Germany is not a nation, but an agglomeration of many nationalities, differing in their origin, their manners, and their religion. The only thing which they have in common is their language; but, should a fortuitous event stop one of the wheels of this immense machine, the whole would fall to pieces and instantly separate. Each country would rise against the master who has brought it under subjection,— would resume its autonomy, and recover the position of which it had been deprived.

Continuing our walk along the Alster quay, we saw on the

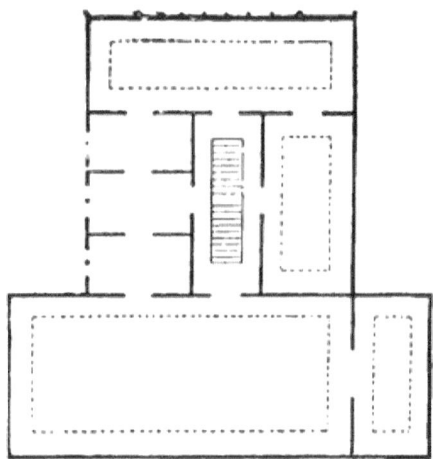

Fig. 143.— Ground-plan of the Museum at Hamburg.

right the new Museum, built entirely of brick, which deserves notice on this account rather than because of its form.

The ground-floor (Fig. 143) is composed of a central building and two wings. A very fine staircase occupies the middle; it is of a single flight, with a wide landing half-way, and seems a miniature of that of the senate-hall at the Luxembourg. On the ground-floor are the sculptures and the curator's apartments. On the first floor there is a large and beautiful room at the head of the stairs, then a smaller one, and a long side-gallery. A fourth division, in three compartments, contains drawings and engravings, light being admitted at the side. The whole of these rooms are not yet filled. The works of art which they contain are but of secondary merit; but they are well arranged, and placed so as to be seen in the best possible manner. Those of greater importance are hung on hinges, which allow the light to be modified, and the position to be altered, according to the hour of the day. There are many seats, and the visitor may sit on a low and wide divan, without fatigue, and examine the picture opposite to him.

Most of the paintings are works of that German school so well known in France by the specimens sent to our annual exhibitions; but the effect produced is not the same when these paintings, instead of being lost in a crowd, are brought together so as to form a whole.

The *Genre* pictures, so much admired by our neighbors, shock our ideas, because of the choice of subjects; some of the details are too crude and too realistic for our refined taste. It was always a subject of astonishment to us to see how openly a German shows his preference for one subject over another. Good taste is as unknown to him as reserve or delicacy. Thus, a group, composed of a husband, wife, and children, who wore the appearance of people moving in good society, were standing by our side convulsed with laughter, and were uttering loud exclamations before a picture representing a soldier too familiar with a servant-girl.

The most favorite subjects of the German artists are interiors, as we have before said; the representation of the ordinary occurrences of citizen life, simple and sometimes trivial family scenes. Such subjects as these are unsuited to the sculptor, so that works in this branch of art are rare. It is not adapted to the genius of the Germans, who only leave the trivialities of life when they lose themselves in the domain of a vague idealism, often difficult to be understood, and which sculpture, with its rigorous geometrical precision, is unable to reproduce.

We have already said that the façade of the Museum (Fig. 144) is entirely built of bricks. These vary in form according to the position which they are to occupy; thus the shafts of the columns are formed by four triangular bricks, united at the

Fig. 144. — The Museum, Hamburg.

centre by a core filled with mortar, exactly in the manner that columns in the Forum of Pompeii, and many other ancient public buildings, were constructed. The bricks used as voussoirs are adapted to the form of the arch; their upper part is wider than the lower, so as to allow the joints to be of the same thickness. Mouldings are formed of bricks of special shape, the inconvenience of which perhaps is, that they have the same profiles as stone, without being able to show such clear and delicate edges. In the upper cornice there are panels filled in with enamelled terra-cotta, ornamented with designs in bright colors. Compartments, formed of bricks of various tints, fill the solid parts of the building, and tend to give it a heavy appearance. We feel that the conception is too labored; the niches filled with unnecessary statues; the combinations of balustrades and of cornices intended to conceal the roof show a striving after effect, a certain embarrassment, and an exaggerated attempt to succeed, while it would have been easy to obtain a better result by the employment of more simple means, and the study of more pleasing proportions.

The Gross-Alster is separated from the Binnen-Alster by a narrow neck of land, on which they have contrived to construct a road and a railway. This connects the Berlin line with that of Sleswig, and serves as a medium of communication between different parts of Hamburg. It crosses, on a level, one of the frequented streets of the city, and yet there is no guard, no barrier placed there to prevent access. When one wishes to pass, he looks if the way is clear, raises a chain, replaces it, and goes on his way. A clock, placed by the side of a notice-board fixed to a post, gives all requisite information, and the precise time of the arrival of the trains, so that large and heavily laden vehicles, which move but slowly, may not pass the crossing without a certainty of having sufficient time. Each person is able thus to secure himself from danger. We do not manage matters so simply in France.

After having traversed without inconvenience the level crossing before us, and passed along the causeway by the side of the Gross-Alster, we found ourselves before the General Hospital, of which we wish to give a short description. Questions relating to the construction and internal arrangement of hospitals are at present of so great interest, that it will be useful to enter into

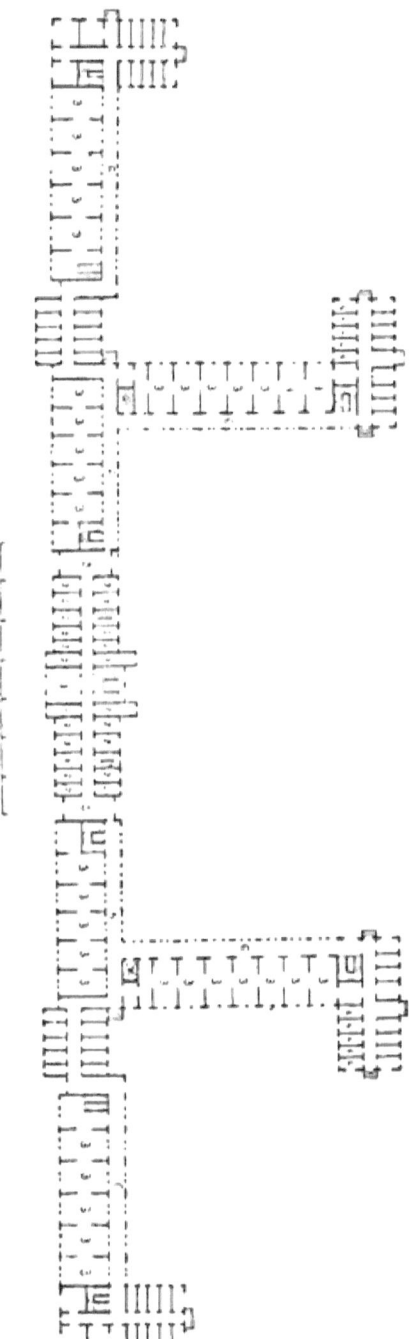

Fig. 145.— Ground-plan of the General Hospital at Hamburg.

1. Vestibule.
2. General offices.
3. Sick-wards.
4. Rooms for separate patients.
5. Passages.
6. Galleries.

some details and explanations respecting that at Hamburg, one of the largest establishments of the kind in Germany.

In a notice issued by the authorities of the hospital, it is said: "We have not here to do with a small establishment limited in its development, and containing but a few hundred beds, but with one of the first rank, organized for the purpose of affording public aid in an unlimited and more perfect manner, and capable of receiving, when necessary, as many as eighteen hundred patients."

Among the hospitals recently erected, that at Hamburg has adopted, in the arrangement of its buildings, one of the forms most usually found in Germany, a quadrilateral, open on one side. Such is, at least, the character of the principal part of the structure; for, since the fire of 1842, which brought to the hospital so large a number of victims, they determined to enlarge it; and in 1848 they added to the original building, and prolonged its façade by two wings, which materially alter the general appearance of the establishment.

The site occupied by the General Hospital at Hamburg is by the side of the basin of the outer Alster. It covers a surface of about 64,585 square yards. It was begun towards the end of the year 1820, and finished three years afterwards. The expense of the works was 1,282,000 marks current (about 76,000 *l.*).

It is composed (Fig. 145) of a central building, and of four annexes. The central part is raised two stories above the ground-floor; the wings have only two, with attics above. Beneath the whole building there are vaulted rooms underground.

On each side of the central building are carriage-entrances, from which staircases lead to the different parts of the establishment. The annexes are divided into two parts, the first of which extends along the front, and the second at right angles. Each extremity is terminated by a rectangular building. The central court-yard is divided into two parts, intended for the patients of each sex. A wide passage crosses it, leading from the principal door of the official department, and ending at the surrounding moat.

Behind the principal building are situated on one side the anatomical hall, and on the other a kind of coach-house, in which the fire-engines are kept. At the side of the outer enclosure is a small building where woollen clothes are washed.

The sick wards are of various dimensions, the smallest being in the rectangular portions at the extremity of the wings. These are allotted to patients who pay for lodging and attendance, and to isolated cases. Each of the ordinary wards, placed on the first floor, is intended to receive twelve patients and a nurse. They are 38 feet long, 22½ feet wide, and about 12 feet 3 inches high; each patient must therefore have about thirty cubic yards of air, which is very insufficient. (See p. 32.) All these wards communicate with the common corridor and with the adjoining wards. They are lighted by three windows opening in the external wall of the building, each of which is 7 feet 6 inches by 4 feet 3 inches. The sill of this window has no projection inwardly at the usual height, but is, on the contrary, recessed from the front wall, so that the patients and attendants cannot look out of the window, or place there vases with flowers, or other ornamental objects.

On each side of the door leading to the corridor are two small rooms, each lighted by an arched window. One of these is reserved for the nurse, and the other contains closets. In the middle of each smaller ward is a stove, and there are two in the larger ones. These stoves, made of brick covered with glazed tiles, are heated by coal or peat. The ventilation of the wards is effected by means of small air-openings made, on one side, in the wall beneath the windows, and on the other above the door leading to the corridor. You have only to tell the air to enter on one side and go out on the other; a very primitive arrangement, and utterly insufficient, since it frequently moves in an opposite direction to that which was expected as the result of its good intentions, and thus occasions great inconvenience. The ceilings are plastered, the walls whitewashed, and the floors rubbed with wax.

In the new wards a system of ventilation is adopted which is less primitive than that used in the old ones. An air-pipe surrounds the chimney of the stove, and carries off the vitiated air brought thither by the draught, while fresh air is supplied in the lower parts of the room by means of orifices at the level of the floor.

The cesspools are not emptied, but the drainage passes directly into the Elbe. The general city aqueduct supplies the necessary purified water. A main drain receives all the water from the smaller sinks, and carries it to the Elbe. The whole establishment is lighted with gas.

The principal and assistant physicians reside in the hospital. There is also an additional branch in the centre of the town, for the examination and reception of patients. Foreign sailors are admitted, in urgent cases, without examination.

The porter at our hotel, who is a Roman Catholic, was intrusted to receive, from his foreign co-religionists, subscriptions towards the construction of a church, the designs for which he showed to us. We gave our mite to this useful functionary, and borrowed from him some drawings, which may, perhaps, interest the reader.

The ground-plan (Fig. 146) consists of a porch leading to the nave, which is bordered by side aisles, and terminated by a square chancel. The wide bays of the nave occupy the width of two of those of the side aisles. All the vaults, both high and low, have bays at right angles to each other. Their angles are without mouldings (Fig. 147), and they are intended to be covered with paintings. The pillars are square, and the edges are chamfered as far as a console, which forms a corbel for the spring of the arch. Small columns, giving additional strength to those of the transept, and placed against each side, support the wall arches. Large isolated windows give light to the narrow bays. In the wider bays of the transept, instead of a single window, a triple one has been made. These windows come down to the string-course above the arches of the side aisles, but their upper part alone opens to the outer air. The lower portion gives light to a gallery, a kind of triforium, covered by

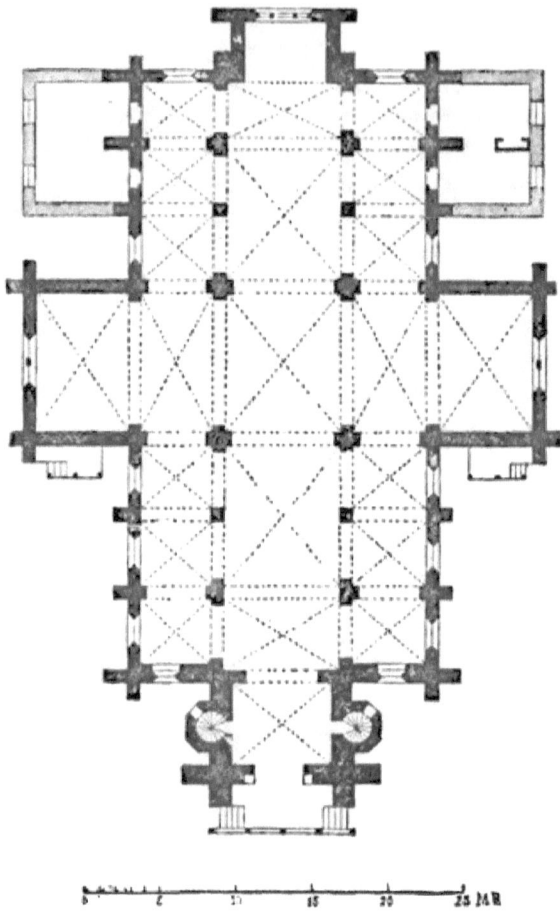

Fig. 146. — Ground-plan of Roman Catholic Church at Hamburg.

the roofs of the side aisles. Arches placed below these roofs, the timber-work of which is supported by them, sustain the thrust of the vaults of the nave.

The steeple is over the main entrance, and forms the great feature of the principal façade (Fig. 148). It is divided into three stories, each treated in a different manner, according to

Fig. 147.—View of the Interior.

the purpose for which it is intended. First, the porch; then, the window belonging to the organ gallery; and above this, the long narrow windows of the belfry, over which is the base of the wooden spire. Triple windows, resembling those of the nave,

Fig. 148.—New Roman Catholic Church at Hamburg.

give light to the transept, and there is a rose-window in the east wall of the chancel at the end of the building.

The materials to be employed are brick and white stone for the masonry, tiles for the roofs, and wood for the framework. Iron is not yet so much used in Germany as in France, and it is but seldom employed.

Having now described the general appearance of this church, an important public building in a city in which there are so few, we must in a few words analyze its form and the nature of its construction.

The person who planned the Catholic Church at Hamburg, having a considerable space to cover, determined to give it a vaulted roof; it was, in fact, scarcely possible to cover a large surface by a ceiling. Metal is not well adapted for decoration under these circumstances, unless it is concealed by a covering of plastering, — a combination in every respect objectionable. Having, therefore, adopted a vaulted roof, the architect made the general plan and its details to correspond with it. The bays of the vault, as we have already said, are at right angles to each other, and are built of bricks without projecting ribs; as the angles are strengthened by a double brick, it is only necessary to make the large triangular bays about four and one-third inches in thickness. The spring of the vaults of the nave comes so low, and that of the side aisles is, on the other hand, so high, that it allows flying buttresses to be formed in the roof of the aisles, supported by external buttresses, and intended to take the thrust of the vaults of the nave.

This arrangement gives the side bays a somewhat heavy and clumsy appearance, but has the advantage of being truly economical, in allowing the height of the nave to be diminished without rendering it dark, since it can be lighted by windows immediately above the roofs of the side aisles.

The danger to be feared in such a case is lest the thrust of one of the smaller arches forming the division of the side aisles should overturn the isolated pillar in the centre of the larger bay; but to obviate this difficulty it is easy to place over the springer of this arch an arrangement which would diffuse the thrust, throwing it not entirely on the column, but partly on the triangular mass of brickwork formed by the meeting of the two arches, which supports the solid part above the sill of the window; this would afford the necessary resistance.

This system of vaulting appears, therefore, very simple and reasonable as to the points of support. Their disposition of the arches is not the result of caprice, but rendered necessary by the part which they have to play. The examination of the plan shows that their dimensions have been carefully adjusted, so as to enable them to sustain the weight to be laid upon them; and these dimensions are increased at the top of the pillars by means of corbelling, intended to give greater surface to the imposts of the wall arches.

Many other arrangements in this building well deserve examination, but it would be necessary to give a great number of plans and drawings in order to enter into these details and explain them. We cannot and wish not to write a complete monograph on each building which we mention; we must be contented with the more modest attempt merely to give our readers some idea of it.

We may here remark that we cannot but notice a certain family likeness between the church at Hamburg and some French churches, — a bond of parentage which is strikingly evident in many respects, — and yet this building is not a copy. It reproduces recollections, reminiscences; it may be looked upon as an adaptation, but it is not a servile reproduction; and if, in studying the details of this structure, we meet with incontestable traces of the influence of a former age or of another country, it is to be found in the principles which have been made use of, and in the rigorous application of a borrowed idea well followed and reasoned out, but not in the barren reproduction of outlines or details, the importance and the true value of which might indeed be ascertained and appreciated merely from the style of their execution.

Since the time when Hamburg began to rise from its ruins, they have replaced, one after another, the churches destroyed in 1842. One of the most important of them, the Church of St. Nicholas, has been built, say the Guide-books, in the *purest Gothic style* by Sir Gilbert Scott, an English architect, whose name has a well-deserved celebrity in the United Kingdom.

The Church of St. Nicholas is an archæological work conscientiously elaborated. There is nothing, indeed, to shock us; but we look in vain for any creative idea, any product of the imagination. It is the exact copy of one of those Saxon churches of the fourteenth century, the types of which are so frequently to be seen in England. The construction suggests nothing but vertical lines. The mullions and dwarf columns are too slight; the gables are too pointed, and are decorated with meagre and flimsy ornaments; the buttresses are surmounted by pointed finials; the arcades are not projecting, and the sculpture is not characteristic; and, besides this, slender flying buttresses pass over the roofs of the side aisles to give support to the vaults of the nave. We have a different idea in France of the architecture of the Middle Ages; yet we must admit that the Church of St. Nicholas has a grand and noble appearance, and has been constructed with the greatest care.

The other public buildings of Hamburg have little worthy of the notice of the architect. The Exchange, for instance, has attracted great attention, but its architectural merit does not justify the notoriety which it has obtained. In front of it is the Bank, constructed on the site of the former Town Hall, of which we will only say that it served in 1810 as the prefecture of the department of the Bouches de l'Elbe, of which Hamburg was then the principal town. It was there also that Marshal Davoust resided during the memorable siege of 1814. The Synagogue, a Moorish edifice, is considered to be one of the largest in Europe. In the Schulgebaude, a kind of professional school, there has been collected a library containing twenty-five thousand volumes, and a museum of natural history and of local antiquities. The buildings in which these various objects are placed are separated from each other by courtyards surrounded by colonnades, — a kind of cloisters, affording an easy mode of communication, and serving to protect the pupils while at play. Unfortunately the internal arrangements of the rooms do not correspond with the good impression given by the external façades.

The construction of dwelling-houses, as may easily be imagined, has been greatly developed in a city which has been partly rebuilt, and which daily increases in prosperity.

The houses in the central district, where the land is dearest, and space is wanting, are lodging-houses of several stories in height. Those erected immediately after the great fire in 1842 have no decided character. They resemble, except in a few details, those which are usually seen in large cities, as in London, Paris, or Vienna. The sketch which we made of one of the Alster quays (Fig. 140) will serve to give an idea of the plan usually adopted; but, on the contrary, the houses more recently erected, and especially those which are being built at the present time, have been influenced on the one hand by the German Gothic school, and on the other by the intercourse with England, with which Hamburg has many commercial relations very important to both countries.[1]

The material of these buildings is brick. These are employed with great care, and in every combination in which they are applicable; they are of various colors, and, in certain cases, of different mouldings and special forms, so as to be suited to the place for which they are destined. Again, enamelled tiles are frequently used, to obviate the monotony caused by the uniform arrangement of these small masses, and thus throw into relief

[1] Hamburg is the principal port in the North of Europe, to which all the merchandise sent from England and America to Germany and Russia comes, either at its arrival or departure.

certain portions of the structure, such as the lower parts of the courses which they trace, the window-sills under which they are placed, or the upper portion of the gables which they embellish.

Figs. 149 and 150 represent the plans, and Fig. 151 gives the perspective view, of one of these dwelling-houses intended to be let to persons engaged in business or commerce. The underground portion is comprised of vaulted rooms, used as taverns or restaurants; they are very warm in winter, and are especially frequented during the evening, which lessens the inconvenience of their being rather dark. The ground-floor, divided crosswise by a series of arches springing from the lower part, contains shops; these are not well adapted to the rich display of goods to which we attribute so much importance, for the sill of the windows is on a level with the heads of those who pass by; the entrance is not directly from the street, as the very severe climate of the North does not permit such an arrangement, which would bring in an enormous quantity of cold air at the entrance or departure of every customer. It is necessary first to ascend a flight of steps, sheltered by a projection, and to enter a vestibule, on which doors open to the right and left, and opposite to which is the staircase leading to the upper floor. The next story is in its general arrangement similar to that below, and on the other floors are dwelling-rooms, in which we must notice the importance given to the dining-room, at the expense of the drawing-room, and the arrangement of the bedchambers with two beds placed in an alcove, forming thus, in reality, a second room, lighted by a window, and which can be divided by a curtain from the apartment properly so called, which may thus be used as a sitting-room for the members of the family.[1]

A covered balcony extends in front of the windows of the drawing-room. We should rather have had it enclosed, for it is evident that though the veranda affords protection from the rain, it cannot preserve persons efficiently from wind and cold. Not

[1] For further details, see "Habitations modernes en Europe," par MM. Viollet-le-Duc et Félix Narjoux, architectes. Morel and Cie., édit. Paris.

a single room is provided with a chimney; they are all heated by the tall earthenware stoves which we have already mentioned, which give an equable, pleasant, and economical warmth, though

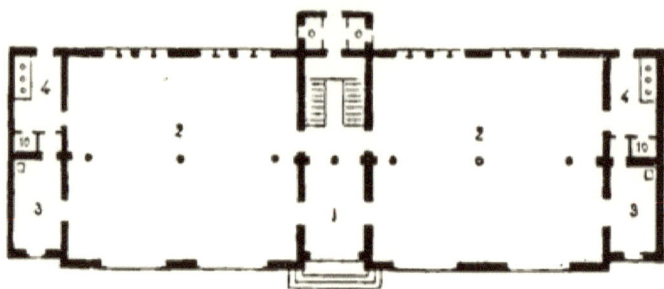

Fig. 149.—Plan of Ground-floor.

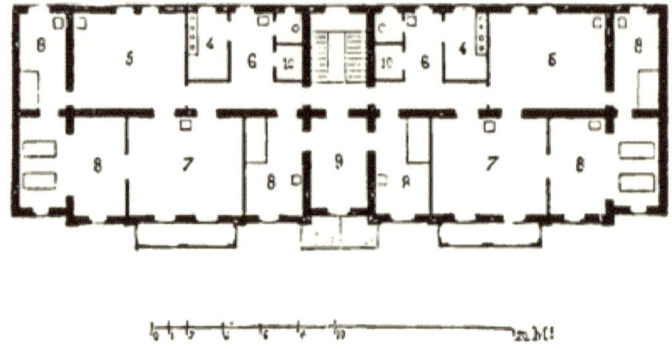

Fig. 150.—Plan of First Floor.

1. Vestibule.
2. Shops.
3. Sitting-rooms.
4. Kitchen for the ground-floor.
5. Dining-rooms.
6. Kitchens for the upper apartments.
7. Drawing-rooms.
8. Bedrooms.
9. Dressing-rooms.
10. Closets.

we should still prefer the sight of a good fire crackling on the hearth. These interiors are comfortable, and resemble our own; with, however, this difference, that the more important rooms, in point of size, are intended for family life and daily use, while the official portions, so to speak, are, on the contrary, arranged in a more unpretending manner. This is quite opposed to what we are accustomed to in France.

The proprietor of the house which we have just described is a

Fig. 151. — External and Internal View.

dealer in artistic porcelain; he directed our attention to the most remarkable specimens which he possessed, and gave us some interesting details on ceramic art, which has been for a long time one of the most important branches of German industry.

The products with which we were most struck were those of

the manufacture of Meisen in Saxony, founded in 1710, fifty years before our manufactory at Sèvres. Meisen more especially produces those well-known figures of the Rococo style; the new specimens are heavy and very pretentious, but the reproductions from ancient models in biscuit and in glazed ware are truly interesting. The favorite subjects are evidently shepherds and shepherdesses, allegorical scenes, and fanciful personages introduced by the sculptor Kandler about the year 1731. After these come well-executed copies of ancient services, candelabras, and mirror frames in foliage-work, either in intaglio, or projecting in a hundred fantastic forms. We must look upon these productions rather as artistic curiosities than works of art properly so called, for the shrinking arising from the heat to which they are subjected in the process of baking modifies so much the original outlines, that it cannot but distort the form given by the artist to his work; nevertheless, such a collection is very curious and rarely to be met with, and therefore well worthy of examination.

The royal manufactory of Berlin, founded in 1760,[1] produces articles of more general utility, which are remarkable for the excellence of the gilding which is "fired" in, and for the brilliancy and uniformity of the colors of the ground. The specimens are heavier, the forms are less elegant and graceful than those of the same kind manufactured at Limoges, to which they are also inferior in the quality of the "dough" and in perfection of workmanship.

There is not the same rage for old and new china among the Germans as in France; however, they copy our modern productions, but with no great success. They have taken the idea of their most remarkable works from their old models of stoves and vases,[2] with or without handles, found in the old castles of Bo-

---

[1] In order to assure the prosperity of his manufactory, Frederick the Great had recourse to a truly German expedient. The Jews could not, at that time, marry without his permission. This was granted only on condition that they should buy all the china for their new establishment at his manufactory.

[2] The Nuremberg vase at the Louvre bears the date of 1578.

hemia and the Rhine; fantastic types, often full of exaggerated details, — faults which are fortunately atoned for by beauty of form, and more especially by brilliancy of color.

When we leave the centre of the city, we find, in the more retired and quiet quarters, the mansions and private dwelling-houses of the rich merchants. These buildings are far from faultless. The façades are either vulgar or overloaded with ornaments, piled over each other without any reasonableness or necessity. But there are some exceptions; and occasionally we meet with houses like those represented in our sketches (Figs. 152 and 153), and before which we stand and admire. The front wall, as in Dutch houses, is separated from the public road by an area, on which open the windows of the basement story, occupied by the kitchen and its offices; on the ground-floor, raised by several steps, are placed, on the right, the dining and drawing rooms; on the left, a waiting-room and a consultation-room, for this house belongs to a physician. Behind is a small greenhouse; the dining and drawing rooms are divided by a movable partition, allowing these two apartments to be thrown into one on reception days, and when they meet to hear performances of chamber-music, — the chief amusement of German citizens. On the first floor are the bedrooms; the principal one has, in front, a glazed iron balcony, completely enclosed, so that the residents may enjoy the view of what passes on the outside, without any fear of the wind and rain. In the attics are the smaller apartments and the servants' rooms.

The façade (Fig. 154) is built of brick; the jambs of the windows on the ground-floor alone are of stone; a few terra-cotta ornaments are placed over the lintels of the windows on the first story. Under the cornice beneath the roof is a row of enamelled terra-cotta tiles, and also in the front of the balcony. Within, there are evident traces of comfort and of British habits, and furniture which reminds one of the houses of the West End, or of the towns in certain English counties.

Along the quays of the Gross Alster, and outside the city

bounds, there are a great number of large houses, which can neither be called mansions nor country-houses, but which partake of the characteristics of both these kinds of habitations. They are the villas of the rich merchants of Hamburg, who in fine weather come thither in the evening, for relaxation after the

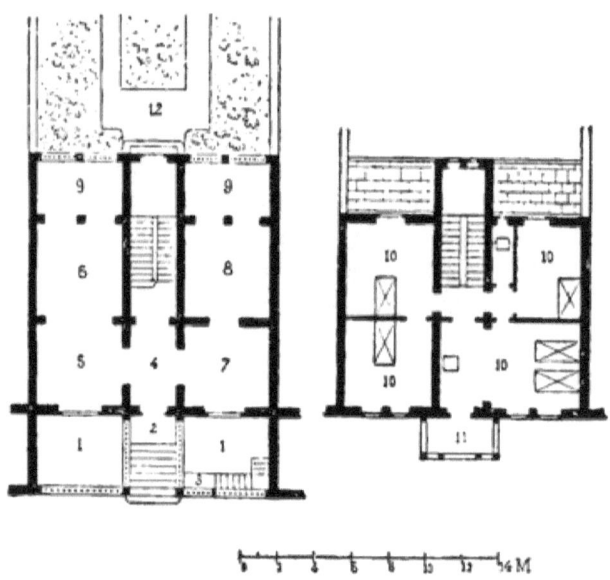

Fig. 152.—Ground-plan of Private House, Hamburg.

Fig. 153.—Plan of First Floor.

1. Area.
2. Principal entrance.
3. Servants' entrance.
4. Hall.
5. Dining-room.
6. Drawing-room.
7. Waiting-room.
8. Morning-room.
9. Winter-garden.
10. Bedrooms.

fatigues of the day's work. We have already entered into so many details respecting these dwelling-houses, that it will be useless to refer again to them. We must not forget that the modern villa bears no resemblance to that of the Romans. It is of recent creation, and is of a new type, which owes its origin

HAMBURG.

Fig. 154.—View of Exterior and Interior.

to our fondness for watering-places and for sea-bathing, and which has been further developed by the facility of communication, by means of which we can transport ourselves, in a few hours, from the place of our abode to the borders of a lake in the midst of mountains, favored with a delightful climate.

ALTONA.

A FUNERAL. — THE KINDERGARTEN. — ALTONA. — BLANKENESSE.

ONE morning, while we were waiting for the departure of the omnibus to Altona, we heard suddenly, in a side street, loud cries of mourning and lamentation; then, at the same moment, we saw a strange procession, which we should certainly have taken for some carnival masquerade, if we had not seen, raised above the crowd, a coffin covered with a long pall, the folds of which concealed the bearers, and swept along the ground. It was a funeral, but the most fantastic that could be imagined. Instead of relatives and friends in tears, those who followed the bier were muffled up in doublet and hose, with swords by their sides, wearing powdered wigs, carrying under the arm a hat with feathers, and on one shoulder a small dress-cloak. These people were hired mourners, and their lamentations were proportionate to the generosity of the families for whom they served as substitutes, when it was necessary to carry one of their relatives to the grave. Their costume and their grief depend on the liberality of the survivors; a silk or velvet robe corresponds with profound sobs and almost inarticulate cries, while a simple cloth garment demands but a few moderate tears.

When the procession had passed, the omnibus resumed its route. It was a lofty and wide American omnibus, and proceeded very rapidly. Our fellow-passengers were principally composed of cooks going to market, or on their return, dressed for the occasion, according to the custom of the country, in their best attire, and concealing under a fold of their shawl the copper vessel in which they carried provisions for the household.

At the end of a few minutes we were opposite to the ancient gate of Altona, on the front of which is the benevolent inscription, *Nobis bene, Nemini male;* and soon after we entered the town, which till lately was the second city in Denmark.

The object of our trip to Altona was to see the Kindergarten (children-garden), which we had been strongly recommended to visit.

The Kindergarten resembles in many respects our orphan asylums. These establishments receive children from two to six years old, at which latter age education becomes obligatory. The resemblance which exists between a plant and a child, and the care necessary for both, form the basis of the principle which lies at the foundation of all these establishments, and gave rise to the name "children-garden," that is to say, the place where their understanding and their affections are cultivated. The premises are large, healthy, and well ventilated. There is a meadow before the entrance, serving as a place for recreation; a schoolroom, and a courtyard planted with trees. One hundred and twenty boys and girls are assembled, the former on the right hand and the others on the left, under the superintendence of a governess, assisted by a certain number of young girls from twelve to fifteen years of age, allowing one to about ten children. The garden is opened at nine o'clock. The children come, after having taken their first breakfast at their own homes; they are examined, washed, and made tidy, and are then arranged before tables, on which they find games of all kinds, — little wooden cubes for building houses, leaden soldiers to be drawn up in battle array, tracings of geometrical figures to be filled in with colors, etc., etc. They are incited by emulation to do better than those around them; their fingers and eyes thus acquire unconsciously a certain amount of skill. After an hour of this occupation, they go out into the meadow and *play at soldiers*, for the German must accustom himself early to the part which he must act during the whole of his life. They there perform many gymnastic exercises, such as stretching out their arms and raising their legs at the word of command. They then go into the garden, and turn over the ground with their spades, or load their wheelbarrows with sand.

They are taught neither to read nor to write; their minds are simply prepared for the lessons which will afterwards be given to them. This system, founded on a just idea and a true principle, gives results the advantages of which have been fully proved by German statistics.

It is said that schoolmasters can recognize at once such of their pupils as have been trained in the Kindergarten. The aptitude which they display, their intelligence, and the free use of their limbs are much more developed than in other children, and they are more readily inclined to follow the directions that are given to them.

Some of these establishments are free, and intended for the children of the lower classes; in others, on the contrary, a greater or less payment is required. But all are managed on the same rules and on similar principles.

Altona is within a pleasant walk. The principal street, the Palmaille, planted with lime-trees along its whole extent, presents a very animated scene; the other streets are quiet, and much more retired than those of Hamburg. The houses stand in the midst of gardens and pleasant groves. Cafés, hotels, and taverns abound; for Altona is on festival days the resort of the Hamburg population, who find there, within their reach, all the elements of pleasure and enjoyment adapted to their tastes and dispositions.

On Sundays, in fine weather, Altona is full of excitement. Dances in the open air, café concerts, and taverns are frequented by crowds of visitors, principally workmen, sailors, and soldiers. Female servants from Hamburg, with their arms bare as far as the shoulders, and a square of lace over the head, meet with the village girls of the neighborhood, and amuse themselves with a freedom of manners of which the public balls of Paris, even of the most advanced type, cannot give the remotest idea. "It is their simplicity," we are always told. Call it simplicity if you will, but our corruption — and there is no doubt of its existence — is a hundred-fold more reserved and less revolting.

The citizens go to Blankenesse, rather farther off than Altona, to seek for rest and pleasure on Sundays. Blankenesse is a pretty little town, or rather a village, on the right bank of the Elbe, situated in a meadow lying at the foot of an eminence, — a refreshing place with abundance of flowers, — and is chosen by German Platonic lovers for their sentimental walks. You may meet them two and two, hand in hand, forming grotesque groups as they saunter along the road. The dreamy lover, with his lustreless light hair curling round his neck, gazes languishingly at his companion decked out in ridiculous and pretentious finery, and with her eyes ornamented with spectacles. They talk but little and think less, but exchange interminable kisses, while they dream of philosophy and ethereal poetry.

HELIGOLAND.

A MORE agreeable excursion than the preceding, full of strange and unexpected incidents, is the voyage from Hamburg to Heligoland. We embark at Hamburg, run down the Elbe as far as Cuxhaven, and then cross the arm of the sea which divides Heligoland from the mainland.

What a pleasant voyage, and what delightful scenes! How refreshing after the works of man! Since we left Dordrecht we have seen nothing but houses and public buildings, which we have been compelled constantly to examine, discuss, and compare. We feel happy as we recline peacefully on the deck of the vessel, looking at the blue sky, watching the innumerable boats which pass and repass around us, or listening to the noise of the water which gently ripples against our prow. We congratulate ourselves that to-day, at least, we have not to draw the plan of a building, to sketch a house, or to study the "logical and artistic employment of building materials."

When Blankenesse has been passed, the river begins rapidly to widen. The two banks differ in appearance: the left is flat and monotonous; the right is more varied, and shows a succession of hillocks, the summit of each of which is surmounted by a country-house. Buoys, placed in the middle of the river, show the channel traced through the shallows and sand-banks. The weather is fine, and the water so limpid that its various tints allow us to distinguish the dangerous passes. Occasionally the channel grows more and more narrow; there are but two fathoms of water, and at the stern of the ship we can see the screw cutting through the thick bank of sand, so as to trouble the water, and send up large bubbles to the surface.

At Cuxhaven some passengers land, and others are taken on board. All the Germans take advantage of this change to get the best places, and we caused great astonishment by giving up our seat to a woman who was standing.

When once the bar of the Elbe has been passed, the greenish tint of the sea-water makes the river-water which rolls by in enormous masses appear yellow. We pass near the island of Newerk, which can be reached on foot at low water, and notice the light-ship, whose fires, lighted every night, point out the shoals along the coast. This ship is moored by an iron chain fixed to an anchor weighing nearly $3\frac{1}{2}$ tons. The length of the chain allows the vessel to yield gradually to the force of the sea; it is rapidly raised by the waves, but, at the moment when it seems about to be carried away, the chain checks it, giving it oscillating movements of extraordinary violence. Its rolling motion is intolerable when the wind blows in a direction opposed to the river current. It strikes the vessel on her beam, and lays her over on her beam-ends without a moment's intermission. The fatigue undergone by the crew is so great, that the strongest sailors cannot occupy, for any length of time, this post, which requires as much courage as devotion to their duties. The tide is going down, and vessels are at anchor at the mouth of the Elbe, waiting for a favorable opportunity of entering the river; but we pass on, and continue our voyage without inconvenience. We had a quiet passage, for the North Sea was propitious. For a short time we lost sight of land — just long enough to feel the curious impression always made on one in the open sea, to see one's self the centre of an immense circle, with the sea bounded as it were by a vast coif, stretching on all sides to the horizon. How powerful man feels himself when brought face to face with that immensity which he is able to control, in the midst of that solitude through which, with so much certainty, he ploughs his way!

The sun was already beginning to descend; but, before it disappeared, it tinged with rays of fire the clouds in the west, and displayed near the horizon distinct zones intensely colored, from the deepest red to the faintest opal. They were so harmoniously blended, that it was impossible to say where one ended, and the other commenced — when suddenly there appeared before us, emerging from the waters, and clearly defined against a splendid background, a point, at first scarcely perceptible, which soon assumed the appearance of an enormous rock, and then of a black compact mass, with sharp crevices and abrupt angles, showing here and there red and white spots formed by houses. This was Heligoland.

Shortly afterwards we landed at the foot of a flag-staff bearing at the top the proud standard which displays on its broad folds the British lion, for Heligoland is one of the English possessions.

In 1807, at the time of the blockade of the European ports, the English established there a depot for contraband goods; then, considering that what was worth while to take was also valuable to keep, they remained masters of this small island, situated at an equal distance from the mouths of the Weser and the Elbe, and which, if it does not command the entrance to those two rivers, would, more especially with the aid of powerful modern artillery, greatly annoy an enemy's fleet either entering or quitting the ports of Bremen and Hamburg. The English government is not, however, a hard master. Its subjects at Heligoland pay no imperial taxes, and are exempt from military service; they live on the produce of their fisheries, and especially on the income derived from the many tourists and sea-bathers who, during the summer, come and live there, to bathe in the waves, which are said to be more powerful than in any other part of Europe.

Heligoland is a triangular rock (Fig. 155), in the midst of the waters, from which it is separated by rocky cliffs nearly 200 feet in perpendicular height. A portion of the shore slopes down, so as to form a narrow tract of sand called the Unterland, the lower land, while the upper part is named the Oberland, the high district. The baths and places of public resort are in the Unterland. There is a finer view from the houses in the Oberland; but it is necessary, every time that you wish to reach the sea, to descend 184 very steep steps, and, what is far worse, to reascend them when you return home.

The great charm of this little island is that one can enjoy there a calm and quiet life, and breathe a pure and bracing air. You can take pleasant walks by the seaside, which are never

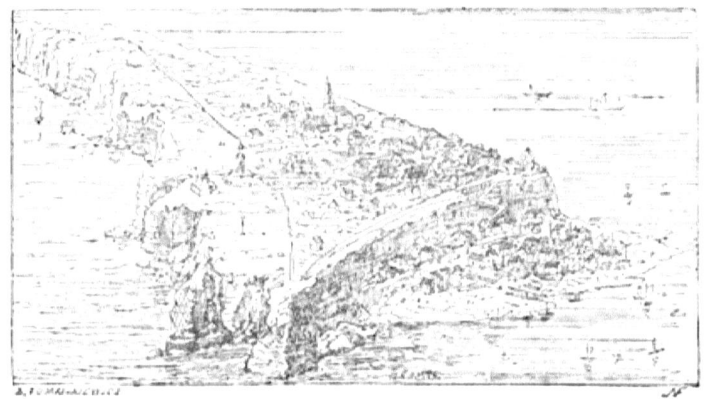

Fig. 155. — View of Heligoland.

long enough to be fatiguing, and can make delightful sea-excursions all around.

The inhabitants have manners and customs peculiar to themselves, and have preserved their original costume. They live happily and quietly, far from the social and political movements which disturb modern society, and strangers to all the passions and interests by which we are governed. When once the bathing-season is over, communication with the mainland is so infrequent and difficult, that it can be effected only at irregular and distant periods.

The national language is Frieslandic, the official language

German, and, during the bathing-season, much English and Swedish are spoken. The habitual visitors of Heligoland are, in fact, Germans, English, and more especially Danes or Swedes, who come thither to enjoy the sea-bathing of the *South*.

We did not go to Heligoland to examine buildings and to trouble ourselves with architecture; nothing was further from our intention; and yet we must describe our lodging, a bathing establishment which, on account of the necessity imposed by its required southern aspect, fulfils in an original manner the most complicated conditions which an architect could be required to satisfy.

It may easily be understood with what violence the winds from every point of the compass blow on this unsheltered rock in the midst of the ocean. The westerly winds especially are very furious; the north-wind is excessively cold; and that from the east, if it is less keen, blows more frequently, even in the fine season; the southern aspect alone is agreeable, and is always preferred, for the sea-breeze moderates the heat of summer.

The proprietor of this bathing establishment required his architect to plan a building capable of containing from twenty-five to thirty bedrooms for visitors, with the usual apartments, dining and drawing rooms, kitchens, offices, etc. It was to be finished in a comfortable but simple manner, and without any complicated decorations and costly accessories — more especially as they are quite unknown in the island. There was one indispensable condition, that all the bedrooms should have a southern aspect, and receive light and air from that quarter only. The building itself was to consist of only the ground-floor and one upper story.

The first idea which strikes one, in order to comply with these demands, is to erect a simple building, with walls of moderate thickness, presenting in one line all the rooms required; but, first, it would be difficult for the servants to attend to the wants of visitors in a house of this description, and a greater number

HELIGOLAND.

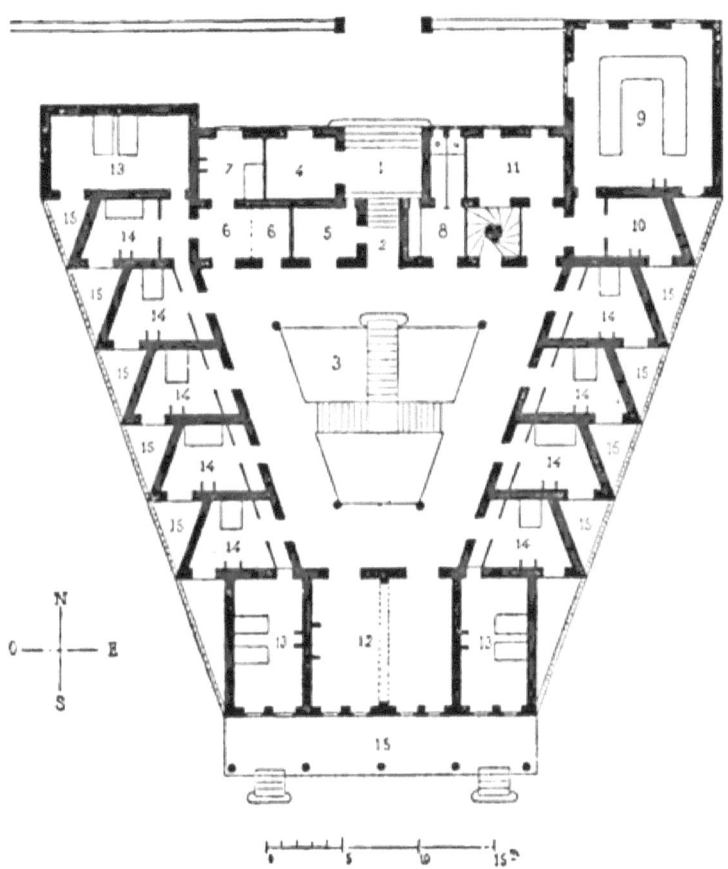

Fig. 156.—Ground-plan of Bathing Establishment at Heligoland.

1. Porch.
2. Vestibule.
3. Hall.
4. Bar-room.
5. Porter's lodge.
6. Office.
7. Director's room.
8. Washing-room and closets.
9. Dining-room.
10. Small drawing-room.
11. Domestic offices.
12. Drawing-room.
13. Chambers with two beds.
14. "   "   one bed.
15. Covered balconies.

must be employed; and then a plot of ground with a frontage of at least eighty-seven yards would be required, and the land at his disposal was not of half those dimensions.

The architect, who is said to have been an Englishman, solved the problem in a manner which it would be difficult to explain without the assistance of the accompanying sketch of the ground-plan (Fig. 156). We do not hesitate to say that this combination is ingenious, and though we should not recommend its adoption by a pupil of the École des Beaux Arts if he wished to be successful in a competition, he might afterwards make use of it in the exercise of his profession. There is no covered entrance for carriages, since they are not used in the island. Under the porch is the entrance to the bar-room, where liquors and spirits are sold, and partaken of by customers while standing there. After this comes the porter's lodge; opposite are the washing-room and closets; then the entrance to the large vestibule, a kind of hall with a glass roof (Fig. 157), and in the centre rises the principal staircase. A projecting part of the rocks which run along the coast shelters from the north-winds the buildings at the extremity, which are only domestic offices and dining-rooms. The bedrooms occupy the two side wings; the sloping direction of the walls gives to all the windows a southern aspect and a view of the sea. In front of each of these rooms is a separate triangular balcony, useful and pleasant during fine weather. The wind may thus blow from three points of the compass, without being felt by the inhabitants of these apartments, which are thoroughly sheltered from the north, the east, and the west.

In the basement story are the kitchens and offices. On the first floor there is nearly the same arrangement as on the ground-floor, only, instead of drawing and dining rooms, there are bedchambers; and above the domestic offices are the linen-rooms, bathrooms, servants' bedrooms, etc. The covered gallery, which forms, on the ground-floor, an annex to the drawing-room, and opens on a garden from which you can go down to the sea-shore, forms also

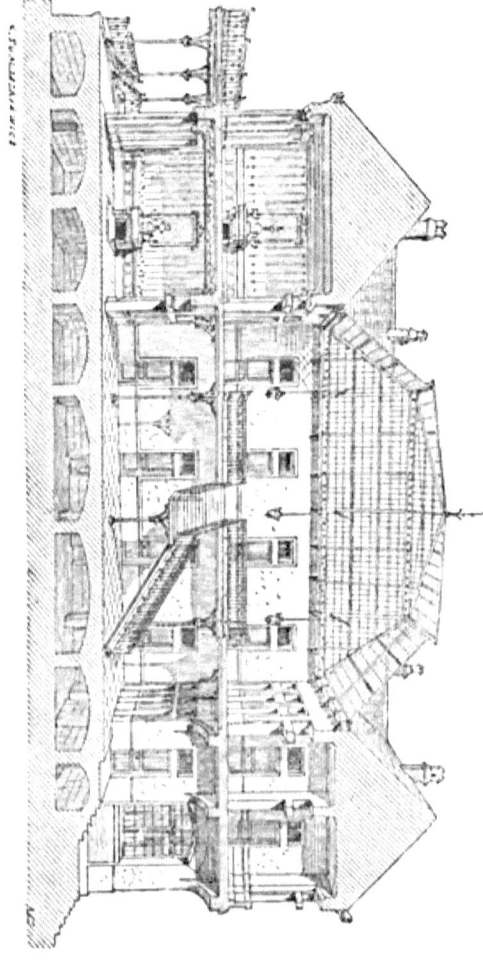

Fig. 157.—Bathing Establishment, Heligoland (Section and View of Interior).

a balcony for the upper rooms, and during the summer it is covered with an awning.

The building is constructed of bricks and iron. The architect does not seem to have thought of ornamenting the fronts in the slightest degree (Fig. 158); his only study and care was to arrange the interior conveniently. The hall, and the staircase which it contains, look rather grand; the rooms appear small, but each piece of furniture has its allotted space. The simplicity of the plan adopted renders communication easy between the different parts of the building. The walls are thick enough to defy the rigor of the climate, so that, though it might be possible to find fault with the problem submitted to the architect, we can certainly find none with the manner in which it has been solved.

We must also remark that this establishment — although primarily intended for the use of those who come for sea-bathing during the summer — is occupied, during the winter, by an increasing number of tourists, especially English, who are fond of deep-sea fishing, and who come and reside on this rock to satisfy this taste, — rich, idle, blasés people, ready to bear any privation, and to brave the dangers of a storm, in the hope of feeling a new sensation; but still willing, on their return, to find in their lodgings the resources of a refined civilization, and the means of satisfying their luxurious, self-indulgent, expensive habits. They can either shut themselves up in their rooms, or enjoy each other's society in the drawing-room. The hall serves as a promenade during rainy or snowy days; and, far removed from those exciting scenes in which their lives are usually spent, each one can indulge in occupations suited to his disposition, and adapted to the degree of cultivation of his mind.

Heligoland offers neither the pleasures nor the amusements of our Norman watering-places. This dull, dreary spot does not appeal to the imagination of every one. In order to enjoy its seductive charms, we must, above all, thoroughly love the sea, and not fear the monotony of an existence free from unforeseen changes. Every morning, at dawn of day, the professed fishermen and the courageous English girls embark and stand out to sea. The bathers stroll down to one of the two strips of coast, and then, beneath the shelter of a rock, watch the tide as it rushes up and washes the foot of the cliffs. In certain parts these are red, and communicate their color to the surrounding water; you might imagine it to be a sea of blood. Then, as the day wears on, they climb to the signal-post, count the sails within sight, follow with the eye the flight of the sea-gulls, whose wings lightly glance on the crest of a wave, or are lost in the mists of the horizon. Sometimes a sudden breeze springs up, sweeps along the sky, and brings on a storm, and every one must hasten to seek shelter. Three times a week, the steamboat from Hamburg or Bremen brings news from the mainland; then the natural disposition for excitement prevails; each one rushes to the journals, and devours the news which they contain, those of France and of Paris more especially, and yet, — a fact which filled us with astonishment, — though among all these people there is not a single Frenchman, there are many readers of the "Figaro."

In the evening they all return to the sea-shore. The phosphorescence of the water is so great, that when the wind raises the waves ever so slightly, and dashes them against the rocks, every drop of water looks like a luminous aigrette, which is reflected on all sides on the surface of the waves. The visitors linger long to enjoy this curious sight, and then every one returns home, prepared to recommence on the morrow the occupations of the previous day.

This calm, monotonous existence has a great effect on certain organizations, on minds fatigued and worn by the struggles of life. There is still to be seen a small house, formerly inhabited by one who had been conquered in the great battle of modern society. He landed on this rock, one day, filled with disgust, and dead to all hope; at least, he thought so. He lived there for some time, calm and tranquil in appearance, thinking of the

Fig. 153.—Bathing Establishment, Heligoland.

past, lost in this deep solitude in which he found repose, in front of this stormy sea, and in the midst of this barren and uninviting land. At last the echoes of some startling event in Europe penetrated even to this spot; the spark was rekindled under the ashes, the old man reappeared, and, rushing afresh into the terrible *mêlée*, made the world resound with his name, and perished at last in a fearful catastrophe.

We were obliged, however, at last to bid farewell to the little island. A vessel which neared the coast of Sleswig, and put into Heligoland for a pilot, took us on board, and carried us to Hussum, a port on the North Sea, the starting-point for the excursion which we desired to make to the scene of the war of the Duchies.

THE WAR OF THE DUCHIES.

PRELIMINARY REMARKS. — THE AUSTRO-PRUSSIAN ARMY. — THE DANISH ARMY. — THE LINES OF DANEVIRKE. — TAKING OF MISSUNDE. — FORTIFICATIONS OF DUPPEL. — TAKING OF DUPPEL. — THE ISLAND OF ALSEN. — CONDITIONS OF PEACE. — THE PRUSSIANS DURING THE CAMPAIGN.

PRUSSIA had, for a long time, cast her eyes on the two duchies of Sleswig and Holstein; she found that they were necessary for the creation and development of her maritime power. In the course of the year 1863 — thinking that circumstances were favorable for the execution of her plan, and under the pretext that Denmark kept troops in Holstein — they pretended that the Danish government wished to annex this duchy. In order to avoid any serious motive for a conflict, Denmark withdrew her troops. Prussia then declared herself the champion of the Duke of Augustenburg, a pretender to the sovereignty of the duchy; and, having taken this first step, she hurried on the necessary preparations, so as to be able to overwhelm her neighbor when the proper moment arrived.

This kind of attempt was then new, and gave promise of what took place afterwards. One of the causes of the power of Prussia is her profound contempt for the trivial considerations of good faith and sincerity. To pretend that feeble Denmark thought of attacking the rights of the powerful Confederation was a bitter mockery; no one could be deceived by it, or feel any doubt of the result of the conflict. Europe did not then suspect the ambitious designs of M. de Bismarck, which, first revealed in 1864, were, six years later, to establish the empire of Germany.

When we look into history, we are utterly astonished that certain events could have taken place without having been foreseen. How is it,—men are always repeating, since 1871, in the reviews and daily journals and in conversation,—how is it that Europe did not, in 1864, anticipate the result of her indifference, and why did she not come to the help of Denmark? How many evils might have been avoided by such intervention! Sadowa would not have existed. The campaign of 1870 would not have taken place, and Prussia would not have been the terrible power which we now see her to be.

But in 1864 France, the great protector of right and justice, yielding to a deplorable policy, remained neutral. The Austrians, to maintain their influence and popularity in Germany, courageously allied themselves with the strongest side. England still felt ill-will against Denmark, on account of the treatment to which the unfortunate Maria Caroline had been subjected. Russia wished to see the issue of events before she took any part, and Sweden was not sorry for the humiliation which she foresaw would befall the neighbor that had so frequently been her conqueror. Denmark therefore found herself alone at the opening of the campaign; but still she did not hesitate to prepare for the conflict, without any boasting, but, at the same time, without despondency. The Danes remembered that they had already beaten the Prussians in 1848; and, although M. de Bismarck boasted that he would soon "make them feel the power of the Prussian arms," they did not despair of the result of the campaign which was about to open. But, alas! they still depended on the help of France, and hoped that, at the last moment, Sweden would remember their common origin. Diplomatists were excited, and rushed hither and thither, assuring the Danish ambassadors of their officious sympathy; but, before they decided officially, they waited to see which side would be successful. We know by experience this situation, and the value of promises of this nature.

The concentration of the Austro-Prussian troops was effected at the end of January, 1864. They were assembled in Holstein, under the command of the Prussian Field-Marshal Wrangel. The reason given for taking up arms was to carry out the wishes of the inhabitants of Holstein to be governed by the Duke of Augustenburg. The allied army had been divided into two corps; the Prussians, to the number of 42,000 men, with 110 guns, formed the right wing, commanded by the Prince Royal, Frederick Charles. The Austrians, who numbered 32,500 men, with 48 guns, formed the left wing, commanded by Field-Marshal De Goblenz; so that there were in round numbers, exclusive of the sick and non-combatants, 158 guns and 60,000 men, prepared long before, perfectly equipped, and well trained.[1]

The Danish army was far from being in such a good condition. The men who composed it were mostly mobilized corps, for the effective force in time of peace is very small, only about 8,000 men. The troops were not fully officered, and the artillery was insufficient; 35,000 soldiers were assembled with great difficulty in Sleswig, under the command of General De Meza. Denmark distrusted her old enemy, Germany.[2] She remembered the war of 1848, and, to guard against an attack, she had long before begun a line of defence, the Danevirke, established at the place where the Fjord of Schley encroaches on the shore, in front of Hussum, and considerably reduces the width of the peninsula. The extreme points of this line were Missunde, on the Baltic, and Friedrickstadt, on the North Sea; the intermediate space was broken by marshy lands, by enclosed portions, and by water-courses, the river Eyder amongst others. This line would therefore have presented a serious obstacle to the march of the allied armies. Unfortunately, the works necessary to complete its defence had not been kept in good order. They were repaired as well as possible, and finished in haste, but in an insufficient manner, and pieces of artillery were want-

[1] "Annuaire des deux mondes." Paris, 1864; Dagbladet, Copenhagen, 1864.
[2] According to an old Danish proverb, Denmark could not fail of being happy if there were no Germany.

ing for the fortifications. The Danish army determined to await the attack behind the Danevirke.

The Prussians passed the Eyder. On February 5 they were before Missunde, and opened fire immediately; the Danes replied but feebly. The Prussian artillery destroyed Missunde without injuring the intrenchments. There was a thick fog. The Prussians advanced, but, being no longer supported by their batteries, the same thing happened as is usual under such circumstances; they gave way and retreated before the Danes. The exploits of this day were confined to the destruction of the village of Missunde; and yet, at the close of the skirmish, Prince Frederick Charles, with that burlesque German pomposity which nothing can equal, ventured to say to his soldiers, parodying the celebrated proclamation of Napoleon I.: "When you return to your homes, you will only have to say, I was at Missunde! and every one will cry, This is a brave man." As to the Austrians, they had advanced on their side, and were at the other extremity of the Danevirke, near Friedrickstadt.

Still the situation of the Danes did not improve. At war even with the elements, they had to endure the severity of such a winter that the Fjord of Schley, in which they trusted as opposing an impassable barrier to the enemy, had to be crossed and recrossed incessantly by a steamboat, to break the ice, and to keep a free passage in the midst of the water.

When affairs were in this state, General Meza, finding himself insecure behind the Danevirke lines, and fearing another attack on his intrenchments, which he knew to be insufficient to protect him, decided on retiring, that he might not compromise, without any chance of success, the safety of an army on which the hopes of his country depended.

His retreat was effected in good order, but the indignation excited in Denmark by this movement was immense. They demanded that the commander-in-chief should be superseded, and they shouted treason, as a nation unfortunately always does when success does not crown their efforts and desires.

Distrust began to show itself in the ranks of the army, and it was under a bad impression that the regiments were re-formed before the island of Alsen, behind the fortifications of Duppel in Sleswig, and Fredericia in Jutland.

They had depended on the line of Danevirke to keep the Austro-Prussians in check till the time necessary for finishing the defences of Duppel. Thus nothing was completed, and the

Fig. 159. — Blindage in the Lines of Danevirke.

sudden retreat of the army disturbed and threw into disorder the plans that were to be adopted. Notwithstanding this, the willingness, courage, and zeal of all, both officers and soldiers, were so great, that the necessary defences were soon, if not entirely finished, at least in a condition to be utilized. The cold was too severe to allow works in masonry to be carried on, but they supplied their place by erections in timber, bound together by iron bolts and wire, and covered with earth; but this earth itself was so hardened by the frost, that it was tedious and difficult to work in it.

We give here sketches of two works of this kind, from models preserved in the museum at Copenhagen. The first (Fig. 159) is a blindage, intended to serve as a covered way between two trenches. The system adopted is composed of a framework covered with a mass of earth, by which means its height may be lessened. The balks, which form the supports, are double. They are more widely separated at their lower extremities, and rest on bearers let into the ground. Cross-pieces, tongued, and securely tied, and iron bands, support and strengthen them half-way up. At the upper end is a cross-beam, on which rest the balks of timber, serving as a roof. These timbers and the sides are covered with earth. The trusses are placed at a distance of 1 foot 8 inches, 2 feet 3 inches, or 3 feet 3 inches from each other, according to the weight which they have to support.

The blindage just described, which was constructed at the commencement of the war, before the Danes had realized the force of rifled cannon, had not been covered with a sufficient thickness of earth to prevent, for any length of time, the chance of rupture or of sudden accident; but in the next example (Fig. 160) the Danes had profited by experience. The supports are double. Two vertical poles, fixed in soles buried in the ground, support two cross-beams inclined at an angle of 45°, which are bound together by a horizontal beam, meeting two other cross-pieces resting on the ends of the vertical poles, and fixed obliquely, so as to unite and cross at the upper ends. These double trusses, placed at a distance of two feet from each other, are firmly bound together by bolts and iron wire. At the sides and on the top are laid balks of timber, forming the walls and the roof. An enormous mass of earth, of from 13 to 17 feet in thickness, is heaped upon the whole. Blindages of this kind have been proved by experience to be possessed of an elastic force capable of resisting the shock of the most formidable projectiles of modern artillery.

In spite of the rigor of the season, the Danes labored without

Fig. 160.—Improved Blindage.

rest or cessation. The works at Düppel, which were necessary to be completed, comprised ten redoubts, eight enclosed and two open ones, disposed round an arc of a circle, and connected together by trenches and works, of which our sketches may give some idea. In front of the salients of the bastions 7, 8, and 9, on which it was supposed that the attacks of the enemy would be made, were outworks and obstacles intended to keep them in check. But we saw, in the siege of Paris, that the mode of attack adopted by the Prussians — by the use of artillery of long range — renders precautions of this kind almost useless. Within the first line of defence there was another, less strong, composed of bastions, covering a trench; the approach to which was defended by a glacis surmounted by pointed stakes and a fence of iron wire. The intention of this second defence was to protect the retreat of the army if routed. This precaution shows an unusual amount of foresight, for unfortunately before the battle people reckon too confidently on victory, and do not sufficiently provide against the possibility of defeat.

The artillery which defended all these works could not contend with the rifled cannon of the Prussian army, of the great range and force of which the Danes were utterly ignorant. When, therefore, they constructed their intrenchments, they did not think it necessary to make them of the necessary dimensions to resist the overwhelming effect of these new projectiles. We ought to make some excuse for them, since after the war of the Duchies, and the Austrian campaign, we did not know much more than in 1870.

In addition to the defensive works on land, the Danes had recourse to an ironclad monitor cruising along the coast, — a new warlike engine, which then for the first time took part in regular warfare in Europe.

The Danish troops, sheltered behind the works of Duppel, or intrenched in the island of Alsen, re-formed their regiments, and filled up the number of their officers; but their equipments and their supplies of provisions had suffered considerable loss during the first part of the war and the retreats that had followed. The soldiers were worn out by their labors in completing the defensive works, digging the trenches, increasing the thickness of the slopes, traverses, and covered ways, forming casements for the guns, and making sorties upon the Prussians, who themselves do not follow up their guns, and never seek to take an obstacle by assault, but destroy it with their artillery before the soldiers approach it. These fatigues caused much sickness. The weather became rainy. When they retired from the trenches, with their clothes saturated with water, and had to run to the advanced posts, they suffered from the sudden cold, and, notwithstanding the energy and the strong constitution of the men, many succumbed to it.

The Danish uniform consisted of pantaloons of blue cloth concealed by large and strong boots, a short vest, and over this a long brown capote; the knapsack unrolled so as to form a kind of skin, which, when spread on the ground, made a dry and healthy bed. Besides this knapsack, each soldier carried a wallet of white cloth, containing provisions for the day; some fresh beef and salt pork, without vegetables, some barley-bread, brandy, and coffee. The muskets were of old-fashioned construction, rather heavy, and consequently very inferior to the rapidly firing guns of the Prussians.

We see, from this, the inferiority of the Danish army in comparison with that of the Austro-Prussians, and yet the latter did not decide on making an attack upon them. The Austrians remained in observation before Fredericia, having thus invaded Jutland, which gave a new aspect to the campaign, and turned it into a war of conquest.

The Austrians had also to contend against a grave complication which arose among the regiments of different nationalities of which their army was composed. The Hungarian contingents had revolted, being ashamed of aiding their conqueror to subdue a nation struggling to preserve its autonomy. It was feared lest this spirit of revolt should affect the Italians, and then the Poles of the duchy of Posen. A terrible act of repression stilled the mutiny in the bud. It is said that 300 Hungarian officers and soldiers were executed, but the hopes excited by this event in Denmark soon vanished.

The siege of Duppel was regularly carried on. The Prussians fortified themselves in their positions, to prepare for a retreat in case of a defeat. They remembered that in 1848 they had been beaten and repulsed before this very city by the same General Meza, and were unwilling to venture on a decisive blow without a certainty of success. For this purpose they occupied the heights all around, placed masked batteries behind copses of trees and slight mounds of earth, not to be removed till the last moment. This is a plan familiar to them, and the bravery of the Danes formed a striking contrast with this prudence. One instance of this may be given. The correct aim of the Prussian rifles astonished the Danes. It was necessary to ascertain the precision of their aim, in order to provide against it and protect themselves. For this purpose an officer ventured alone to a distance of about sixteen hundred or two thousand feet in an open space, thus serving as a mark for the balls of the enemy. He observed the discharge and noted the deviation of the ball, which at this distance was about a yard.

The bombardment of Duppel commenced on March 27. The Danes abandoned the town after having burnt it, and retired behind the fortifications, which up to this time had not greatly suffered.

On March 29 the Prussians attempted an assault, but were repulsed with loss. The soldiers, as soon as they found themselves within range of the enemy's projectiles, threw themselves flat on the ground, refusing to advance, in spite of the commands of their officers.[1] After this check, the Prussians did not quit their lines, leaving the artillery to do its work. In such contests as these, the valor of the soldiers counts for nothing. It was out of their power to approach the Prussian batteries; their strength rendered it impossible that any attempt of this kind should succeed, and surprises in such a contracted space were

---

[1] "Le Danemark," par Oscar Comettant.

impracticable. The Danes, whose guns could not reach the enemy's batteries, now only made use of them to repel an assault. As to the Prussian cannons, they were never silent. It had been hoped that they would spare Sunderborg, an unfortified town. This was a strange delusion, for the town was destroyed. On April 2 the bombardment was resumed with greater vigor. By the 14th the Danish intrenchments had already received 50,000 projectiles. The defensive works had been destroyed. The garrison, worn out by disease and privations of all kinds, diminished by their losses, which amounted to from 100 to 200 men per day, were exhausted, and were no longer in a condition to continue the struggle. The *psychological* moment seemed to have arrived; none of the hoped-for and expected reinforcements came, and yet the Prussians, fearing a reverse, dared not attempt the assault. The enemy, deprived of all their resources, weakened by months of privations and physical and moral sufferings, still appeared to them too formidable. They waited till the 17th, and, thinking that by this time the Danes could no longer even hold their guns, they recommenced the bombardment with extreme violence. In the course of thirty-six hours they threw 30,000 projectiles into the enemy's intrenchments, and then at last decided on forming the attacking columns. But even then — a thing which is scarcely credible — the Danes, whose strength and courage might have been thought to be utterly prostrated, roused themselves with fresh energy, instead of surrendering, and, though without hope and certain of defeat, they all fought like heroes. Out of 10,000 men who were engaged, 2,000 fell, 2,000 were made prisoners, and the rest crossed the Little Belt and retired to the island of Alsen, after having cut the bridges which connected the island with the mainland,[1] the extremities of which bridges were defended till the last moment by a body of brave men who sacrificed themselves for the common safety.

[1] This manœuvre was very skilfully executed, by means of gunners fastened by chains to the movable bridges. At a given signal these men set themselves in motion, dragging the bridges after them.

This was the last effort of the Danes. They attempted to fortify themselves in the island of Alsen, but they had lost all hope and all ardor. The soldiers, having no longer any confidence in success, saw traitors and spies everywhere, and the struggle was thenceforth continued only to sustain to the last the honor of the national flag.

The Prussians did not profit by the advantages gained. They dared not attack the island of Alsen, which the Danish fleet could still effectually protect, and perhaps retake if they were to gain possession of it. They preferred to extend their conquests, and a part of the allied army combined with the Austrians to take possession of Fredericia, which could not resist, but fell into their hands on April 28. Three days afterwards the Austrian fleet allowed itself to be beaten by that of the Danes off the coast of Heligoland, where it had been compelled to take shelter under cover of the English guns. But this success could have no influence over the issue of this disastrous campaign, the result of which was already considered desperate; therefore a suspension of arms was agreed upon on May 12.

The situation of the Danes was deplorable; the fourth part of their army had been destroyed; they had now only twenty rifled cannon left. On the other hand, the Austro-Prussians occupied Sleswig, Holstein, and a part of Jutland; their army of sixty thousand men lived at the expense of the conquered country. This is one of the laws of war, and we know well how conscientiously the Prussians carry it out.

A conference was held in London to arrange terms, but no result could be obtained before the end of the armistice. Hostilities were therefore resumed on May 26, and on the 28th the Prussians took the island of Alsen. This conquest was not difficult, since the Danes could no longer defend themselves; men, rations, and ammunition were wanting. They abandoned the island, and retired into the island of Funen, whither the Prussians did not pursue them. No more Danes remained on the mainland. The Germans completely occupied Jutland, and prepared to cross the Little Belt, to invade Funen; but on July 20 an armistice was signed. It was changed on August 1 into a final suspension of arms, and afterwards a treaty of peace was imposed upon Denmark.

The Duchies were to be annexed to the Confederation under certain conditions; the payment of that part of the Danish debt which referred to the Duchies was still to be paid by them. Prussia had the right to make a canal between the Baltic and North Seas, a condition of immense importance to them, since this canal would open a free communication with the ocean for their fleet, without compelling them to pass the Sound through the Danish and Swedish waters. As to the Duke of Augustenburg, whose pretensions to the sovereignty of the Duchies had served as a pretext for M. de Bismarck to commence hostilities, his name was not mentioned during the debate.

A year afterwards, a misunderstanding arose between the joint proprietors of the Duchies; Austria and Prussia declared war against each other, and came to blows.

The consequences of the annexation were deplorable for Sleswig. Though the inhabitants were greatly attached to Denmark, they saw themselves violently severed from it, and united with Germany, which they detested. The proceedings of the conquerors were also not calculated to gain the affection of the conquered people; the exactions and the enormous taxes so violently imposed were the prelude to vexations of all kinds. The simple and unsophisticated feelings of this courageous people were constantly hurt by the gross instincts and rough manners of their new masters; yet, notwithstanding the misery endured by the whole country, not a single inhabitant would take advantage of the aid sent from Berlin. Societies were formed to facilitate emigration *en masse* among the peasants who wished to quit the country, and meetings were held in the towns imploring the assistance of France. Unfortunately, France remained unmoved, keeping in its scabbard that sword which had so often protected the feeble and the oppressed, and which in our own times had defended Turkey and created Italy. Then silence fell on this great catastrophe, and Prussia had, unsuspected by the whole of Europe, taken the first step in her career of fortune. Might had overwhelmed right.

We will now finish this sketch with some details of the manner in which Prussia behaved during the war.

They almost entirely destroyed Sunderborg, an unfortified town, which was not exposed to the fire of the batteries directed against Duppel. In the island of Alsen, they burnt detached farms, destroyed Kjer, Ronhavis, and all the villages along the coast, merely for the satisfaction of doing mischief, and thus going back to the state of civilization and morals of many centuries ago, — a crime with which they have been openly reproached.

At each suspension of hostilities both sides made an exchange of dead. The uniforms of those sent back by the Prussians had been stripped of their buttons and lace; the officers had been deprived of their decorations; all their jewelry, money, and other valuables had disappeared, and their pockets were turned inside out.

Towards the end of the campaign the Danes stood on their ruined intrenchments, waiting for an invisible enemy who had hidden behind their cannons; in fact, it is a plan always adopted by the Prussians never to show themselves openly, or to give any signs of their presence. They hide themselves in a hole or behind a tree; you may be close upon them, and suspect that they are there, but you do not see them. There is never any fire in their camp, the smoke of which might betray them; they go forward, working slowly, without rest or intermission, till at last one day a "rideau" of turf is thrown down, an "épaulement" disappears during the night, and unmasks a new battery. All these precautions are fair in war; they show great prudence, and a perfect knowledge of the character of the German soldier, who could not stand against the impetuosity of the charge of a French regiment, but who could remain for hours together crouching at the bottom of a ditch. The instincts of bravery and chivalry, noble, delicate, and elevated sentiments, excite a smile in a German. They would never have said to the English at the siege of Fontenoy, "Gentlemen, pray fire first."

During the whole of this long and terrible campaign the energy and resolution of the Danes never failed for an instant; the patriotic feeling with which they were animated was so powerful that it caused them to do wonders; but they sought in vain to contend against an enemy whom they could not discover, but who from a distance thundered upon them with his terrible artillery. No reverses daunted them, but they marched against the enemy, raising their heads aloft in the midst of a shower of projectiles, while the explosion of a shell made the Prussians fall flat on their faces, with Prince Frederick Charles at their head, in the island of Alsen on April 27, 1864.

The Germans were armed with superior rifles and cannon; they were four to one in number, and in many cases they were beaten and suffered great losses when they were no longer protected by their batteries. But their rodomontades and their inordinate vanity exaggerated the slightest advantages gained, coolly changing defeats into splendid victories. One day three Danish officers and sixteen soldiers went to a small island near Alsen, and spiked two of the guns of a battery which, since the preceding evening, had annoyed the Danish force. This bold exploit so astonished the Germans, that the next day they took the credit of it to themselves.

The Danes bore with the most noble firmness the misfortunes which befell them. The soldiers, as well as their officers, had a high sense of their duty and their dignity; astonished to see the Prussians always well informed as to their plans and preparations, they supposed themselves to be surrounded by spies and traitors. Such is, unfortunately, the impression of every soldier when defeated; yet their discipline did not for an instant relax, and after their retreat into the island of Alsen, in the midst of the general disorder, an eyewitness[1] declares that he never saw a single drunken man.

It was not our intention, in thus referring to some of the events of the war of the Duchies, in which the Prussians commenced the series of their conquests, to have the puerile satisfaction of exciting the reader's feelings. We will no longer proceed to draw inferences which every one will doubtless do for himself; but it seemed necessary, when passing through the country which had been the theatre of this memorable struggle, to recall the remembrance of contemporary facts, which seem already to have happened long ago in comparison with those of which we have so lately been the victims.

It is not our business now to deal with political questions; nevertheless, it will not be out of place to show the similarity of the means employed by Prussia against her enemies in 1864, 1866, and 1870. The same plans preceded the declaration of war; it was always Prussia that was attacked, and that acted on the defensive.[2] Then, when war was declared, it was found that these people, taken unawares, were in an admirable state of preparation,—that their troops were concentrated, their soldiers trained, their arsenals full, their arms perfected; while their opponents had not a man or a piece of artillery to employ, and, during the time so valuable to them for making preliminary arrangements, they were compelled to fight without being able to find an ally or a supporter.

There is no doubt that this is excellent warfare. Perhaps it is better to see others use such means than to do so ourselves; at all events, the best way to lessen their influence in the future is to speak of them, and to make them known.

How is it that at a period like the present, when railways, steamboats, and telegraphs enable people to know so well and so rapidly what passes in other countries, we are so completely

---

[1] "Le Danemark," par Oscar Comettant.
[2] Prussia and Austria contained, in 1874, 70,000,000 inhabitants; Denmark only 1,600,000.

ignorant of what the Germans are doing, while they know so thoroughly all that happens amongst ourselves? The thing is easily to be understood. We never visit them, we do not read their books, and but seldom translate them; they are constantly in France, they read and make translations of all that we write. It is easy for us to follow their example, and, in doing so, we shall be more and more convinced of the advantages which we may derive from a thorough knowledge of the good qualities and faults of our adversaries, so as to be able to imitate the former and avoid the latter.

DENMARK.

DENMARK.

JUTLAND. — THE LITTLE BELT. — A FERRY-BOAT. — A FARM. — FUNEN. — THE GREAT BELT. — THE ISLAND OF ZEALAND.

"Since we have begun to go beyond our own frontiers and look around us, we have as yet no thorough knowledge of any country, except of England and Germany.[1] When we shall have gone a step farther, and visited Denmark, we shall be surprised to find that there are treasures amassed in a city to which we are accustomed to attribute but little influence, and learned men dispersed through a country which one of our journals lately called a land almost barbarous." — X. Marmier.

AS soon as we pass the new frontier which divides the empire of Germany from the kingdom of Denmark, the country changes its aspect; it is as flat as ever, but seems less dull and monotonous. The peat-bogs are intersected by large woods; animals are seen feeding in the meadows, tied to separate stakes at regular intervals, as in Holland. Here and there appears, like a colored dot in the midst of a gray or green ground, a red hut, a blue farm, and the picturesque costume of a peasant-girl, who, with her large eyes wide open, gazes placidly, from a distance, on the crest of smoke hovering over the passing train.

The costume of these peasant-girls is, however, that which especially attracts attention (Fig. 161). The head-dress is shaped like a Persian cap, tied by ribbons under the chin; they wear a short cloth cape, trimmed with colored embroidery or metal ornaments of various forms, sewed upon it. The sleeves

---

[1] M. Marmier perhaps goes too far when he asserts that we are thoroughly acquainted with England and Germany.

are narrow and short; the arm is left bare as far as the
elbow in summer, but in winter it is covered with long and
thick leather gloves; bracelets of metal or black velvet surround the wrist; the petticoat is made of thick brown or
deep red stuff; and the apron, made of silk or woollen material, is either red, blue, or green. The colors are rather gaudy,

Fig. 161. — A Peasant-Girl, Jutland.

but the pale light of the North harmonizes and softens, instead of exaggerating them, as under the brilliant sunshine
of the South.

On the right of the road appears the extremity of a harbor,
with green transparent waters; this is Fredericia, where we are
to embark in order to cross the Little Belt.

This passage is effected by means of a ferry-boat, which

THE LITTLE BELT.

conveys the train — a method of transport common enough in America, but still rare in Europe.[1]

The Little Belt is not 1¼ mile wide; yet this short passage is sometimes difficult, and even dangerous, during the prevalence of certain winds, on account of the currents, shallows, and reefs which obstruct the strait; so that large vessels avoid this

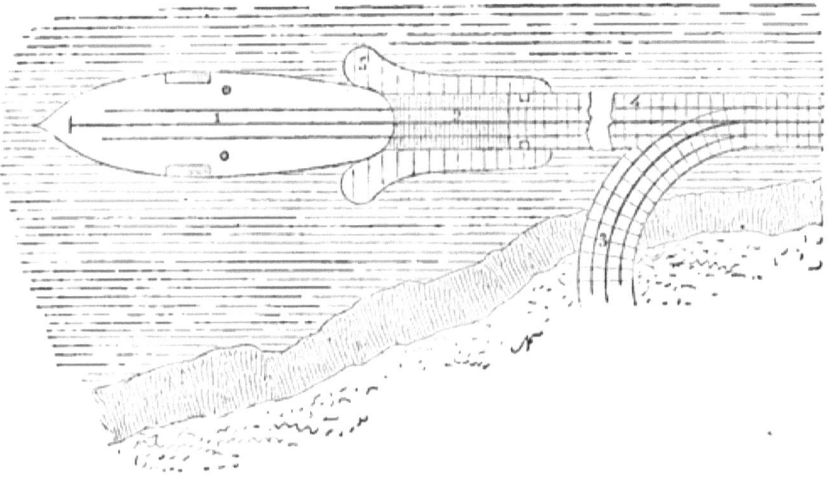

Fig. 162. — Plan of the Approaches of a Ferry on the Little Belt.

1. Railway ferry-boat.
2. Movable pontoon.
3. Rails for leaving the pontoon.
4. Rails for approach.
5. Pier.

passage, which is almost always effected by means of coasting-vessels and fishing-boats.

The landing and embarking of luggage formerly caused great waste of time, for so short a passage, and involved tedious and fatiguing labor; so that a considerable improvement was introduced by the Danish railway company, when they conveyed the

---

[1] We think that there is no railway ferry-boat in Europe, except on the Lake of Constance and at the Little Belt. It has been lately proposed to start one between Calais and Dover, on the system of Dupuy de Lôme.

carriages directly to the ferry-boat, which carries them to the opposite coast, where they are again placed on the rails,—a result which is obtained by a very simple contrivance.

The railway, which follows a direction almost at right angles to the sea, passes obliquely as it approaches the shore, so as to become parallel to it; then, advancing or backing, according to the direction in which the train arrives, it reaches the pier terminated by a movable pontoon, at the extremity of which the ferry is moored.

The Baltic, like the Mediterranean, is not subject to tides; the level of the pier and that of the deck of the vessel are, therefore, almost always the same. The difficulties which would arise from the rise and fall of the tides might easily be avoided by bringing the ferry-boat into an enclosed basin, in which the level of the water could without difficulty be regulated, so as to coincide, at first with that of the movable pontoon, and afterwards with that of the sea. When the two rails—that of the ferry, and that of the pontoon—are placed exactly in a corresponding direction, the carriages are shunted in by an engine, which does not enter the boat, but remains outside. The carriages thus placed on board, generally two or three in number, are sent forward in succession, one at a time, so as to allow the level of the movable pontoon to be adjusted according as the boat sinks more deeply after each fresh load. When once on board, the carriages, which are firmly secured, are left uncovered on the deck of the ferry-boat; the plan adopted in America, on the contrary, is to convey them in the covered part of the vessel.

These carriages are usually only goods-trucks or luggage-wagons. Those allotted to travellers are forwarded only when the sea is sufficiently calm; but in all cases passengers are permitted, when once on board, to leave the carriages and re-enter them as they please, and have every facility afforded them for walking on the deck, or remaining in the cabin during the passage. As the rails occupy the centre of the ferry-boat, the engine cannot be fixed in its usual place, and it has been found necessary in its construction to have recourse to a system of horizontal cylinders, arranged in such a peculiar manner that we cannot intelligibly give a description of them.

This system of making the passage by sea, without unloading and reloading the carriages, offers great advantages; but it is often impracticable in rough weather, the necessary manœuvres, both at the departure and arrival, being then very difficult. On the other hand, in spite of the opinion given by a man of un-

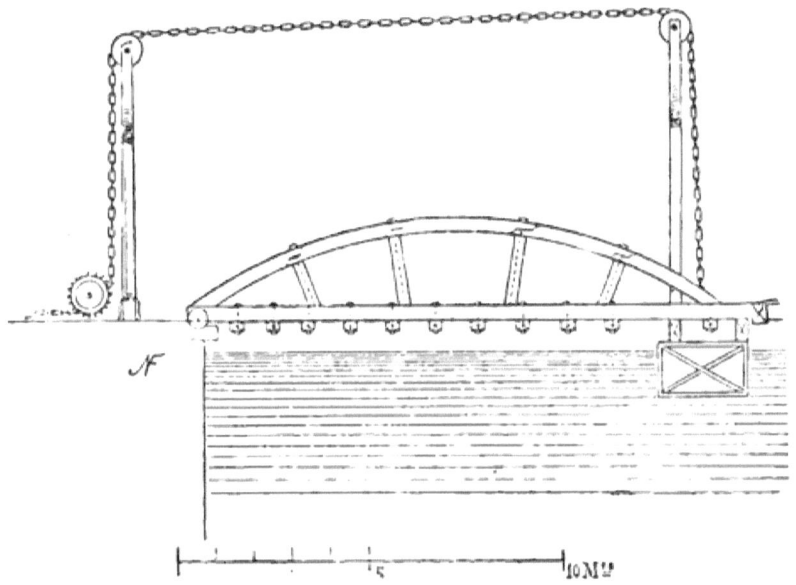

Fig. 163.—Section of the Movable Pontoon.

questionable ability, we consider that a voyage of any length would be very dangerous in a vessel too heavily laden on the deck. Fig. 162 shows the plan of the approach to the station, and to the landing-quay on the shore; Fig. 163, the movable pontoon or drawbridge, forming a connection between the pier and the ferry-boat.

Our passage was rapid, and without any inconvenience. When the ferry reached the other side, a similar manœuvre, in the opposite direction to that adopted at starting, brought the carriages to the pier, and they were placed on the rails which led to their destination.

At the moment that we were taking our places in the train we saw some one advancing toward us with a smile, and with extended hand. We recognized in him a former travelling companion, with whom we had made acquaintance as we were going from Rome to Viterbo, shut up in a pontifical mail-coach with a yellow body, and escorted by two of those magnificent carabineers, with a terrible and martial air, whose presence reassured the traveller when he thought of the consequences of some unfortunate encounter which might befall him; but who, by their lofty plumes, served to inform the brigands, if there were any, of the importance and quality of those who were on the road.

We renewed our acquaintance while the train was preparing to start. Several years had passed since our last meeting. We had left Paris after a long evening spent together, while he related, and we listened to, the many changes of fortune which had occurred during the struggle between Denmark and Prussia in 1864. We now met again in the island of Funen in 1872; but we, alas! had in our turn to relate the disasters of 1870.

Our friend was a Norwegian, a native of that land which professes the greatest admiration of France, and the warmest sympathy for it.

"Whence do you come?" we immediately inquired. "From the South." "You are then on your return from Italy?" "O no! from Jutland." "Do you call that the South?" "Certainly, when you live in Christiana." "Yes, of course. And where are *you* going? To the North?" "Yes; to Copenhagen." "Do you call that the North?" "Certainly, when you come from Paris." "Ah! well," he replied with a laugh; "it is all right when we understand each other. Well," said he, "instead of reaching Copenhagen this evening, you will have to delay for a few days. You would not care to stop at Odensee, where even the cathedral has but little to interest an architect. I will take you with me to a farm near Nyborg, which belongs to me. It is now occupied by a friend, a fellow-countryman, who has just completed and furnished it in such a manner as would astonish a Frenchman. You will there have a curious glimpse of our Scandinavian customs, and an interesting specimen of those wooden structures which you Europeans, as they say at Christiana, are too much inclined to consider huts of savages built of trunks of trees."

There was but one reply possible, — to thank our friend and accept his invitation.

Shortly afterwards the train stopped. We were at Nyborg, on the shores of the Great Belt. Instead of going on board the vessel which crosses the strait, we took our places in one of the large cars of the country, drawn by three horses abreast, which started with us at full trot along the coast road.

This was the first time that we had seen a real Northern landscape. The green-tinted sea was gently rippling on the sandy shore; extensive and unvarying plains were stretched before us, surrounded by woods of beech and birch. Here and there cultivated fields relieved the pale verdure of the meadows or the dark trenches of the bogs. From time to time were to be seen a park, with its lawns and well-kept flower-beds, an elegant house half hidden behind a grove of trees; then farms and agricultural buildings surrounded by fields of thin and short-stalked corn; an orchard of fruit-trees; and herds of cattle returning from the pasture. We passed, on the sea-shore, a lively fishing village, full of small houses with roofs nearly flat; the bricks as well as the woodwork were painted with gaudy colors, the windows glittered in the sun, and on the ridge of each roof was a carving rudely representing the prow of a vessel. Through the half-open doors you could see neat and clean rooms. The fishing-nets were spread on the shore to dry; the boats were drawn up; the women and children looked at us with curious eyes, and the men raised their woollen caps to salute us. They are robust and vigorous, and look quiet and good-natured. These excellent people, who enjoy such a calm and orderly existence, who live honestly on the produce of their fishing, and practise all the virtues of domestic life, are nevertheless descended from those bold pirates whose terrible exploits were the terror of the seas; who, in the ninth century, sailed up the Seine as far as Paris, and, in the twelfth, seized upon the Crown of England. These men, whose honesty and loyalty remind us of the Golden Age, seem to have no idea that their ancestors were such audacious corsairs.

We have now left the coast, the road turns inland; we traverse a forest, with solitude all around us. An old woman passes, bending under an enormous bundle of grass mixed with flowers, on which a small lean cow feeds, as she walks behind her.

On the doorstep of a cottage are three children, eating, with a good appetite, some coarse black bread. Nothing is heard among the large trees but the footsteps of the horses, and the harsh and hoarse shouts of the driver; we ourselves are silent. All is quiet and tranquil; a sweet melancholy and an indefinable feeling of sadness pervade both man and nature. The light is softened, as if it passed through a screen of gauze; the effects of light and shade are toned down; there is nothing to arrest the eye, nothing to attract or detain it. The silence is deep and profound; no cries are to be heard, no songs, only a slight twittering of birds hidden in the foliage, the lowing of an ox, or the noise of a cart whose wheels grate on their axle. Then, all at once, the prospect widens, our team starts off more rapidly, the conductor cracks his whip loudly, and, just as the sun is about to disappear beneath the horizon, we see a group of habitations regularly arranged. The roofs are red, the last rays of the setting sun glitter on walls of varnished pine-wood; a bell rings to announce our arrival, the carriage passes through the large gateway, turns into the courtyard, and stops before a house, under the veranda of which our hosts are waiting to welcome us.

We ascend a flight of steps sheltered by a small wooden

porch; and, conducted by the master of the house, pass through the veranda, which serves as a hall, and enter a room which is at the same time a drawing-room, a dining-room, and a reception-room. The floor is strewn with green twigs covered with red, blue, and yellow flowers, which form a rich carpet of brilliant colors. The sideboard, at the end of the room, is surrounded by garlands of flowers, and on the walls are festoons of foliage; the eye is charmed with this decoration, for which they are indebted to nature alone. Everything is pervaded by a sweet smell of resin and wild plants. When we have been introduced, we are conducted to our chamber. We occupy the spare room, a very large apartment on the first floor, with a wide bed, placed high above the ground. The furniture is of pine-wood; there are windows on each side, some opening on a gallery over the veranda below, the others on a covered balcony. But we have no time to examine everything; we must go down quickly, for it is the dinner hour, and we are soon seated at the family table.

The dinner, for we must speak of it, commenced with some *sweet soup*, a mixture composed of small pieces of meat swimming in a broth, in which were prunes, slices of orange-peel, pieces of licorice, dried currants, barley, pepper, and salt. Fortunately, to aid in the digestion of this alarming dish, they gave us some excellent beer, served in small glasses placed before each guest, and some rye-brandy, which removes from the palate the flavor of everything which it may have previously absorbed. Then came *steaks* of sturgeon, *rog-brod* (rye-bread), slices of black bread spread with butter and mustard, rolled round ham and smoked beef, and *rod-grod*, a kind of pudding; very solid food, but at the same time very acceptable.

After dinner, we had, with our friend and our entertainer, a long conversation full of recollections of the past and anecdotes, till the evening drew to a close. We retired to our apartments; the night was clear and fresh, and the breeze brought vague intimations of the pine-forests, the sweet perfume of flowers, and the distant murmur of the sea on the sandy shore; while through the half-open windows came the somewhat harsh accents of a woman's voice, who in the courtyard, in the midst of a group of men-servants, was singing an old Runic chant.

On the following day they showed us, in detail, the farm and its dependencies. Our host was a native of Norway; peculiar circumstances had induced him to quit his native country; so he came to settle in a corner of the island of Funen (Fionia) with his wife and children, — two pretty little fair girls with gray eyes, who never ceased to gaze at us, seeking to divine the meaning of our words from our looks and gestures. This family had brought with them all the habits and customs of their native land, and their dwelling was, in many respects, the reproduction of old remembrances which they loved to retain and perpetuate.

We first left the enclosure (called in Norwegian the *guard*), which contains the courts and buildings, and we looked about us. The whole is comprised in a large rectangular space (Fig. 164), covered with buildings of various heights and dimensions, all fronting in the same direction, having a narrow gable at the north and south ends. Each of these buildings, being allotted to a special purpose, is separated from the next by a considerable space, a kind of wide road around each of them. The only material employed in their construction is wood, with the exception of the tiled roofs. In front of the entrance is the first building, higher (Fig. 166) and more ornamental than the rest; this is the dwelling-house of the farmer. On the ground-floor is a porch, which, as we have already mentioned, shelters the outer flight of steps, and a large veranda serving as a vestibule, on which all the rooms open. This veranda is closed during the winter by glazed sashes, and serves for the reception of persons who are not expected to enter the private apartments. It opens into the *hall*, a large family room, where they usually live, and in which they take their meals. By the side of this are the kitchen, the closets, and the staircase leading to the first floor; on which are a gallery over the lower veranda, two large rooms, and one smaller one. On the side opposite to the veranda, and facing the farm buildings, is a balcony supported on cantalivers. This balcony is enclosed with sash windows, and together with the lower gallery is a part of the house used as a play-room for the

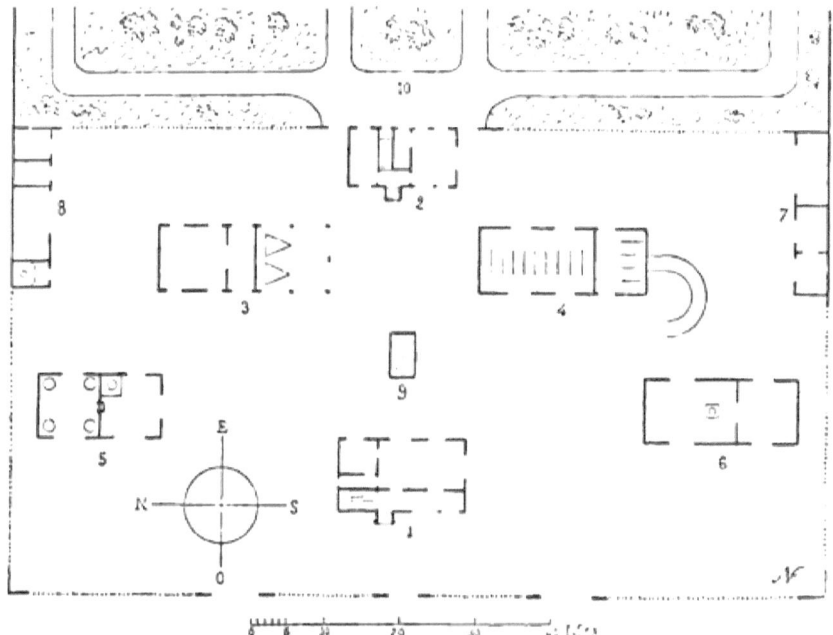

Fig. 164.—General plan of a Farm in the Island of Funen.

1. Master's residence.
2. House for servants.
3. Barns and coach-houses.
4. Cattle-house and stabling.
5. Wash-house and bake-house.
6. Workshops.
7. Dairy and sheds.
8. Fowl-house, pigsties, water-closet.
9. Slaughter-house.
10. Kitchen-garden.

children, and as a place where the family can walk when, being detained at home by cold and snow and by the nights of eighteen or twenty hours long, they cannot leave the house. This balcony serves also as an observatory for the farmer, and enables him to see every part of the various buildings, and to superintend his laborers.

The buildings are, as we have said, entirely of timber, and are composed of wooden bays, very different from the framework concealed under a coating of cement, which is usual among ourselves. They are constructed by means of slight uprights, of 7 inches by 7¾ in scantling, connected by horizontal cross-pieces,

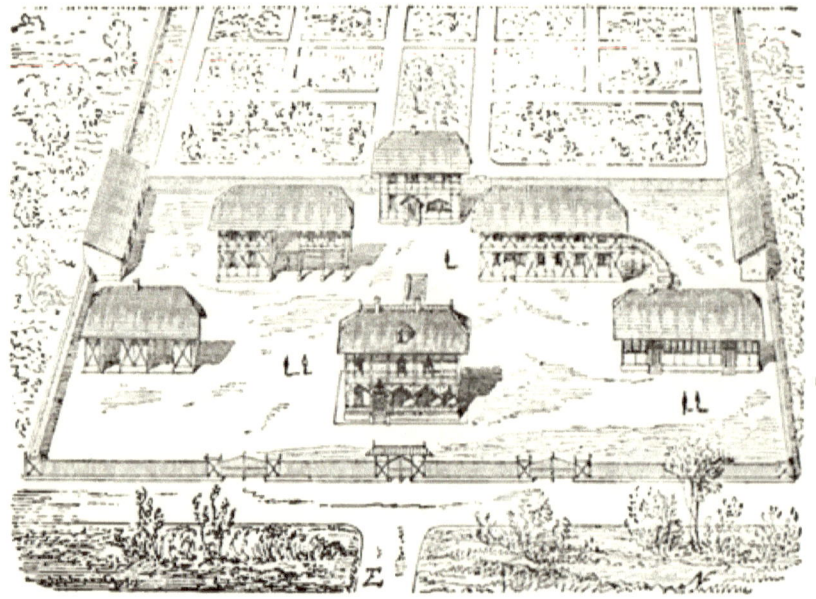

Fig. 165.—General View of a Farm.

connected by plough and tongue joints, and rabbeted into jambs. This framework is covered on the outside with deal shingles. The inner cross-pieces are from 2 to 2¾ inches in thickness; the wainscoting is nearly 1½ inch thick; the shingles 2 inches wide, nearly 5 inches long, and about ½ inch thick. The end of these shingles is flush with the projection of the vertical side-posts. The woodwork of the roof is composed of rafters with trusses;

that is to say, that each rafter forms in itself a principal. The whole structure, in fact, is a perfect casing of pine-wood.[1]

Fig. 166. — Exterior of Farm-house.

The interior (Fig. 167) of this dwelling-house and its furniture are of the simplest kind, and show no striving after luxury or

---

[1] This manner of working in pine-wood is not the only one employed in Denmark and Sweden. See "Encyclopédie d'Architecture," 1872; and "Compte-rendu de l'exposition des pays du nord de l'Europe." Félix Narjoux. Lib. Morel, 13 Rue Bonaparte.

DENMARK.

mere appearance, but, on the contrary, the love of home and domestic life.

The walls are covered with very thick felt, fastened to the

Fig. 167. — View of Interior.

partitions by lattice-work made of crossed laths; and small triangular pieces of wood, attached to this, form combinations both curious and ingenious. In the principal room the portion of the stuff which is shown is decorated with a flower or a geometrical figure. These ornaments, which are colored, relieve the surface, which otherwise would appear cold and too uniform.

The cornice is ornamented with a carving in pine-wood, the ground in which has been painted of a deep color, on which the ornamental part stands out uncolored. The ceiling is formed of bare joists united by cross-beams, thus forming compartments, in which are fixed centre-pieces of carved varnished wood, which relieve the blue or red of the groundwork.

The furniture also is made of deal. The seats, we must confess, are not very comfortable; but the beds are large, with thick hangings, and placed at some considerable height above the floor. In the dining-room were two large sideboards, surrounded by garlands of flowers, for which they substitute, during the winter, paper wreaths of various colors. The windows are double, the panes of glass brilliant, with no curtain to obstruct the light; blinds are not in use. Large gilded and painted earthenware stoves diffuse everywhere a pleasant and equal warmth, but deprive those who sit near them of the sight of the bright flame which sparkles and crackles in the chimney-corners of our country-houses.

The sitting-room is employed for many purposes, not only for the ordinary use of the family, but for festival occasions, and the feasts which are given after hunting and fishing excursions. Northern manners, which are less polished than ours, have preserved certain rude traditions which have disappeared among ourselves; and it is not uncommon, even now, to see these festivals degenerate into orgies. In former days they almost always ended in a fight.

Buildings of this kind are more especially adapted to the demands of a climate which requires, above all, that a dwelling-house should be dry and warm in winter; but they have this inconvenience, that they are an easy prey to fire. In order to guard, as far as possible, against this danger, each building is destined to a different purpose, and is separated from the rest by a large space serving as a courtyard and a passage (Fig. 165).

A relic of ancient Northern traditions does not permit servants to sleep under the same roof as the master; they have a separate house, built opposite to that intended for the head of the family. This building includes, on the ground-floor, a common sitting-room, a kitchen, and a room serving as an office; on the upper story are bedrooms.

To the right of the servants' house are the stables, in which there are, on the ground-floor, stables for the horses, and stalls for horned cattle. The first floor, which is approached by an inclined plane, is reserved for goats and sheep. Opposite to this, and at the other side of the enclosure, is the barn, containing the threshing-floor, and, above this, the granary. In front, and at a considerable distance, for fear of fire, are the wash-house and the bakery; and, opposite to these, workshops for the construction and repair of all tools, implements, and furniture necessary for the farm and the household. Denmark, an essentially agricultural country, is deficient in manufacturing establishments, and, therefore, every one is obliged, in certain cases, to construct such implements as he may require. Some of the peasants are skilful enough to make wooden clocks quite sufficient for their purpose. To complete this assemblage of buildings, of which our figure will give some idea, there rise, on each side of the court, sheds and other shelters, and at the extremity is a large kitchen-garden.

All these buildings are covered with tiles, and the ridge of the roof of each is decorated with one of those carved beams which slightly resemble the prow of a ship,—the last recollection of the existence of those maritime populations who had no other dwelling than the deck of the vessel in which they passed their lives.

The agricultural produce consists of wheat, black corn, and food for cattle,—a crop which is often compromised by sudden heat or late frosts. Field-work is completed in a shorter space of time than in more southernly countries. Sowing and reaping must be begun and finished within a few months. The more rapid cultivation in this climate is productive of less favorable results. Spring and autumn have scarcely any existence, and the heats of summer succeed almost immediately to the long and cold nights of winter. The return of the sun, the time when it comes again to render the earth fruitful, are days of joy, welcomed and celebrated in the country by festivals and public rejoicings, in which all, young and old, rich and poor, take part.

On May 1, when the cold north-wind has ceased to blow, when the snow melts under the first rays of the sun, and when the thick mists, which have enveloped the earth for long months, have at last disappeared, the peasants dress themselves in their best attire; the boys tie ribbons of bright color round their hats; the girls adorn the body of their light gowns with spring flowers; and then in long files, preceded by bands of music, they go, on foot or in carts, towards the place chosen by each group of villages for the celebration of the *return of the spring*. The day is passed in amusements of every kind, especially dances, and is ended by an immense feast, to which every one contributes his share, and which is prepared by those whom more advanced age detains from more active enjoyments. Then, before they leave, all who are present choose among themselves a king and queen, whom they crown with flowers, and who, during the whole year, bear the title of king and queen of the spring, and enjoy certain privileges, of which the final result is very frequently a happy union.

But the time of this festival has long gone by; we are on the eve, not of spring, but of winter. We are only in the month of September, and yet already the nights are cold, a slight hoarfrost covers the fields and the sea every morning, so we must hasten on, and not linger on our journey. We therefore return by the way that we came, and, provided with warm letters of recommendation to friends at Copenhagen, we embark on the "Great Belt," to resume the journey so pleasantly interrupted; our friend accompanied us, and, as we went along, we spoke of Denmark and her population.

Notwithstanding the disasters which have befallen this country, it is evident that it still enjoys a certain amount of prosperity. Agriculture prospers; the Dane is more fit for field labor than for commercial pursuits. Honest, laborious, intelligent, and very much attached to the country, he is prudent, and but rarely risks in any enterprise the money which he finds it so difficult to earn; so the industrial pursuits of the country make but little progress. Large fortunes are as rare as extreme misery, and public education is developed more and more every day. The Dane, thick-set, robust, with projecting cheek-bones and square chin, the signs of force and resolution, does not possess the lively, supple, and graceful characteristics which constitute the great charm of the Latin races. They atone for this by their energy and perseverance; and their bold mariners have made the national flag known in the most distant seas, as far as the extremity of China and Japan.

France has no influence in this country, and yet its name excites the warmest sympathy; we frequently found this as we proceeded on our journey. Formerly, Hamburg had a preponderating prestige in the whole of Scandinavia and Denmark; but since the annexation to Germany, the German and Scandinavian races grow every day more alienated, and English influence prevails in their stead.

A great project, which would secure for Denmark the transport of all the merchandise brought from Sweden into *Europe*, and *vice versâ*, is at this moment seriously contemplated; it is to unite Copenhagen with Vordingborg by a railway, and then to reach, by means of fixed bridges, the islands of Falster and Laaland, a packet-boat from which would cross the strait of Fehmern to the island of that name, which would be connected directly with the mainland by a new series of fixed bridges. The execution of these works would certainly change the face of the country, and modify its tendencies, by substituting for English influence that of the southern European nations, with which they would be placed in easy and rapid communication.

The "Great Belt" was not favorable to us; the passage, always difficult on account of the shallows, becomes very unpleasant when the wind blows directly through this narrow channel, so that we hailed with delight the green coast-line of the meadows in the island of Zealand.

As we approach the shore, we are struck everywhere with the adventurous life of the mariner, which develops the strength of these brave Northern races. On the sea were to be seen numerous barks struggling against the waves; not large vessels, for their greater draught of water obliges them to pass through the Sound; but a number of small coasting-vessels coming from the Cattegat, and thus establishing a communication between the ports of the Baltic. There are many villages on the shore, near to each other; we could distinguish the fishermen's cottages, and their nets drying on the strand, the boats drawn up and placed under shelter from the storms of the night; and, beyond, rich enclosures of fruit-trees, parks, and country-houses, the summer villas of the nobility or the rich merchants of the town.

When once seated in the railway-carriage, we proceed rapidly; the country has always the same melancholy and miserable appearance. There is nothing bright or luxuriant in the landscape; the land is flat, the vegetation fresh and humid, the horizon shut in by forests of oak and beech trees; everything around looks cold and stern, and inspires sadness rather than ennui.

We soon perceive, on the left, the deep indentation of a fjord, at the extremity of which is Roeskilde, formerly a royal residence, and the episcopal town of Denmark, until the introduction of the Lutheran religion. Roeskilde, which contained twenty-six churches with their cloisters, the palace of the kings, and that of the princes, which was surrounded with the splendor and magnificence of a court that swayed the sceptre of the three Scandinavian states, retains nothing of all this glory except the cathedral of Canute the Great, the silent resting-place of the kings of Denmark.

This cathedral, the most beautiful structure of the kind in Denmark, was founded in the middle of the twelfth century; its plan is long and narrow (Fig. 168). Its side aisles are separated from the nave by a number of arches of unequal width;

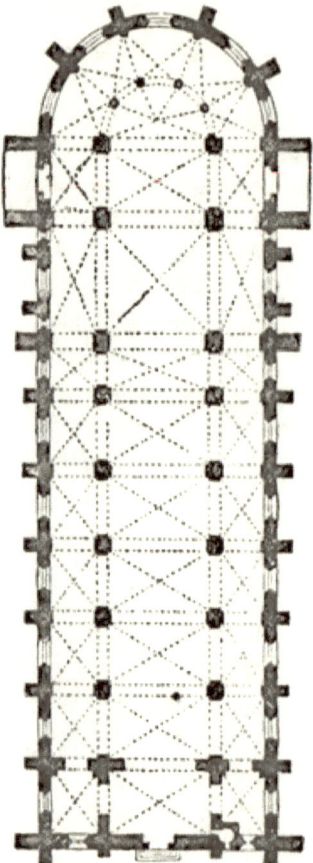

Fig. 168.—Ground-plan of the Cathedral at Roeskilde.

the building is terminated by a circular apse; and, by an arrangement very frequently adopted, the thrust of the vault of the nave is counteracted by arches placed under the roofs of the side aisles. Like all the edifices of this period, raised in the extreme North, the cathedral of Roeskilde is disfigured by additions of greater or less importance, which have altered its original form, and modified, not only its details, but its proportions. The large, wide, and lofty chancel, and the transept and its aisles, with galleries which lessen the apparent height, give some idea of what this building must have been at the time of its splendor, alas! how long ago; and, to crown all, the whole of the internal decorations have been lately cov-

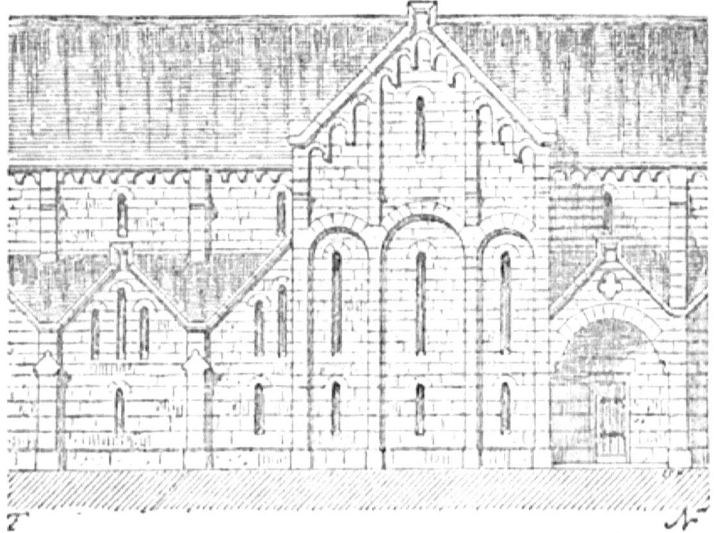

Fig. 169.—Geometrical Elevation of the Façade of the Transept.

ered with glaring paintings representing flowers, branches of trees, and verdure, which have completely destroyed the grand and noble effect of the building.

The façades (Fig. 169), built of granite wrought with great care, are rather primitive in style, the effect of which is not without its charm, and reminds us of our churches in Auvergne and Limousin, erected at the same period, and with materials of a similar kind.

The tombs of the kings are numerous. They have been compared, with some amount of exaggeration, to those of St. Denis. One of them, however, attracts attention; it is that of Christian IV., surmounted by a statue by Thorwaldsen.

The surrounding country is filled with tombs, funeral monuments, and Runic stones, and abounds with souvenirs of mythological history, poetry, and the paganism of the North, of which this country was the birthplace. Altars, on which human sacrifices were offered, are to be seen at Lethraborg. The legend of Hrolf and his twelve giants is connected with Leira. At Illeidra was the sacred wood of the goddess Hertha, with the lake, into the waves of which she plunged the incautious men who had surprised and gazed upon her while in her bath. It was over this land that she drove in her chariot drawn by cows; and under the shadow of these beech-trees were offered those horrible sacrifices of human beings, tied to each other before they were put to death. But if the monuments which recall these recollections possess an archæological interest, they have none in an artistic point of view; and we must also own, in all humility, that the most beautiful Runic inscriptions are but a dead letter to us.

Nevertheless, as it is not possible to be in Denmark without speaking of Odin and the Runes, we must say a few words about them. Odin is said to have been the inventor of these Runes. As they were cut and engraven in stones, it is asserted that their name was derived from a Gothic word having the same meaning, or from another word Rona, which signifies *secret*,—an explanation derived from their mysterious character; but as the Germans pretend to have discovered everything, and to be in themselves the origin of all things, they will have it that the word Rune comes from one in their own language, *Raunen*, which signifies a murmur,—a rather *German* allusion to the part assigned to the Runes, which, thanks to the explanations of the learned, murmur almost whatever they wish.

The Runic alphabet is composed of sixteen characters, supposed to be of Phœnician origin, each of which has a name and signification peculiar to itself. These characters are grouped, intermixed, and interlaced; they are read either from left to right, or from right to left, and thus give rise to translations which vary among every nation, and according to the taste of every individual.

These Runes were not only graphic signs, but they had a mysterious power, and a charm to which the initiated had recourse under certain circumstances. They attributed to them the power of inspiring love, raising the dead, curing diseases, lulling tempests, extinguishing fires, etc.

Runic chants are full of a strange and mysterious poetry, which strikes the imagination and carries it away to the realm of dreams and improbability. It is difficult to forget these accents when they have been heard, even for once, so profound is the impression made by these mystical words, whose meaning is unknown, when they are chanted to a rhythmical air filled with strange power and harmony.

COPENHAGEN.

GENERAL ASPECT.

THE terminus is a wooden building, covered with a roof on the plan of Philibert Delorme, and which cannot be compared with the magnificent halls of the French railways, built of iron, and covered with glass; but, as some compensation, the police and the custom-house soon set us at liberty, and we found ourselves outside, in a large avenue planted with trees, facing an extensive park, and the Norrbro (the Northern bridge), passing over which we entered the city.

The sunshine was delightful, the air pleasantly warm, the sky clear; and throughout the day we walked on and on, gazing on the right hand and the left, on persons and things, being intent on seeing as much and as thoroughly as possible.

When we had passed through the environs of the city, we walked down one street, traversed the square, entered a second street, and found ourselves in front of an enormous building. It was the Christianborg (the palace of Christian, the royal palace), which resembles a fortress or a state-prison. Close by there was a canal thronged with boats laden with vegetables, fruits, and fish; and then came a labyrinth of small streets, and a large open space, the Kongens Nytorv, an irregular square, bordered, in some parts, by lofty narrow buildings, with fantastic gables (Fig. 170). At the extremity was a palace; at the side, the Opera-House; at the other end, a canal; and in the middle, a statue, hidden in a clump of rose-bushes. At the corner of one street we read: "Restaurant des Dames françaises." There was a great crowd of persons in this square; carriages, horses, omnibuses, crossed in every direction; a detachment of soldiers were passing with their drums beating; the men look strong, but their step is rather heavy; their equipment and uniform resemble ours, and they are armed with rifles. We begin to sketch;

Fig. 170. — The Kongens-Nytorv, at Copenhagen.

a crowd gathers round, an officer comes to us from the neighboring guard-house. We do not understand what he says, but still, full of deference for discipline, and thinking that he came to forbid us to continue our sketch, we close our book and rise to go on our way; but it seems that this was not what he wanted.

He had thought that we were German. He asked what we had been doing: we showed him our sketch-book, in which were some remarks in French, and our address in Paris. The officer reads: Paris, French: the bystanders repeat, French, Paris (it sounds in Danish something like *Frensk*, *Parisk*). The expression on the features of those around us at once entirely changes, and they look on us with kindness and sympathy, two soldiers are sent from the guard-house to clear a space around us, and we are allowed to finish our drawing. We know not how to express our thanks; but, without being able to understand each other, we exchange the most friendly words and cordial compliments.

In the Ostergade (West Street) there are many shops, in lofty houses of several stories, built of stone or brick. Some, of an unusual shape, have an original and grotesque appearance, but the greater part are uninteresting, and of an ordinary kind. The footpaths are paved with red Norwegian granite, which, when recently washed, is of an agreeable color, and the particles of mica glisten in the sun. By the side of the path is a wide and deep gutter, covered with strong deal boards, serving both to limit the roadway and to act as a drain. People pass quietly, and without haste; they do not press on each other, and keep scrupulously to the right hand. We reach the Gothergade, the Regent Street or the " Rue de la Paix " of Copenhagen, where there are beautiful, large, lofty, well-built houses, with shops over each other; that is to say, on the basement and ground-floor. Those below the level of the ground, to which the approach is by steps made in the area which separates the houses from the street, are used as taverns, beer-shops, restaurants, and shops for eatables. When we set our foot on the threshold, the step gives way, the visitor feels as if he were losing his equilibrium, and a bell tingles at the farther end of the shop; this is a signal to announce the arrival of a customer. In the shops on the ground-floor, which might, indeed, be as well called the first story, are sold articles manufactured in Paris, London, or Vienna, such as gold ornaments, jewelry, and stationery. There are also shops of a more modest, but no less useful kind, such as those of tailors, shoemakers, and dealers in cigars. The goods are not displayed, as the sill of the window is nearly on a level with the heads of passers-by. There are no splendid shop-fronts; large panes of glass merely protect the wares, not from ill-intentioned persons and robbers, for these are unknown in Copenhagen, but against wind and rain. Tradesmen, who are more distrustful, leave the gas alight during the night, so that it is impossible that any robbery should be committed without being seen from the public street.

We see many persons at the gate of a large garden, the Rosenborg-have. We enter; bands of music are playing in the open air, and people are walking about. There are many young and pretty women, with bright complexions, blue or gray eyes, and fair hair; they wear white or light dresses, with a bright-colored band round the waist. Their figure is slender, their hair falls in long curls over their shoulders, and is only confined at the back of the neck by a ribbon of the same color as the waistband. A kind of small head-dress with feathers is placed jauntily on the top of the head; the neck is left bare, and under the transparent material of the body of the dress there is a glimpse of the rich carnation of the shoulders. The hands, tightly gloved, carry an immense parasol, and, as they pass by, they occasionally draw round them, with a graceful and coquettish air, a long scarf, when the keen breeze from the North raises the ringlets of their hair, or gives them a momentary shiver. The fine season is, in fact, so short that people must enjoy themselves as much as possible while it lasts, and display their bright summer dresses whenever there is the least interval of sunshine. These women are gay and merry; they are always ready to smile, in order to show their beautiful teeth; they exchange greetings, and shake hands energetically with the friends whom they meet; which is often the case, as every one here seems to know everybody else, and they look more like the promenaders of a provincial town, than the inhabitants of a capital city. The men exaggerate the Parisian fashions, want what we call distinction, and have rather a heavy and clumsy gait.

Passing through Dronningenstvergade, we arrive at a complete "faubourg St. Germain," with wide quiet streets, lined with palaces and rich mansions separated from the public road by courts and wrought-iron gates. There are but few persons passing by. The nobility are at their country-seats, and their town residences are deserted. This quarter has a grand appearance, but these solidly built mansions have not the architectural character that you might expect. They remind us of our *rococo*, of the period of Louis XV. You must look at them in their entirety, and not notice the details. At the farther end of this quarter is an octagonal space, with four broad and four narrow sides. At the four smaller sides are four similar palaces, with wings extending along the larger sides and down the streets which open in the middle of the shorter ends (Fig. 172). Two of these palaces are united by arches crossing one of these streets, and forming the royal residence. The square, if it may be so called, resembles the grand courtyard of a palace. In the middle is an equestrian statue; the whole has a cold aspect, but nevertheless looks rather grand.

Some masons were at work in a side street; they were building a brick wall, and placed their bricks methodically, but slowly, paying especial attention to the regularity of the joints, adjusting their bricks before they laid them, fitting them gently, and employing a thousand precautions lest they should break them; steeping them in water, and covering their hands with tar to protect them against the rugged surface of the materials they employed. Their task was well finished, but they did not work quickly, and a great number of men must be employed to build a house during the short space afforded by the fine season. Some other men were constructing a front wall built of large ashlar stones, which were all of equal size, and consisted of granite with the surface rendered slightly smooth. The joints, which were very projecting, were of cement, and gauged to the same width. The work had the appearance of being carefully finished; the gray stone is surrounded by joints, which, in process of time, become black, and give the houses a rather gloomy look. The wages of the laborers must be low, or else this kind of work would be very costly. They were employed, a little farther on, in forming an arch with blocks of stone; the voussoirs, prepared beforehand, were too long in proportion to their breadth; they were laid without sufficient precaution, and their form was not adapted to the purpose for which they were intended, so that the joints had not a regular width; they were too close together at the base, and too far apart at the top; the skill of the workman was at fault.

We have not met a single beggar; and we begin to believe in the reputation possessed by Copenhagen of being the best-built city in Europe. We have not yet seen, and do not expect to see, any of those dilapidated dwellings, those unwholesome hovels, of which too many sad examples are to be found in the largest cities. Even in the suburbs there is no vestige of those wretched habitations in which the dregs of the population of a large town pass their miserable and abject lives.

There is a view of the sea from the Amaliengade. Here is to be seen the harbor with its ships, large and fine steamers which are bound to stations in the extreme North; there is great activity, but little noise. The language spoken is harsh, rapid, abrupt. The Russian sailors, tall, strong, and with broad nostrils, are distinguishable by their rough appearance and their violent gestures. A tavern established in the underground story of a house is the favorite resort of laborers and sailors. We look in at the open door, and see regularly arranged upon the counter large glasses full of milk, and, near each, smaller glasses filled with *Kirsch;* the Danes drink, emptying each glass one after the other, pay their money, and go away without noise and tumult. On the other side, gin and *Kummel* are served out to the Russians; they are noisy, boisterous, and rough; many of them are scarcely able to stand. This sobriety on the one hand, and excess on the other, form a contrast all the more striking, as it is circumscribed by so narrow a space.

We now reach the sea-shore, and find there a long promenade, the Lange-line, which is sometimes compared to the Chiaia at Naples. There, however, we perceive in the midst of the beautiful bay, islands bathed in the blue waves of the Mediterranean, the smiling scenery of Pausilippo, groves of orange-trees and oleanders, the heights of Vesuvius, and the whole country flooded with that brilliant light which makes so many and such various objects unite and blend so exquisitely. At Copenhagen we see the many ships traversing the Sound, sharply defined against the green sea waters, and the coast-line of Sweden lighted up by the pale Northern sunshine. The Chiaia and the Lange-line are therefore by no means alike, but still each has its peculiar merit and beauty. Thus, during the winter at Copenhagen, when the strait is covered with a thick coating of ice, and when the snow conceals with its winding-sheet both the land and the sea, this immense white plain, which extends as far as the pole, and is wrapped in a dense mist, must unquestionably present a spectacle the grandeur and severe majesty of which may well vie with the splendor of the lands of the South, where, as at Naples, Nature has shown herself most prodigal of her gifts and favors.

At this end of the city stands the citadel, a castle more gloomy than dangerous, more terrible than useful, constructed on Vauban's system, protected by two outworks, which modern artillery would soon demolish; then close at hand is a quarter formed of long streets lined with small low houses, all similar in form and dimensions, and completely uniform in all respects; this is inhabited by sailors and other persons connected with maritime occupations.

We cross the harbor in a boat, and land on the island of Amok, where are large dockyards for ship-building, and in a side street there are modest-looking shops, in which Jews sell, at a moderate price, lacquered ware, curiosities, and porcelain from China and Japan. At the end of this street we notice the grotesque tower of the Church of the Trinity; and, returning by the same way, we see the spire of the Exchange, the form of which can neither be understood nor described. At last, by the Langebro, we come again to the Wester-allée and the new quarters of Frederiksborg, lined with cheerful hotels, small houses, and places of public resort, which minister to the pleasures of the lower classes during the summer fête days.

This was the result of our first walk in Copenhagen. We must now examine in detail that which we have only observed in the mass in this rapid survey.

COPENHAGEN.

II.

KONGENS-NYTORV. — AMALIENBORG. — RONDE-KIRK. — FRUE-KIRK. — CHRISTIAN-BORG. — ROSENBORG. — EXCHANGE. — CRYSTAL PALACE. — HOSPITAL-SCHOOLS. — FREDERIKSBORG. — THE OLD AND NEW FORTIFICATIONS.

THE Kongens-Nytorv, the Place Royale, or new market, serves as a connecting link between the commercial quarter and that inhabited by the nobility. It is very large, and of an irregular form. The palaces, which extend along one side of it, are not devoid of architectural interest. Their destination is various, but their character remains the same; and one cannot understand at first why, for instance, the Carlottenborg is not used as a military school, — the military school for a museum of the fine arts, and *vice versâ*.

Two old houses of the seventeenth century still remain standing on one of the sides of the square (Fig. 170). They belong to that period called the German Renaissance by the Germans, who, in their inordinate vanity, wish to persuade themselves that they have originated a school of architecture, because they have exaggerated the forms and disfigured the proportions of foreign works.

These houses, built of stone and brick, are of considerable height; the small space occupied by the town, enclosed as it is within the fortifications, did not allow the buildings to be extended, and they were therefore obliged to raise them to a greater height. Each story is marked out by a moulding, which serves as a support to the windows of the floor above; all the lintels are protected by arches; the gables are pointed, with retreating portions ornamented with grotesque pinnacles; the water-courses and the iron clamps in the walls still remain.

In the centre of the square there is a statue erected in honor of Christian V., which has been judiciously concealed behind a clump of trees. It is intended to be equestrian, but it is difficult to ascertain positively on what animal the hero is mounted; he treads under foot a woman, *the symbol of envy*. Around the pedestal several personages are arranged, who seem much astonished at being together, and look as if they were asking each other the reason of their meeting; these are Alexander, Hercules, Artemisia, and Minerva. All these grotesque and ridiculous figures are cast in lead.

The Amalienborg (Fig. 171) is a series of palaces surrounding a beautiful square. Taken separately, these palaces, which have a gloomy and cold appearance, seem mean; but, seen together, their mass is imposing, and we must only look at them in their entirety, for their details and arrangement show no originality, novelty, or evidence of careful study.

The middle of the square, or rather of the palace-yard (Fig. 172), is occupied by a leaden equestrian figure, like that of Christian V., and representing a Frederick or a Christian, but which of the kings known by those names, we will not venture to say for fear of mistake; but, at all events, this liberal and witty monarch certainly deserved something better, if only on account of the interesting anecdote of which he is the subject.

One of the privileges of the nobility, at that time, permitted any noble to get rid of a *villain* who had offended him, on condition of placing a crown piece on his dead body. This privilege appeared to the monarch to be excessive, and he suppressed it. There was great discontent and complaint at court; the nobility combined, made protests, which were not well received, grew angry, and retired to their country estates, — in short, acted with such vigor that the *tyrant* was obliged to yield and cancel his decree. He did it, however, most graciously, and assembled his high and mighty lords to announce to them the restoration of the right which they claimed; and at the close of his speech he added, by way of peroration: "But if I am not allowed to deprive you of any privilege, no one can forbid my granting one to

Fig. 171.—The Palace of Amalienborg.

my other subjects; and I have therefore decided, that in future any man belonging to the lower ranks may get rid of a noble who displeases him, on condition of paying two crowns, for, as you have justly said, we must maintain a proper line of demarcation between the social classes in the community."

The churches of Copenhagen are not very interesting. The most remarkable have been destroyed in the great catastrophes that have befallen the city. The Runde-Kirk, built in the seventeenth century by Steenwenkel, a pupil of Tycho Brahe, who was not only a great astronomer, but a skilful engineer, is the oldest that is still remaining. It was built in the style which

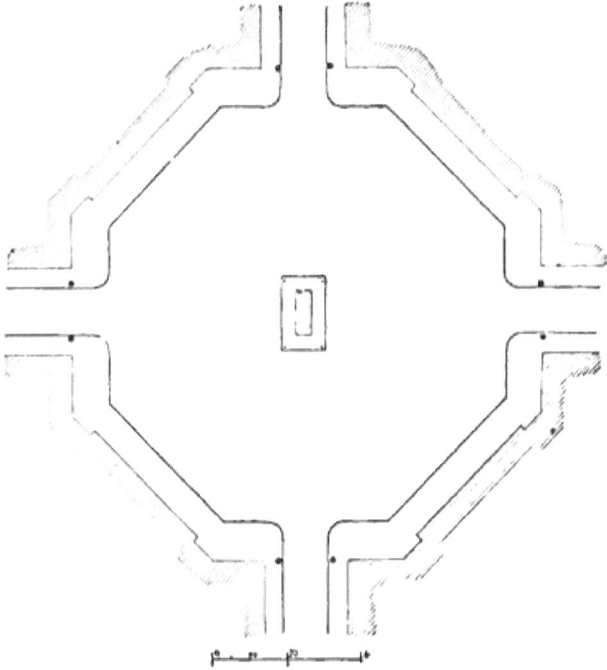

Fig. 172. — Plan of the Amalienborg-Slot.

is called, in France, Jesuit architecture; and there is nothing worthy of notice in it except the pyramidal spire on the top of the tower (Fig. 173).

The base of this spire stands on a low circular vault, supported by the tower, — an enormous base, lofty, with thick walls, and great force of resistance. An open spiral path, leading to

Fig. 173.—Runde-Kirk, Copenhagen.

the very top of the building, is hollowed out of the mass of the tapering spire, thus allowing one to ascend, on the outside, to the highest point, from which there is a magnificent view. Ordinary people go up simply on foot, keeping close to the wall or clinging to the hand-rails; and notwithstanding these precautions, there is some danger for persons whose heads are not very steady; but some sovereigns, as Christian IV. and Peter the Great, are said to have made the ascent in a carriage-and-four, — an extravagant feat, which inspired an early writer with great respect for the coachman and the horses.

It is evident that it is a great mistake to compare the spiral of the Runde-Kirk at Copenhagen with the inclined plane of the Campanile of Venice. The former is a very picturesque external pathway of a very unusual form, which could not be modified without being entirely destroyed; the latter, on the contrary, being concealed in the interior of the building, gives no idea, from without, of its form and arrangement, which might be quite different from what they are, without materially altering the form or the plan of the structure.

The second of the Copenhagen churches, worthy of a visit, is the Frue-Kirk, the Church of the Virgin. The original edifice was destroyed in 1807 by the English bombardment; that which exists at the present time dates from 1829, and is the work of Hansen. It is not the architectural merit of this Greco-Roman building which attracts the notice of the visitor, but the sculptures of Thorwaldsen with which it is adorned. The most remarkable are those in the tympanum over the principal entrance, and in the pediment of the façade. They represent our Saviour's entrance into Jerusalem, and St. John preaching in the wilderness; we see also, in the interior, the statues of the twelve Apostles, and under the altar, placed in a niche, the well-known colossal head of Christ. As we shall have occasion, when describing our visit to the Thorwaldsen Museum, to study the works and the genius of the great Danish artist, we merely mention here the sculptures in the Church of the Virgin, to which we shall subsequently refer.

The Christianborg is not, properly speaking, a palace, but rather the union of several palaces of various forms, and of different importance and destination, erected at various periods, partly destroyed by fire and war, and rebuilt without any idea of uniformity, or any settled and definite plan.

It is possible, by simply comparing a few dates, to judge of the transformations undergone by this palace. Bishop Absalom built in 1168, on the site now occupied by the Christianborg, a fortress which, after it had become a royal residence, fell more than once into the hands of the enemy, and was, at last, utterly destroyed. Frederick IV. in 1726 constructed on these ruins a castle, six stories high, which could not have been a very pleasant dwelling-place, and did not last long, for Christian VI. caused it to be pulled down in 1740, and replaced by a new castle, one of the finest in Europe, if we may believe the chroniclers; but this, unfortunately, was destroyed by fire in 1794. At last, in 1828, the edifice which we see standing at the present time was finished. It is more remarkable for its great dimensions than for its form or appearance, for it has the greatest faults that can incontestably be found with a work of art; it is common and vulgar.

The palace-yard looks gloomy; grass grows between the stones of the pavement; the base of the walls is green with damp. At the back is a kind of courtyard, which is a thoroughfare for the public, like ours at the Louvre; it is surrounded by porticos, and terminated by two wings covered with a terrace walk, from which there is a beautiful view of the country and the sea. Before the principal gate there is a porch, surmounted by a pediment, in which Thorwaldsen sculptured Jupiter in the midst of Olympus; on one of the sides of the gate may also be seen his Hercules.

This edifice is used for various purposes; it contains state apartments rarely inhabited, and drawing-rooms for grand court receptions. One of these rooms, the hall of the knights, contains, in the entablature of a gallery which surrounds it, Thorwaldsen's famous frieze, — the expeditions of Alexander. The rest of the palace contains a riding-school, stables, a theatre, a chapel, the ministerial offices, the treasury, the high court of justice, and the hall of the Reichstag.

One of the most agreeable places of residence in Copenhagen is the Rosenborg, a château constructed in the midst of the Rosenborg-have park, having in front of it a large space used for reviews and military exercises. The approach to it is by a street, the Danish name of which, the Kronprindsessgade (the street of the Princess Royal), deserves mention, since it shows how easy this beautiful Danish language is to be understood,

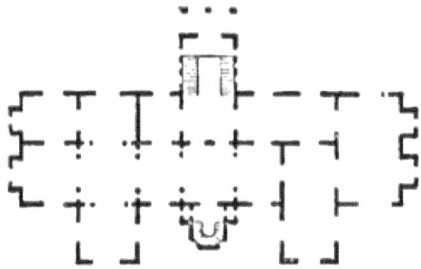

Fig. 174. — Ground-plan of the Rosenborg.

and how conveniently it can be used by foreigners. The Rosenborg was built in 1604 by Christian IV., whose statue stands in the courtyard behind the principal façade. This building is of small dimensions for a royal château (Fig. 174); the staircase is placed in a separate tower projecting beyond the rest of the building. With the exception of a few large rooms, the whole is used for the preservation of the archives of the kingdom, and contains documents precious, in an historical point of view, concerning the monarchy and the charters of Denmark.

The architecture of the edifice takes a certain character from the nature of the materials employed, red bricks embrowned by time, and long regular courses of freestone, forming cornices, plain mouldings, and the parts around the bays. From the side walls project bay-windows, which, if other proofs were wanting, attest the Anglo-Saxon origin of this building. Quaint gables, tortured like those of the Netherlands, deprive the façades of the appearance of unity, which is noticeable in the lower parts. The whole, shown in Fig. 175, is not an architectural creation; it is an agglomeration of incongruous elements, good and bad, united without any reason, and appearing dissatisfied at finding themselves connected with each other. However, as to its resources and its pleasantness as a habitation (which is, in fact, the main object to be attained in any dwelling, whether a palace or a cottage), this château is, of all those to be found in Copenhagen, that which, both by its situation and its general arrangement, must be the most agreeable and the most convenient. Its appearance, doubtless, has not been considered sufficiently imposing, for the Christianborg, a kind of fortress, has been preferred to it, or the Amalienborg, which is narrow and confined, but has façades adorned with pilasters and column.

The Exchange (Fig. 176) is a long and grotesque building, which occupies almost the whole of one side of the Slotsholmsgade. The entrance door is in one of the gables; it is approached by a rather steep inclined plane, which, seen from below, adds to the grandeur of the front. This gable, which is very pretentious in its form, has at the top a large niche, which is still vacant, waiting for a hero. Behind this is the Exchange, properly so called, which is installed on the first floor, with reference to the level of the quay, on which opens a ground-floor occupied by depots and shops of all kinds. The façades, extending along the quay, contain wide mullioned windows; dormer windows, arranged along the roof at certain distances, and surmounted by stiff and grotesque gables, break the monotony of the longer lines, and produce a varied outline, which, seen from a distance, has a good effect. But the most important feature of the building, that which has more especially rendered it noticeable, is the spire above the central tower. This spire is of timber, covered with lead, to which has been given the form of four

Fig. 175.

monsters, whose nature it is difficult to determine. Their heads rest on the four corners of the tower, and their tails are curled upwards round the spire, and terminate in a sharp point. It is impossible to explain this strange conception, and to under-

Fig. 176.—The Exchange, Copenhagen.

stand its meaning. Even its origin is uncertain, for it is said not to be of Danish workmanship, and Christian IV. is reported to have brought it from Kalmar, as a trophy of his victory over Sweden.

This is not a remarkable building, artistically considered, but its unusual character excites curiosity.

The interior of the Exchange is not in keeping with the outer part. It seems almost a deception to find there only one or two ordinary rooms kept very clean, wainscoted with deal painted so as to resemble oak, with a deceptive ceiling divided into sham compartments, and false projecting joists which support a false floor.

The exhibition building was erected in 1871 to receive the Universal Exhibition of the Northern European states; this is the most important modern building in Copenhagen. It stands outside of the town, near the Norrbro, at the extremity of a vast

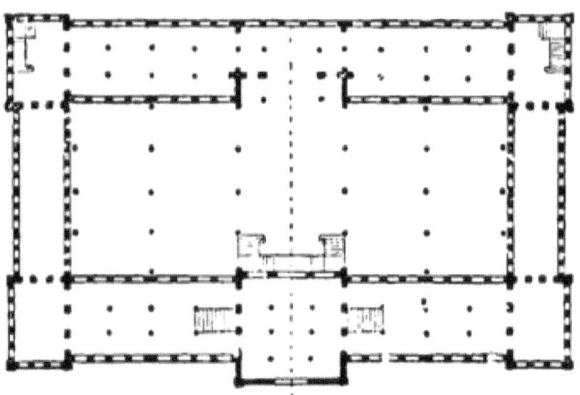

Fig. 177. — Ground-plan of the Exhibition Building.

park, varied by occasional slight elevations, and pieces of water, both salt and fresh, — real lakes, which allow certain special exhibitions of objects to be made under conditions peculiarly appropriate.

The palace forms a rectangle whose longer sides are 492 feet, and the shorter ones 295 (Fig. 177); this rectangle is divided into four compartments, surrounding a central court covered with glass.

A crystal palace like those at Paris, London, and Vienna, was impossible at Copenhagen; the snow, which would have accumulated on the large roofs, would have been productive of rapid injury; and, on the other hand, the Industri-borg was to be preserved, and afterwards utilized for several purposes. It was therefore necessary to render it habitable at every season of the year, and capable of being warmed, either entirely or in parts. The Danish architect has surrounded his central court with buildings having thick walls, the comparatively narrow apertures in which, either towards the public road or the internal courts, can easily be closed by glass windows. He afterwards

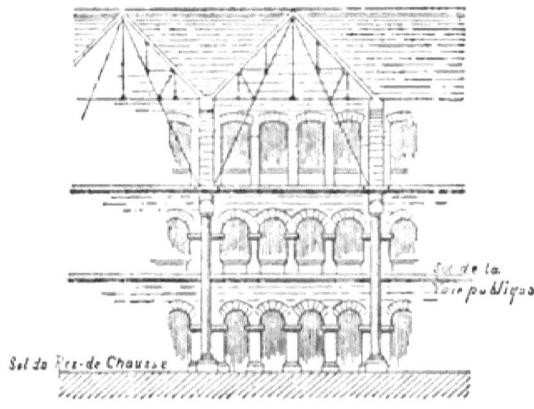

Fig. 178. — Transverse Section of the Exhibition Building, Copenhagen.

covered the interior, not with a single roof, which, extending over the lateral buildings, would be exposed to the terrible blasts of the north-wind, but by five successive roofs (Fig. 178), resting on supports rising from the foundations; these are placed sufficiently near each other, and strong enough to sustain the weight of snow that might accumulate in the intervening spaces. This division into five parts also has the advantage of throwing any occasional addition of weight on a much larger surface than could have been done if the roof had been single.

The façades are rather monotonous (Fig. 179); they might perhaps have laid the bricks in a more ornamental manner, and it would have been possible to avoid the monotony of all those windows of equal size, and those similar pilasters. Even the entrance-door is not of sufficient importance, and does not look grand and noble, in spite of its dimensions; but the whole building is judiciously constructed. We have already explained the plan of the large hall covered with glass; the same idea is carried out in the façades. Thus, the pilasters which ornament

Fig. 179.—General View of the Industri-borg.

them, far from being a mere decoration, form, on the contrary, firm and stable supports to the walls, while the intervening space is filled in with slighter work.

The materials to be found in the country have alone been employed. The floors, the steps of the stairs, and the partitions are of deal; iron is used in some parts of the roof; bricks constitute the whole of the masonry work of the walls, and even of the isolated points of support of the grand nave, which have the form of columns of 1 ft. 8 in. or 2 ft. 3 in. in diameter.

The primary schools are lofty and very large, and the children are not so crowded as in ours; but these buildings, both in their external and internal arrangements, are not to be preferred to those in France. There is one exception as to school furniture, not with respect to its form, but to the manner of its construction.

The Danish schoolmasters were struck with the evils resulting to the health of the child from its being badly seated, and having the reading-book or copy-book too near or too far from the eyes, during the school hours; and with the inconvenience of placing great and little children on the same form; and therefore they prefer that each child should have a seat proportioned to its height, and made, in some respects, to its measure. The class-rooms are therefore filled with rows of small pieces of furniture,[1] comprising a chair furnished with arms and a back, to support the body during the hours of study; before this is placed a small desk, with a top which opens to hold books and paper. Each child is seated at the place assigned to it according to age and height; and the seats are brought nearer to each other according as the class is great or small, thus never leaving an empty or unoccupied space.

This arrangement requires much room, and would be very costly in any country where the furniture would be required to be less roughly made than in Denmark, and in Sweden, where it is also common. A precisely similar plan would not seem practicable in France, but the idea might be adopted, and we might find it advantageous to remedy somewhat our school furniture, which is so inconvenient.

The large Communal Hospital (Fig. 180) is built almost in the country — where all hospitals ought to be located — between the outer wall and a large canal which surrounds the city on

---

[1] See "Construction et installation des écoles primaires," par Félix Narjoux. 1 vol. 8vo. Morel & Co., 13 Rue Bonaparte.

this side. The wards are of great size, and occupied by a restricted number of patients; they open on a gallery connected with the various domestic offices. The rooms appropriated to the officers of the establishment extend along enclosed courts, while the sick-wards have open courts around them. This establishment is therefore well arranged as far as salubrity is concerned, but the internal appointments are not so comfortable as are required in hospitals of this character.

We have still to pay a visit to another palace, that of Fred-

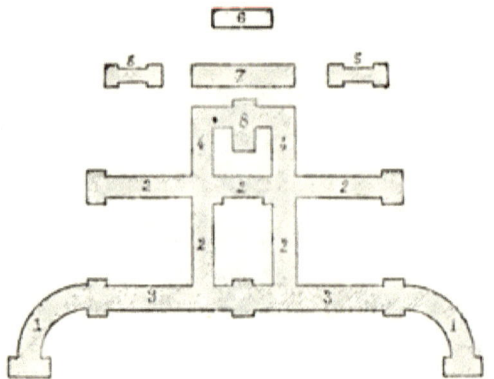

Fig. 180.—Ground-plan of Communal Hospital.

1. Director's apartments.
2. Sick-wards.
3. Rooms for separate patients.
4. Domestic offices.
5. Wards for contagious maladies.
6. Lying-in ward.
7. Surgery and Amphitheatre.
8. Chapel.

eriksborg, at the gates of the city. We enter, at the Kongens Nytorv, one of those large omnibuses which are just beginning to be used in Paris, and in which forty persons can sit with ease, and can enter or leave the vehicle without pressing or interfering with each other. The omnibus is full; a woman presents herself, and immediately a man rises, gives up his place, and stands upon the platform. Each passenger, when he pays the conductor, takes as a receipt a little square piece of paper, which he holds in his hand, and thus avoids all dispute. You pay by tickets instead of money, and these are sold beforehand at the offices. When any one wishes to alight between two stations, the horses slacken their pace without entirely stopping. The carriages cannot turn on their springs, so that when they reach the end of their journey, the horses are unharnessed and put in at the opposite end. There is but one tramway, so all the carriages must wait for each other at the crossings. This causes long and frequent delays, but no one is disturbed by it or grows impatient.

We alight at a large iron gate, at the end of a road planted with trees. This avenue has on each side cheerful houses, surrounded with gardens, lawns, and beds of flowers. At the extremity is the Frederiksborg-have, a very beautiful park, though of no great extent, well laid out, so as to appear larger than it really is, and traversed by a *Serpentine River;* but the flat and level soil is not well suited for such picturesque conceptions. The palace, which stands in the front of a large court and a green lawn, is an ugly building, of a kind of Italian architecture, uninteresting and with no originality. This park and the avenues which lead to it serve as a drive for carriages during certain summer nights, when the sun remains above the horizon till ten o'clock. Then popular fêtes are held there; and performances in the open air, café concerts and noisy balls give extraordinary animation to the scene. It is said that these fêtes are very curious for a foreigner to witness; but unfortunately we are far from the time when they take place, but the amusements which are offered by the Tivoli Garden may give us, as we are told, a good idea of them.

The old city is surrounded by ramparts which cramp it; while the new one, on the contrary, spreads and extends without restraint. It passes into the country by wide and beautiful avenues, builds its houses in the midst of gardens, and surrounds them with verdure and flowers.

The fortifications of the old city are insufficient; they would not now protect it, even provided that they could protect anything but a very small portion of the habitations. A bombardment would soon demolish the lines, if they were exposed to the fire of the besiegers, and the city might be entirely destroyed by means of cannon of long range, placed in batteries at the distance of 6,500 yards, and firing at random. It has, therefore, been necessary to provide against this contingency, and to insure a safe defence if required.

The attacking batteries, according to modern warfare, would be composed of guns of long range, and, as we have said, would probably be placed by the besiegers at the distance of from six to eight thousand yards from the place to be taken, and they would fire either directly or vertically. In either case certainty of aim would not be possible at that distance, since an inappreciably small difference in the training of the gun would give a considerable divergence from the mark at which the shot is aimed. For this reason one can rarely attain accuracy of aim by direct fire; on the contrary, the projectile almost always passes over the ramparts, and falls at a greater or less distance beyond, so as sometimes even to go over the opposite parapet of the town or fortress. With vertical fire, relative success, at least, is more certain. In fact, taking as an example a place defended on Vauban's system, still in use even in modern times, we see that, though the projectile very rarely strikes the ramparts, it is not difficult to make it fall within the lines, and do irreparable injury to the barracks and magazines of all kinds crowded together there, and often to a whole city. The enemy, carefully firing into a circle of large diameter, is thus always certain of doing sufficient damage to cause the surrender of the place within a certain time.

But if, instead of an enceinte fortified by fronts and salients enclosing a large space, the defence presented only a succession of very extended fronts of but little depth, and if these fronts were connected with each other by splinter-proof passages, traverses, and covered ways, and were also sufficiently distant from each other, so that the projectile intended for the outer line of fortifications should not reach the second, and so in succession, the efforts of the besiegers would be singularly neutralized. In the first place the quantity of projectiles required would be enormous, since it would be an exceptional case when those sent would reach their aim; and the line of defence, being extended over a considerable front, would be very effective. As to towns, instead of being surrounded by walls, they would, on the contrary, be open and free, sheltered from a bombardment, and beyond the range of projectiles, because of the distance of the outer lines of defence from the inner enclosure.

It is this system which is to be employed in the defence of Copenhagen. Forts, presenting an extended front with but little depth, will be erected at a great distance from the town on the heights of Vigersbev and Utterslev, to protect it on the land side; while a fortress, defended in the same manner, and built on a part of the coast which is not yet definitely determined, will defend it from any attack by sea. These forts, connected with each other by covered ways and secondary works, will prevent approach, and defy the terrible projectiles of modern artillery. In addition to this, the line of defence thus obtained will be too considerable to be blockaded, and the complete investiture of the town will thus eventually become impossible.

The siege of Paris in 1870 has afforded experience to the Danes, as we have already seen; why did not we profit in the same manner by the lessons which they had received during the war of the Duchies?

The inhabitants of Copenhagen have good reasons for taking these precautions. They find, in the history of the city, records of great disasters that have befallen them; and without going back farther than the beginning of this century, they remember the attack attempted by Nelson in 1801, and, six years afterwards, the bombardment of their city by the same English, who, without any previous declaration of war, destroyed, in three days, three hundred houses and public buildings, and took possession of the Danish fleet.

COPENHAGEN.

III.

THE MUSEUMS. — THORWALDSEN MUSEUM. — THE MUSEUM OF NORTHERN ANTIQUITIES. — THE ETHNOGRAPHICAL MUSEUM.

THIS morning it rains; later in the day it will be very hot; and in the evening we shall be frozen by the north-wind. This is a climate which has nothing settled except its variation, and it is sufficiently trying to foreigners. Therefore we get under shelter whenever we can, and spend our mornings in the museums, where we are fully compensated for our disappointment in not being able to examine the public buildings of Copenhagen.

THE THORWALDSEN MUSEUM.

On one of the sides of the Christianborg stands a long square building, the front of which is ornamented with Etruscan paintings, which it would be more correct to call grotesque. These represent the principal events in the life of Thorwaldsen, of whom Denmark is so proud, and in whose honor the museum which bears his name has been erected. This museum contains a great many original works of the illustrious sculptor, and the moulds, models, or sketches of almost all the others.

Thorwaldsen was born at Copenhagen in 1770; he gained in 1796 the first prize at the Academy, and was sent to Rome at the expense of the government. This journey was made at an unpropitious time, which was very unfavorable for study; the political agitation into which Europe was thrown at that period occupied the minds of all men so entirely, that the feelings of the citizen allowed but little scope to the inspiration of the artist; so that the time allotted for his stay there closed without allowing Thorwaldsen to give much promise of what he would one day become. The generosity of Hope, the banker, gave him an opportunity of continuing his studies, and the works which his genius inspired were from this time produced without any further delay or relaxation.

After his first attempt, Jason carrying off the Golden Fleece, the marble copy of which is in London, the bronze in the possession of the King of Denmark, and the plaster model at the Thorwaldsen Museum, there followed rapidly a vast number of busts of all the important personages in Europe, and at that time there were indeed many. All those heroes who had recently acquired glory wished to transmit to posterity their features sculptured in marble or cast in bronze. At the same time as these works, which were produced from day to day, appeared the Lion of Lucerne; the monument in memory of Poniatowski, erected in front of the bridge over the Vistula at Warsaw; the Triumph of Alexander, ordered by Napoleon, which we saw at the Christianborg; the bas-relief of Priam and Achilles, one of his most popular works; the medallion of Night; the statues of the Graces, of Hebe, Adonis, Venus, and Hope; those of Copernicus, Maximilian of Bavaria, Byron, and Christian IV.; the tomb erected in St. Peter's to Pius VII., etc., etc. Any account of a visit to the museum must necessarily be to some extent a mere catalogue of names.

After having accomplished these laborious tasks, Thorwaldsen was seized with an irresistible desire to return to his native country. He quitted Rome, after having lived there forty-two years, and in 1838 came back to Copenhagen, where he was received in triumph. Notwithstanding his advanced age, for he was now sixty-eight, the great artist set to work, and still gave proofs of his skill. The decoration of the Frue-Kirk at

Copenhagen was intrusted to him; this was his final important work, and the last scintillation of his genius. Thorwaldsen died in 1844, six years after his return to his native city. His tomb was erected in the court of the museum which is devoted to his memory, which bears his name, and where he rests in the midst of his works.

Thorwaldsen disputed with Canova the glory of being the first sculptor at the commencement of this century; there were many controversies to establish the superiority or inferiority of the Danish sculpture when compared with that of Italy. This was a barren discussion, since the premises of argument were incorrect. Thorwaldsen was not a Danish, but a Roman sculptor, like Canova, from whom he received lessons. He did not create a school or a style peculiar to himself; his productions do not form a distinct branch of art, but, on the contrary, belong to the Italian school, which he studied, and the tendencies, forms, and results of which he so happily assimilated to himself.

An indefatigable laborer, Thorwaldsen produced many works. The most remarkable were all originated at Rome, under the influence of the surroundings in the midst of which he lived. Except the bas-reliefs of the Frue-Kirk of Copenhagen, sculptured in the decline of his career, his works were all executed far from the scenes of his native land; and not one, except a few busts and statues, was inspired by the manners, the nation, or the men of the country where he was born. His imagination revelled in the ideal world, and all his most remarkable compositions have for their object the reproduction of an allegorical idea, recollections of mythological ages, or of so distant a period of history that it may be ranged among them. When, on the contrary, he wishes to reproduce a purely human idea, and to represent a contemporary personage, with respect to whom the ordinary details of life are of importance, he becomes inferior to himself. It is for this reason that his Cupids of every kind, his Gods of Olympus, and the Triumph of Alexander are far superior to his statues of Schiller, Gutenburg, Pius VII., Poniatowski, and others, whatever the incontestable merits of these works may be.

The chief characteristics of the works of art of the countries beyond the Rhine are the careful working out of detail, and their servile and often trivial copying. Purely ideal conceptions are not formed by these artists, and the productions of Thorwaldsen are remarkable for results diametrically opposed to these. He had the germ of his genius within himself, in his soul and his nature; but it was under the sky of Italy, and by the study and the contemplation of the productions of Rome, that this divine essence was developed, and acquired its power and perfection; the seed was sown in Denmark, but it put forth its full blossom only in Italy.

Thorwaldsen was not, therefore, a Danish, but a Roman artist; if he was born in Denmark, he lived, formed his artistic character, and became what he was only in Italy.

The tombs of Canova and of Thorwaldsen plainly show the difference of sentiment between the races and countries which have given them birth. They are evident proofs of the distance which separates these two countries, which distinguishes their tastes, their feelings, and the manner in which they receive impressions.

The tomb of the Danish sculptor is a complicated monument, both in form and dimensions; for it is not merely the mound and the sepulchral stone erected in the midst of the court. His tomb is rather the museum, the halls and galleries, the works of all kinds, sculptures, inscriptions, symbols, the triumphal car, the laurels; each minute detail is carefully carried out, each souvenir appeals to our attention, excites our curiosity, and satisfies it; it insists upon informing all, as if they were totally ignorant of it, who it was whose loss is so much deplored. Nothing must be left to be guessed or interpreted by the imagination of the people of the North.

What a difference between this funeral monument and the

tomb of Canova in the Church of de 'Frari at Venice! When we disregard the rather complicated assemblage of persons and scenes, which are independent of the general conception, and render it pretentious, we see only a pyramid of marble. At the base stands a winged genius, who is extinguishing a torch and opening the door; through the opening we perceive the gloomy horror of darkness, and on the top of the pyramid are these words: "To Canova." The spectator is astonished, disturbed, and excited. This is not effected by the multiplicity of the means employed, by novelty of invention, or complicated details; but these blocks of stone, and this door of eternity left open, sufficiently tell the tale. The impressionable Italian needs but a word, a sign, and an indication.

MUSEUM OF NORTHERN ANTIQUITIES.

The museum of the Antiquities of the North is installed in the palace of the princes.[1] This is richer in prehistoric antiquities than any other in Europe; there we find collected, classified, and explained, all the discoveries obtained from excavations made in the islands of the Baltic, and in the peat bogs of Funen, Zealand, Gothland, Rugen, and elsewhere. The different ages of the world are there represented by objects illustrating the various degrees of civilization. We may thus follow, step by step, the formation of the social ages of the globe. The classification is so well made, and the objects so skilfully displayed, that we go from one glass case to another without fatigue or ennui, studying, comparing the various transitions and the handiwork of men who succeeded each other, generation after generation, in a regular, constant, and uninterrupted gradation.

We pass by the ages of polished stone; all these little flint implements, whether round, sharp, or worked into a pointed form, or one resembling a hatchet, give us but little informa-

---

[1] See "Musée des Antiquités du Nord à Copenhague." Engelhardt, Kiobenhavn, 1870.

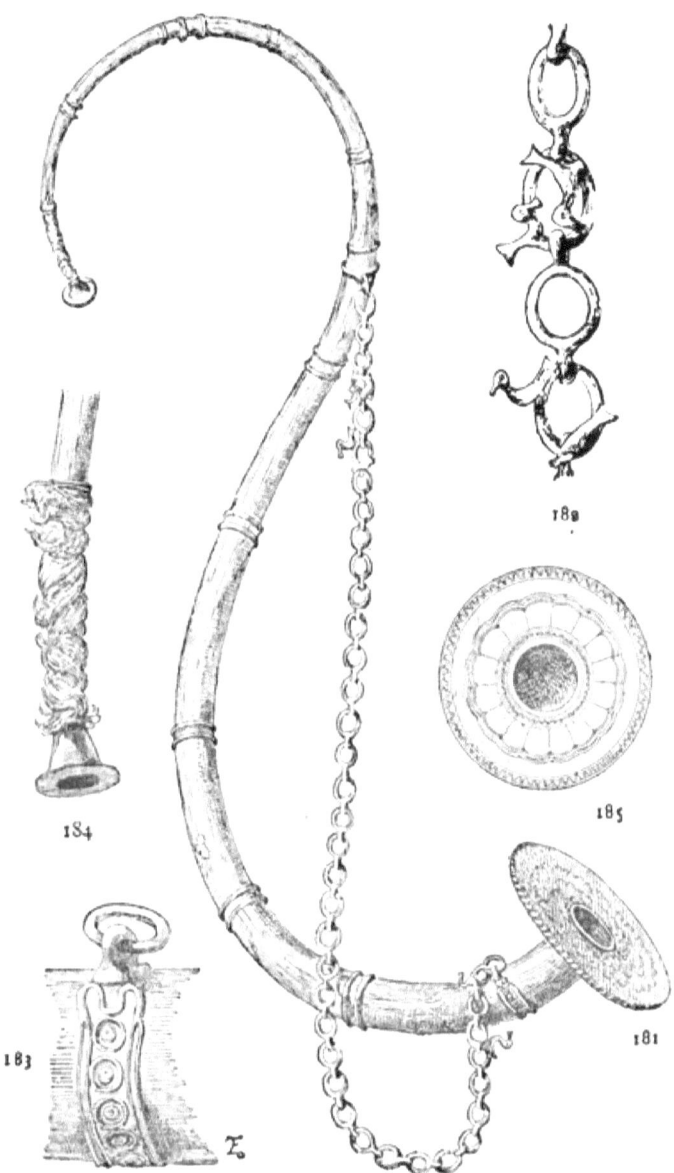

Figs. 181 to 185. — Trumpet of the Age of Bronze.
(Prehistoric period.)
From the Museum of Scandinavian Antiquities, Copenhagen.

tion; and we reach the rooms allotted to the bronze age, that period when arms and cutting instruments were cast in bronze, an alloy of copper and tin. Gold was already frequently used in the manufacture of jewelry and ornaments, but they did not yet understand the working of iron and silver; and they were also ignorant of the process of soldering. They were, therefore, much restricted in their productions, and the forms obtained could vary but slightly. Yet the results are very astonishing; we may judge of them by some ordinary articles selected from among those which struck us the most.

A bronze trumpet (Fig. 181), composed of several parts joined together, but cast separately, the form of which resembles the letter S. A small chain connects the two ends, and from the links of this chain project small birds (Fig. 182), the first attempt to represent living creatures. Projecting rings (Fig. 183) on the body of the trumpet show where the chain was attached; the mouthpiece (Fig. 184) is still surrounded by some threads or the woof of some kind of stuff, intended to be grasped by the hand of the person who wished to use the instrument; on the mouth (Fig. 185) are traced in intaglio some perfectly regular geometrical designs. It would certainly be curious to place this trumpet to one's mouth, and to ascertain what sounds it would give forth, and what melody it was formerly able to produce.

Fig. 186 represents the handle of a drinking-horn, made of bronze.

There is also a bronze dagger about 13 inches long and $1\tfrac{1}{5}$ inch broad; on the handle there are designs engraved, very simple geometrical figures, but very regularly traced; the sheath is made of wood, covered with carving; the care shown in the fabrication, the choice metal, and the finished touches of the ornamental parts, show that this poniard was a valuable weapon. It was found in a wooden coffin, formed of the trunk of an oak, hollowed out without the aid of the saw, no traces of which could be found. The bottom of the coffin was covered with the hide of an ox, on which the corpse was laid, dressed in gala costume, and surrounded by his weapons. The other articles discovered in this coffin were very curious; there was a fragment of a dress composed of woollen cloth, a small box, a horn comb, a bronze knife, and a hatchet, also made of bronze. This hollow hatchet is filled with clay; one of the sides has been broken, but the other, which remains intact, has on its surface ornaments in deep intaglio, incrusted with gold.

Fig. 187 represents a bronze pin, of the natural size, and of a regular design; the plan by which the pin is moved is very simple and ingenious, and is still in use in modern jewelry. Some other very rich golden ornaments, but heavy in appearance, and of no very complicated workmanship, are by the side of the first; these are diadems, bracelets, rings, and armlets, ornamented with engraved work and spiral or geometrical de-

Fig. 186.—Handle of Drinking-vessel.

signs. There are in every instance the same simple patterns, easily traced and uniformly repeated.

The iron age improves slightly on these early productions of human industry. We will mention some specimens of this period.

Coins with Cufic[1] legends, of the ninth, tenth, and eleventh centuries, which have enabled us to distinguish three distinct periods in the iron age. Articles of the toilet or the riding-school, earthen vases, etc.

Fig. 188 represents a bronze pin, of the natural size; the spring which is adapted to the pin is of a spiral form, scarcely different from those used at the present day. At the extremity, near the broken portion, is the inscription "Hiriso," which re-

---

[1] Arabic characters used before the fourth century after the Hegira.—Tr.

minds us of those of the same kind which are now engraved on ladies' ornaments; all round this are small ornamental circular depressions. The body of the pin was evidently intended to represent a ribbon or some kind of stuff tied in a bow.

Another very curious bronze pin, of simple but very original form, is shown in Fig. 189, two thirds of the natural size; the spiral which gives motion to the spring is similar to that used in pins of English manufacture (Kirby).

Many other ornaments of the same kind are to be seen, with inscriptions, which are most probably Runic.

Fig. 190 represents a bronze cup, half the natural size, of remarkable workmanship; the outlines are sharp, well defined, and free from stiffness; the handle is curiously curved, and of

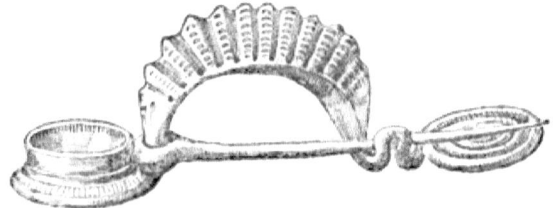

Fig. 187. — Bronze Pin.

original form; in the upper part is an attempt at the representation of the head of some animal. This vessel came from a tumulus discovered in Jutland, which was formed of two concentric circles of stone; in the middle were found other goblets of silver, enriched with plates of gold, and a kind of saucepan covered with a strainer, intended, as is supposed, to receive the blood of victims after a sacrifice.

There are also other ornaments of Byzantine workmanship for women; these are heavy and clumsily formed, and on many of them Runic inscriptions are engraved.

There is a boat, discovered in the peat-bogs of Sleswig (a vessel more than 78 feet long, and 11½ feet in its greatest breadth), in which there is an oar still remaining, in such a state of preservation as to allow us to study the mode of construction, and the manner in which wood was employed. We see also spearheads, swords whose blades are damascened with wonderful care

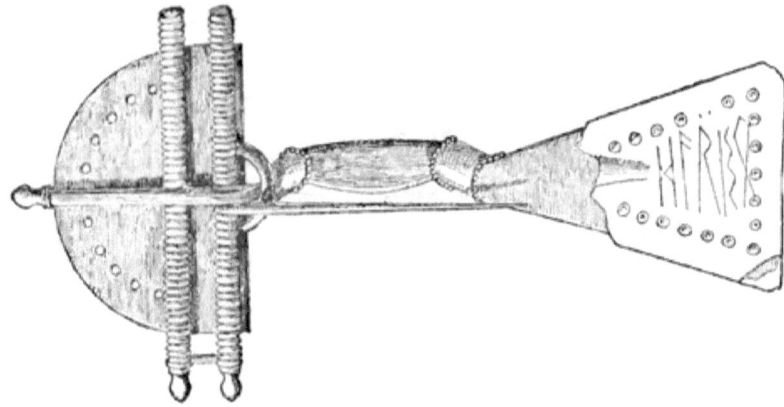

Fig. 188.— Bronze Pin.

and art, fragments of coats of mail, and clasps to fasten them. A helmet made of *repoussé* bronze, and plated with silver; the visor allows the mouth, nose, and eyes to appear, the hinder part

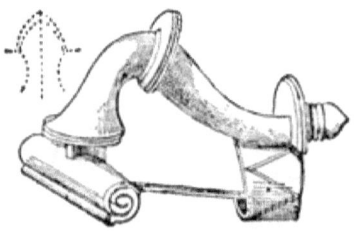

Fig. 189.— Bronze Pin.

was enclosed with bars of openwork; between these two parts is a rich band embellished with gold, and decorated with engraved designs.

In Fig. 191 is shown part of the harness for a horse, of the later iron age, which came from a tumulus opened in the island of Funen. It is composed of an arched cross-piece of wood, ornamented at the upper part by a projecting piece through which the reins were passed. The ends are enriched by the heads of fantastic animals (Fig. 192), and the ornaments, made of *repoussé* bronze, engraved and gilded, are wrought with extreme care; they show one of the earliest examples, of so successful a character, of the reproduction of allegorical figures, resembling, in some degree, beings endowed with life. There are also fragments of woollen and silk stuffs, of an odd design, easily understood, but difficult to describe; as well as Runic

Fig. 190. — Bronze Cup.

stones, covered with inscriptions, which appear to possess a high archæological interest, but which we are unable to understand or discuss.

We now come to the Middle Ages.

The new kind of architecture, introduced into the North at this period, and derived from Rhenish recollections or those brought from the Isle of France by monks of all orders, does not manifest its influence by large public buildings or edifices of great size. Examples of this kind are very rare; those found in Scandinavian lands are, with few exceptions, dark, low churches,

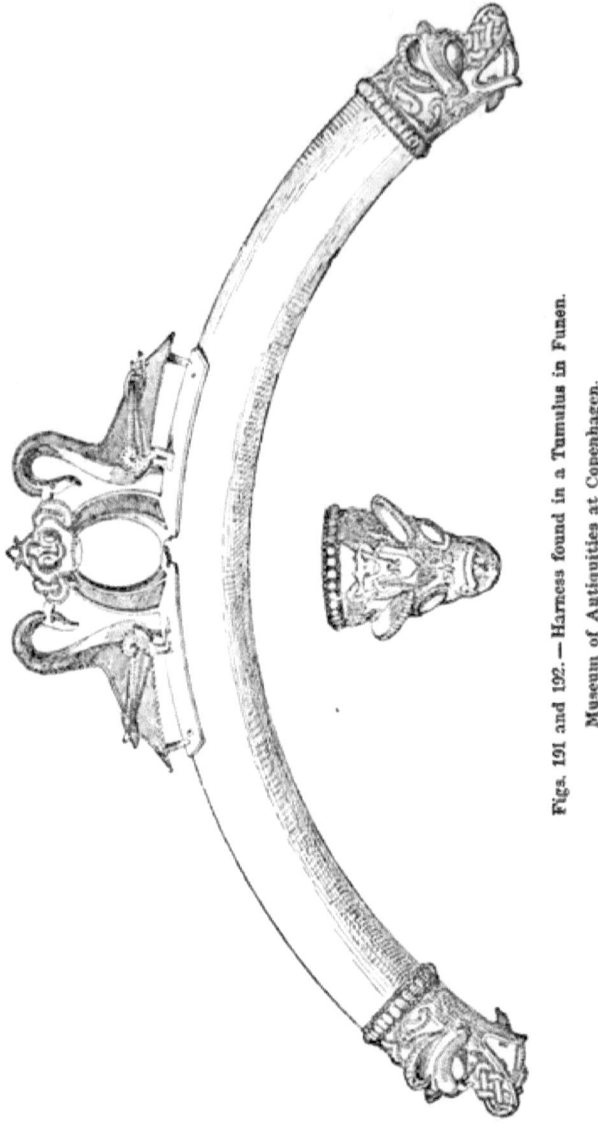

Figs. 191 and 192.—Harness found in a Tumulus in Funen. Museum of Antiquities at Copenhagen.

without towers or steeples; often with a flat wooden ceiling instead of a vaulted one. The interiors are meagre, and in the few decorations that we find, Pagan ideas predominate, adapted to the requirements of the new worship. But still, the gradual improvement of Middle Age art may be seen and ascertained in the monuments of this period which are still preserved.

Fig. 193.—Granite Tomb. Front View.

We will mention a few of these.

A tomb made of granite (Fig. 193) shaped like a roof; the ridge, the sloping side, and the base are surrounded by a moulding, forming a kind of frame. The tomb was supported by two

Fig. 194.—Opposite Side of Tomb.

stones, having grooves cut to receive it, and placed at each end.

On one side is sculptured in relief (Fig. 194) a man, armed with a bow, fighting with a centaur, behind whom stands an angel carrying a child in his arms. On the opposite side is a fanciful animal (Fig. 193) devouring a man, whose head alone is still protruding from its jaws.

The Danish archæologists, as ingenious as those in France, suppose that the former subject represents the deceased striving against evil, under the figure of the centaur. The angel on the other side is St. Michael, opening his arms to the soul, victorious in the fight to which his fleshly body has been exposed. The second subject is an allusion to the words of the Apostle St.

Fig. 195.—Granite Font.

Peter, "Your adversary, the devil, as a roaring lion, goeth about, seeking whom he may destroy."

Granite baptismal font (Fig. 195). In the front of this is the figure of a woman between two imaginary animals, who are gnawing her arms; the manner in which, according to Danish archæologists, they expressed the fact that man is always a prey to evil passions, unless he watch against them.

The sculpture of these two small monuments of the past is in good preservation, and its execution is distinguished for its remarkable simplicity, which is shown, not only in the workmanship itself, but also in the expression of the figures, and the manner in which they are depicted and grouped. These works, of archæological rather than artistic interest, are very inferior to those which our Middle Ages produced at the same period.

Fig. 196. — Chancel Candlestick.

A century later, the arts had made sensible progress. There are shrines of the twelfth century, made of metal or wood, and adorned with enamels and wreathed work, executed with great skill. There are also a considerable number of other enamelled articles, and among these a chancel candlestick (Fig. 196) of copper, enriched with enamels, the designs of which are very fine, and show great freedom of execution, being formed of scrolls around a central pattern.

We find here a great number of objects used in public worship (thirteenth century); some tolerable painted windows, statues and groups of figures, censers, pyxes, and other sacred vessels; also carved stalls and seats, in every respect very inferior to our productions of the same period.

There are other curious objects of a more recent date, — ancient Scandinavian calendars, domestic utensils, drinking-horns ornamented with copper and silver both engraved and gilt, arms and ancient armor, and pieces of artillery.

Fig. 197. — Terra-cotta Taper-stand.

There are some taper-stands made of terra-cotta (Fig. 197), nearly eight inches long by seven in height, rudely representing a castle defended by gates, with towers separated by a gable; on all sides of these are irregular designs, applied before the material was baked. There are, besides these, tapestries of the sixteenth and seventeenth centuries, an altar of ebony and silver, clocks, watches, nuptial crowns, etc.

We see, by this too rapid survey, what riches are deposited in the Museum of Northern Antiquities at Copenhagen; it may easily be understood how many things interesting and worthy

of attention we were obliged to leave undescribed. One ought
to be able to devote a considerable time to this museum; and
the student, who has leisure to do so, will not regret it, and will
find there an enormous quantity of rare and curious articles.

THE ETHNOGRAPHICAL MUSEUM.

Another museum at Copenhagen, the Ethnographical, is less
learned, but as useful and interesting as the museum of antiquities.

It comprises a collection of typical objects, characteristic of
human civilization in every part of the world; and, in order to
arrive at this result, it gives such details as are best suited to
illustrate the nature and the degree of advancement of each form
of civilization. The most curious and amusing portions of this
museum are those which relate to Greenland and Japan, countries of which we know very little, and which consequently
excite greater curiosity.

Instead of rags hanging on the walls, and articles, lying side
by side, without any link to show the connection between them;
in fact — instead of objects dispersed over a large space — the
Ethnographical Museum at Copenhagen exhibits, on the contrary, collections which attract and arrest the attention, and in
which every one seeks immediately the points in which he is
interested; details which differ in each individual, according to
his tastes, his tendencies, and his education.

Thus, instead of furniture, dresses, and utensils arranged separately and scattered here and there, we find a dwelling of the
natural size, with actual furniture, and with the masters of the
house at home, and under the circumstances of ordinary life.

And, first, we have the habitations of the Greenlanders —
huts built of earth and moss, from 13 to 20 feet in diameter,
covered internally with skins of animals. The entrance is
effected by a low and narrow passage, through which it is
necessary to pass in a creeping posture; at the top of the hut

is an orifice, which can be opened in case of need. Within is a family, installed, as they would be in their snowy desert; two men, three women, and four children are partaking of a meal. An earthen saucepan is on the fire, and others are arranged in a corner with some dishes and lamps; the usual combustibles are wanting, but their place is supplied by oil, which warms the frosty atmosphere and cooks the food.

The perfumes which exhale from this interior, and which, to render the illusion more complete, have been conscientiously respected, will not allow us to make too long a stay. The figures, of life-size, are dressed in skins of animals; some furs, stretched on a low and wide settle, indicate what serves for a bed. The women are preparing the food, and putting the saucepan over a lamp furnished with a wick made of moss, the size and length of which are adjusted so as to be sufficient to cook the meal; and then all lie down and sleep. When the family wake, the feast is ready, they eat, fill the pot again, place it over the lamp, the wick having been renewed, and then they lie down again and sleep, resting and eating alternately. These people have no idea of days or hours; they make no distinction of time except between periods of light and darkness.

There are also a team of dogs, which, in that country, supply the place of horses; sledges drawn by seven dogs ready harnessed; one of these animals serves as leader; it is he who excites, leads, and encourages the others; his marvellous instinct guides him, and secures the confidence of the travellers.

Then, there are fishing-dresses made of skins with the fur on, inflated with air, so as to be buoyant in water in case of accident, and to avoid damp, the consequences of which are fatal in these latitudes. The men, thus dressed, look like the figures of gold-beater's skin, filled with gas, which serve to amuse children. There are also hunting-dresses, woven from the intestines of the dog-fish.

We next see a Cajak fishing-boat, rowed by women,—twenty of whom hold the oars; they are not handsome; those who wear red head-dresses are married; the others with green ones are unmarried; those with yellow caps are neither married nor virgins, and make no secret of it.

There are some fishing-implements; and as the fish lurk at the bottom of the sea, and often far from shore, in order to find warmer water, it is necessary, when they wish to catch them, to make a hole in the ice, and to let down a net from 2,300 to 2,600 feet in length. These nets are made of whalebone, and have great strength.

We notice also the marriage trousseau of a young Greenland woman — a carpet of dog-fish skin ornamented with minute colored designs, some thread made of the fibres of animals, a thimble, a little instrument used for tracing the designs with which the skins are ornamented; there are also dresses and furs.

We pass over America, Africa, and Oceania, which are represented in a manner less striking and original, and contain but little to attract the attention, and we arrive at the empire of the rising sun.

There is a Yeddo house, built of fir-wood and paper; the principal supports are four posts, the intervals between which are formed of frames covered with paper. In the daytime these frames are removed, and the roof seems supported on stilts; when night comes, they push in the side scenes, and the house, lighted within, resembles a gigantic Venetian lantern. Every house of this kind is inhabited by a single family. On the ground-floor is a shop; on the upper one a sitting-room, divided, at night, into a certain number of little rooms by means of sliding partitions. The furniture is very simple: a cupboard to contain the mattresses during the daytime; a small stove hidden in a corner; a series of little tables slipping into each other; and, arranged on shelves, a collection of cups or dishes of lacquered ware. In the middle of the room are the chibot or brasier (*brazzero*), and the tabacco-bou (tobacco-box); on the floor is a very fine, thin, and flexible mat made of straw, on which no one is allowed to tread till he has taken off his shoes.

The house which we were examining had the front removed, so as to allow us to see a very cheerful scene within, — five or six persons together, squatting on their heels, drinking and smoking around the teapot. The women are dressed in a kind of cloak, confined at the waist by a very broad girdle of green and yellow silk, tied in a large bow at the back. Their lips are gilded; their black hair, smoothed and waxed, is confined with large pins, by which it is built up to an extraordinary height. You may see at the door the little wooden shoes in which they hobble along in the street, and which they have now taken off, in order to lie down on the mat. One of the men is standing, to show his splendid costume, — an overcoat with sleeves of extravagant width, under which appear two sabres, the insignia of his rank as a Yakonine, or officer of the Daïmio, whose arms are embroidered in gaudy colors on his back, and around his neck. He wears a large hat of a dark crimson color; at his waist is the whole apparatus of a smoker, a pipe as small as a thimble, a tobacco-box made of paper, a flint and steel, etc., etc. On his feet are stockings made with a special compartment for the toe, and sandals of plaited straw, which he keeps on with difficulty.

There is a Norimon, or Japanese cab, a very inconvenient box, into which the traveller squeezes himself, with his legs bent under him; air is admitted by a small opening in the roof, similar to that in the Hansom cabs in London. At each side of this box are two poles, which are supported on the shoulders of two bearers, very slightly clad. When they are fatigued, they allow the norimon to rest on two short poles with which they are furnished, so as to avoid the trouble of lowering and raising their burden.

We noticed a specimen of Japanese paper, a kind of parchment, but thicker, and at the same time more pliable, a tissue which cannot be torn, is impermeable, and whose uses are manifold. They make of it the walls of houses, great-coats, napkins, and umbrellas, and it has nothing in common with the idea which the word "paper" awakens in our minds.

Japan detained us for a long time; we cannot, however, describe all that we saw, or the many curious and interesting things that attracted our attention, such as a Daïmio with his attendants, and the view of a Yankiro, one of the quarters of Yeddo or Yokohama, where the tea-houses are situated. We cannot give an idea of all the costumes, and the attitudes of these full-sized dolls so splendidly dressed, representing persons in every social position in Japan. We must not describe their large public buildings and immense temples, or relate the legend of the forty-seven Yakonines who disembowelled themselves on the tomb of their Daïmio, so terribly represented in a series of colored pictures; but we must say a few words about the remarkable productions of industrial art in Japan, and examine the furniture, ivories, porcelain, lacquered ware, and bronzes, of which there are so many examples around us.

The oddness of these objects is not their most remarkable characteristic. It is more apparent than real; it strikes us, because some of their customs and ideas are so opposed to ours; and it suggests so great a dissimilarity between their surroundings and those to which we are accustomed. We are also not always willing readily to suppose that others can think and act in a different manner from ourselves; but still this discrepancy between our ideas and theirs is not necessarily to the disadvantage of the Japanese, and, on the contrary, it is sometimes in favor of their tastes and usages. After all, we must not judge of the peculiarities of the Japanese from the specimens displayed in European bazaars, the unusual forms of which have been exaggerated by the manufacturer in order to attract more strongly the attention of the purchaser.

The Japanese, unlike ourselves, make no distinction between high art and that which has recently been called "industrial." They look upon both these branches of art in the same light;

and the artist who models a vase of an elegant form, or designs a graceful decoration, is considered to be as truly an artist, and to possess the feeling of his art in the same degree, as he who decorates the façade of a temple, or sculptures a statue in honor of Buddha.

The result of this is that articles in common use are brought to a higher state of perfection, which astonishes us, and would surprise us still more if we knew that the delicate porcelain and lacquered dishes, which are used by us only on grand occasions, and are considered as exceptional, are employed in Japan for the ordinary purposes of daily life.

The peculiar characteristics of all these works, those by which they are distinguished from our productions of the same kind, are the absence of symmetry, the entire correspondence of form with the nature of the material employed, and the method of coloring.

We must not understand by the absence of symmetry a disproportion between the various parts of the same whole, or imagine that we shall meet with a bandy-legged or maimed figure; we must not confound harmony with symmetry. If, for example, we place two vases on our mantel-shelf, they will be exactly similar, not only in form, but in decoration. They are in reality the same vase, and when we look at them we have no double pleasure from this twofold possession. If, on the contrary, we examine two Japanese vases, we find them similar in their general form; one is not tall and the other short and wide, but still the sweep of the outline is not identically the same in both, although the difference between them is not sufficient to shock our taste. Then the decoration on each is different, the color of the ground in one is often that of the design in the other; the birds and flowers vary in their tints; the figures are of a different character; and the scenes represented are not the same. These observations refer not only to vases, but to everything,— paper-hangings, lacquered boxes, cups, plates, etc., etc.

The complete correspondence of form with the nature of the materials employed is still more easily explained. We have only to compare the smooth and unvaried surfaces of porcelain, which is a material essentially fragile, with the irregular projecting surfaces given to bronzes, the substance of which is extremely hard. Ivories are carved in intaglio, without allowing any projection to rise above the level of the ornamentation and thus to be exposed to injury; and, a circumstance which strikingly illustrates our observations, the teacups have no handles, and those of the vases are merely small thick hoops, so as to give the least possible chance of inevitable accidents.

Again, the manner in which all these articles are colored differs essentially from that practised by ourselves. The painting is not in relief; no transition, except that of the harmony of colors, produces the contrast and difference of the tints, and yet, notwithstanding their intensity, this harmony is so great that they never offend the eye; the colors employed are always definite and but few; yet, owing to the variety of designs employed, their number seems infinite.

But we must stop, or we might be accused of imitating those travellers whose enthusiasm increases with distance; and as we are already in Japan this might carry us too far.

These museums are not the only ones to be seen in Copenhagen. We may mention the museum of antiquities, that of engravings, and the gallery of the Moltke Palace. During the Exhibition of 1872 a number of pictures were collected, consisting of the modern works of Swedish and Danish artists. It must be confessed that there was no great artistic merit to recommend these paintings; but they were very interesting to a foreigner, since they depicted, almost exclusively, scenes relating to the manners and customs of the daily life of Scandinavian society, and thus afforded a striking contrast to those treated in our annual exhibitions.

There were many winter landscapes; a boundless horizon, an immense white sheet, enveloped in frozen mist; and there, lost in this desert, you could just perceive a sledge drawn by reindeer, whose furious gallop threw up the whirling snow; this dark point was the only object which told of movement and of life in the midst of this white immensity. By the side of this picture were to be seen, under a serene sky, sledges full of handsome women, who shiver under their furs, as they pass over a carpet of snow tinged by a pale ray of light; others are looking at a group of skaters in bright costumes, or striving to catch the harmony produced by a band of musicians, whose notes seem to freeze in the air. This picture is a recollection of Lapland; it is the Melar, on a festival occasion, on a *beautiful* cold day.

In contrast with these scenes is the Gustaf-Adolph Platz at Stockholm on a winter's night, when at midnight you can still distinguish the outlines of the ships outward-bound for the Baltic. In other pictures we see the islands of the Archipelago of Aland, covered with trees whose verdure mingles with the greenish hue of the water; or the dark rocks of Norway, against which some monstrous iceberg is dashing; or, again, the Djugarten, filled with gay and loving couples clinging to each other; and, still farther on, the portrait of a Dalecarlian woman in her picturesque costume, or that of some frail and enticing coquette. But, as we have already said, the interest of this exhibition was, unfortunately, to be found only in the choice of subjects, and in their novelty, rather than in the manner in which they were treated.

COPENHAGEN.

IV.

THE DANES. — THE THEATRES. — AMUSEMENTS.

THE men are of middle height, strong, and well knit; they have pronounced features, light hair, and blue eyes. Their gait is heavy, and is wanting in ease and gracefulness. They have no elegance or distinguished air. They dress badly; they scarcely look like gentlemen, or else greatly exaggerate our fashions. The materials of their dress are usually much coarser than those which we use, and they seem altogether ignorant of the resources and refinements of the toilet.

The women have bright complexions, white teeth, blue or gray eyes, and long fair hair; but they are not graceful, in the Parisian sense of the word. They are economical in their dress, and we scarcely remember having seen ladies in silk dresses except at the theatre.

The Danes are intelligent, as you may see by their features; if you speak to them, you find them polite and affable. Instead of walking on, when a traveller stops them to ask for any information in a language which they do not understand, they make a thousand efforts to discover what he wants, and to assist him. They are always hospitable; and even now, when a customer enters a shop, and it is clearly ascertained that he is not a German, the tradesmen, after a thousand friendly protestations, which are unfortunately in Danish, and before they show him any of their goods, offer him, on a waiter, a glass of Kirsch to counteract the effects of the fog. The Danes are well informed, and there is no country in Europe where public education receives more attention than in Denmark.

The women are *the angels of the house;* they know nothing but calm and peaceful home life. Their amusements in winter are family parties, and the theatre, to which they often go without escort; and in the summer they take country walks.

The young people marry early, and are engaged beforehand. The *fiancés* enjoy privileges which might cause inconvenience among other people, — ourselves, for example, — but which are harmless among the Danes, who are calmer and less impressionable. It is very unusual for those who are contracted to each other to break their engagement, for the blame which they would both incur is sufficient to prevent their taking such a step.

Their out-door pleasures possess but little variety, and boisterous amusements are unknown; their family and friendly meetings are not prolonged to a late hour. The theatres are closed at nine o'clock, the lights extinguished, the streets deserted, the taverns empty, and every one is snugly ensconced under the bedclothes.

The manners of Copenhagen have not always been so simple and exemplary. The examples of the court of Louis XV. of France were regarded at one time with great favor. We shall presently see what traces of this epoch have been left, in certain quarters, in the dwellings constructed in the eighteenth century.

Statistics prove that suicide is more prevalent in Denmark than in any other country in Europe. The cause of the development of this mental malady is unknown, but it is a proof of the love of the Danes for the family and for domestic life, that this madness prevails especially among the unmarried and widows; and it is by no means unusual for a woman to hang herself when she is placed in one of these positions.

By a contrast, which is difficult to explain, Brigham Young still gains the greatest number of Mormon recruits among the

Danes, and a new Copenhagen is now rising near Salt Lake City.

Education is very general in Denmark; it is obligatory, and the father of a family must send his children to school, under penalty of a fine. The students at the university are numerous, but so great a proportion of them study theology, that it is impossible to find positions for all who seek for them; so that, while waiting for a cure, future pastors sometimes exercise a profession whose functions seem but little compatible with those which they hope hereafter to fulfil. All the students of a college unite in a club, where they find every opportunity for study and amusement: a library, a theatre, concert-rooms, and a tavern, which are always open to them; they eat and drink there, and more especially smoke incessantly. The large dining-room is always filled, and between two lectures or repetitions there is a great consumption of rog-brod and of bocks of Bavarian beer. Those who frequent it are concealed by clouds of smoke issuing from large pipes which are never allowed to go out.

The love of their country is strongly developed in all classes of society, and their hatred of Germany, far from being extinguished, increases every day. To call a Dane a Prussian — a Berlin Prussian — is the greatest insult that you can offer to him.

One day we went into a stationer's shop to buy a small sheet of drawing-board. While we pointed out to the shopkeeper the article that we wanted, as we knew not how to ask for it, he grumbled in a low voice, murmuring incessantly between his teeth certain words which we could not fail to understand as expressions of ill-humor. At last, wishing to eke out the dumb show which we found so ineffectual, we uttered a few words in French. The expression of his face instantly changed. "Not Prussian, French!"[1] he exclaimed, and, jumping over the counter, he seized our hands, opened the door of the back shop, and

[1] We cannot give the exact Danish expressions corresponding with these words, as we are not able to depend on our memory.

called out his wife and children, crying out, "French! French! Paris!" We were obliged to shake hands with them all, to kiss the children, to drink a glass of Kirsch to the health of France and to the confusion of Prussia; and at the close of the interview the stationer, seizing a hank of string, wound it round his neck, imitating the position of a man who was hanged, putting out his tongue like one at the last extremity, and crying, "For the Prussians, for all the Prussians!"

Compared with the Germans, the Danes are gay and excitable. In the North, they have the reputation of resembling the French. It is from Denmark that they procure recruits for the theatrical companies of Stockholm and Christiania, and the performers at the café concerts, so common in Scandinavian towns.

There are but few manufactures in Denmark, their productions being almost exclusively agricultural; but glove-making has increased lately. The Danish gloves are supple, strong, and well sewn; they may even be washed, but they are very dear. Commerce carried on by sea is in a very flourishing state. Every one gains his living modestly by continued and incessant labor, in which there is nothing exaggerated. Our feverish ambition is unknown, and no one desires or seeks to increase his store immoderately, or to make a rapid fortune at the expense of his neighbor. The Dane is excessively honest, loyal, and trustworthy, and robbery is almost unknown in the country. The shops and warehouses do not require to be protected by shutters of wood or iron; and the goods are exposed within reach of the hands without its being thought necessary to watch over them. Great fortunes are as rare as excessive poverty. It is true that at Copenhagen few people keep their carriage; but, on the contrary, you never meet a beggar.

We spoke of the cookery during our stay in Funen; it is similar in the other provinces, and is not always satisfactory to a French taste; but the hotels and restaurants, when you can make yourself understood, are very excellent and exceedingly cheap. You get the same dishes as elsewhere, and you drink exquisite tea and good beer; but the wines, on the contrary, especially those from France, are shamefully adulterated, and are execrable.

Danish literature is known to us only by certain translations of novels, the *naïveté* and simplicity of which form their greatest charm. Hans Andersen is known throughout the whole world by his popular tales, full of such acute observations and profound views, under a guise so simple and familiar. The theatrical repertory is composed of pieces written by native authors, which are few in number, and, as ought to be the case, of translations of our French literature.

This evening we are going to the theatre. It is five o'clock; we hasten in order to be there when the doors are opened. The price of seats is very moderate. They are going to give a translation or adaptation of Octave Feuillet's "Romance of a Poor Young Man"; so we shall be able, by our remembrance of it, to guess, if we cannot comprehend, something of the dialogue, and see what impression is made on the spectators.

The house is very large, but very simply decorated. There are two tiers of open boxes, a gallery, some orchestral stalls, and at the bottom a large pit. The seats are not comfortable, they are rapidly filled, and not one is left empty. There are many children there who evidently could not be left at home alone. The spectators belong to all classes; the women are predominant, forming at least two thirds of the assembly. Their dress is very simple; they are all, with few exceptions, in woollen dresses or white muslin. They come wrapped up in large waterproofs, in groups of two or three, sometimes accompanied by a gentleman, but more frequently alone. No one, however, is astonished at this; it is a recognized thing, and, however young and pretty a woman may be, she may come to the theatre, remain there, and go away unattended, without any risk of enraging a jealous husband, or of being exposed to the annoying attentions of a too gallant admirer. In the pit many persons place provisions by their side on the seats, even solid provisions, a bottle of beer, and slices of rog-bród.

After some kind of overture the curtain rises, and at the same time the chandelier is entirely lowered, so that the house is left in complete darkness. The spectators have nothing to distract their attention, and must therefore, whether they will or no, look at the stage, which is very brilliantly lighted. The actors are pretentious, the actresses pretty, and their costumes very rich and elegant. The performers seem to speak too rapidly, but this is always the impression produced on the ear by a dialogue uttered in an unknown language. The action of the men is monotonous and rapid, that of the women more correct and moderate; that which we call stage business is exaggerated and false. Two innovations were introduced into the piece; the first was to substitute for the *bal champêtre*, in the second act, a very outrageous cancan, in which all the company took part in the most serious manner; they called it the *national* French dance, accompanied by appropriate songs. There is no doubt that all these good Danes are fully convinced that our men and ladies of high rank are in the habit of indulging in these fantastic exhibitions of themselves. The second novelty consisted in bringing all the actors in front of the footlights, after each important scene, to chant a chorus, which was unintelligible to us, but which seemed to connect the various parts of the piece together; it reminded us of the ancient choruses.

The darkness did not allow us to ascertain the effect produced upon the spectators, except by their applause, which occurred in the right place, and proved that a great impression had been made. The good feeling of the *portière* was much applauded, and the manifestations of the evil disposition of Mademoiselle Hélion were received with prolonged hisses. After the scene in the tower, the actor who took the part of Maxime returned in a black coat to bow to the assembly, and assure them of his safety. The principal actor, indeed, always wears this dress-coat, which seems to be the privilege of his part, as the Italian tenors "di primo cartello" are allowed to come on the stage with cloaks over their shoulders.

Between each act the gas is turned up, and all the spectators, both male and female, rush out at all the doors, invade the buffets, and return at the first sound of the bell with their hands and mouths full.

All was over by nine o'clock, and we returned to our hotel, with our overcoats buttoned to the chin, and shivering as we listened to the flapping of the flag on the Christianborg under the influence of the keen north-wind.

A new theatre is to be built at Copenhagen; the only information that we could obtain respecting it was that the expense would amount to nearly 600 rix-dollars, about 40,000 *l*. This will be called the Theatre Royal, which will give to the artists the privilege of being appointed by the king, engaged for life, and considered as state functionaries. The first stone of this building has been laid, but when will they lay the last?

The next day was fine; so, instead of going again to the theatre, we went to the Tivoli. The Tivoli is a place of amusement very similar to the Djugarten at Stockholm, though of much less importance; we have nothing of the same character. All the inhabitants of Copenhagen congregate there, especially during the long summer evenings, which, in fact, are not evenings, as it is broad daylight.

We see at the Tivoli, boat-houses, café concerts, theatrical performances in the open air, balls, restaurants, games, and amusements of every kind. The crowd of people is very great, and composed of all classes; but, whatever may be said on the subject, it is not likely that mothers would take their young daughters there; and they are quite in the right.

The good people who are there go for the purpose of amusing themselves, and they attain their end conscientiously; without constraint, without scruple, and entirely at their ease. We remember especially a fat young fellow with a merry face,—

a student, no doubt; he kept on waltzing for a long time quietly and peaceably, then on a sudden he sat down to a table with his partner on his knee, devoured rog-brod and drank beer, between every two mouthfuls kissing his companion, who was as hungry as himself, and then both returned to the dance, coming back to eat again shortly afterwards; and this was done with an eagerness and a regularity with which nothing could interfere. Close by was a person in authority, a sort of a "Prud'homme," in a long blue coat; awkward, but smiling, he swam round with a satisfied air, uttering from time to time a sonorous laugh, a kind of clucking, much to the admiration of his partner, — a pretty girl, who, with her hand resting on his shoulder, looked at him beatifically, throwing round his neck her bare, round, white arms. And so with all the rest; and then, to complete the picture, some German couples with spectacles on and faded hair, looking ridiculously pretentious, and all outrageously ugly.

What a difference between these silly and somewhat coarse amusements and the popular fêtes of Provence and the Bay of Naples!

There the sky is deep blue, intensely blue, and transparent; the sea is blue also, but of a paler tint. It is crowned with wavelets tipped with white foam; sometimes it sinks into a hollow, and utters a deep sigh, which dies away on the shore. Everywhere, as far as the eye can reach, in the sky and over the sea, are the same calm and the same color, broken only, at the edge of the horizon, by Ischia and Capri, enveloped in a slight mist. The intense light of the sun filters through the branches of the orange-trees which perfume the air, and scatters over the ground minute luminous spots, on which the lazy lizards come and warm themselves.

But, as the sun goes down, the evening breeze, so anxiously longed for all day, begins to come in from the sea; the fishing-boats are drawn up, and the fishermen rest. Then come in, from the country, the peasants and the young girls with their bright eyes, and petticoats glistening with copper ornaments and sea-shells. An improvisator mounts on a platform, guitar in hand; a circle forms around him, and his song commences, and with it the gay and loud laughter of the crowd. How well they all seize and understand his allusions, and the various points of the recital! How pleased they are with trifles! how satisfied with their rags and their naked legs, even with the vermin which devour them! and how readily they encourage and applaud him! But they needs must sup; so the songs cease, and, stretched on the sands still warm with the heat of the day, they try their beautiful teeth on tomatoes, and fruits that grow by the sea, quenching their thirst with a glass of water iced and flavored with anise-seed. Soon after, the dance begins; the groups form, and pass through long slow rhythmic movements, to a melodious and well-marked air. What poses, what attitudes, these men of the people fall into, without being aware of it! with their waistcoats turned back over the shoulder, their long red caps hanging down, their shirts thrown back from their bronzed breasts. Their feet beat the ground with a strength and agility which scorn fatigue, while, with one arm, they support their strong and active partners. And these women! how noble and elegant is their step, what simple grace is in their every movement; how voluptuously they bend, showing the roundness of their forms beneath their coarse dress, and throwing back the tresses of their long black hair! What eagerness, what gayety, what shouts of laughter, and what noise!

Close by are the morra-players,[1] lighted by a smoking lamp with three burners, of antique form. What rapid movements of arms and shoulders! what groups are formed around them! what shouts are heard, and how excited they become! The handle of the knife is sometimes drawn from the right-hand

---

[1] The *morra* is a game played by two persons, each holding up the fingers of one hand, some being closed and the others open. Each player calls out a certain number, and if this is equal to the extended fingers of *both* persons, he scores a point. — TR.

pocket, but their anger cools as rapidly as it breaks out; friendly words succeed to angry speeches, and soon — But a breeze springs up from the north. We are not on the shores of the Mediterranean, but on those of the Sound. No one seems to notice the cold, but we shiver and go home as quickly as we can.

COPENHAGEN.

V.

THE DWELLING-HOUSES.

WE may easily guess, from what we have said of the calm and peaceful manners of the inhabitants of Copenhagen, of their retired life, and calm and tranquil existence, what their houses must be. How little they must resemble those of other countries, and how, on the contrary, they must possess many peculiarities which our visit and the examination which we are about to make will render apparent.

There are many lodging-houses in the old city. The fortifications prevented the extension of the streets, and it was necessary to economize space. The houses have now, for the most part, lost the primitive character which they had when they were first built, and which they owed, more especially, to the quaintness of their gables. The tradition of these extravagant gables, of which we have already given an example when describing the Kongens Nytorv (Fig. 170), has not died away, and certain proprietors still wish to reproduce them on the houses which they are now building. The modern gables (Fig. 198) are, however, less unreasonable than those of the last century. They seem to be subject to some conventional rule, and are divided into irregular compartments, separated by white bands which are thrown into relief by the red background of the bricks. The effect is always exaggerated; but under a sky which is so often gray, and, for months together, obscured by thick mists, the more simple results, which would satisfy us, are evidently insufficient.

They might, however, have recourse to less exaggerated plans; and the remains of ancient gables, now half demolished, give proof of this. We give an example in Fig. 199, now in a very incomplete state, but easy to be understood. The two sloping

Fig. 198.—Modern Gable.

sides of the gable are very decided, and, except the central part, which is terminated by a square projection, follow wholly the lines of the roof. Perpendicular lines on the façades indicate the main and party walls; other bands, running parallel to these, strike the eye as they run upwards through all the stories, and are connected by oblique bands with the sloping sides of the roof.

The elevations show no great complication in their details. There are a few pieces of stone, and bricks of different colors to distinguish the projecting from the recessed parts; and the lintels, protected by relieving arches, sufficiently point out the mode of construction, and ornament it at the same time. The

Fig. 199. — Elevation of a Lodging-house.

shops are distinguished by large bays. At the top of the gables is a pole, serving to raise or lower, to and from the upper stories, heavy and cumbrous packages. Cellars are not in use in Copenhagen; the soil, too damp and permeable, and too slightly raised above the level of the sea, renders them quite insalubrious.

The basement story, which is reached by means of steps in the area, is usually occupied by tavern-keepers and dealers in

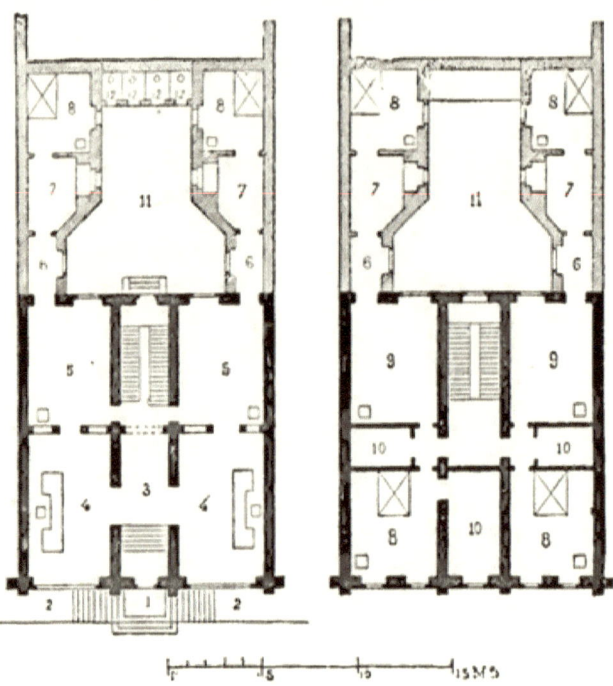

Fig. 200.—Plan of the Ground-floor. Fig. 201.—Plan of First Floor.

1. Entrance.
2. Area.
3. Hall.
4. Shops.
5. Back shops.
6. Sitting-rooms.

7. Kitchens.
8. Bedrooms.
9. Dining-rooms.
10. Smaller "
11. Courtyard.
12. Closets.

eatables. A large room for the shop, another for the back shop, and three or four rooms at the back, form the almost invariable distribution of this lowest story. On the ground-floor (Fig. 200) is a large passage; then a hall, at the end of which is the staircase leading to the various floors. The ascent from the street is by a flight of steps, a portion of which is within the house. The shops, placed to the right and left of this hall, have no direct opening to the street; behind each are a second or back shop, and a kitchen and sitting-room placed in each wing. Between the two wings is a courtyard of moderate size, at the end of which are closets. Each inhabitant has his own, situated not on the floor on which he lives, but in the courtyard; and you may perceive from the street a row of little buildings of wood or brick, the doors of which are opening and shutting at all hours of the day or night. As the houses are rather lofty, it may be easily understood how much trouble and annoyance such a custom, which nobody seeks to infringe, must entail on those who live on the upper floors of a house; but, as it has always been so, no one thinks of adopting a better plan.

Each of the upper stories (Fig. 201) comprises two sets of lodgings; a large apartment fronting the street, and behind this, receiving light from the courtyard, the sitting-room and the kitchen, with sometimes a bedroom for children or servants. These apartments are intended for persons of the middle class. There is no drawing-room. The dining-room serves as a family sitting-room, and as a place where the meals are taken. The principal bedroom is lofty, being at least 13 feet high. The floor is of deal; there is a wainscoting of deal up to a certain height. The ceilings are either bare or plastered; the paper-hangings are simple, not to say common. There is no gilding or *pie-crust* decoration, so common in France, but instead of this they use varnished wood. There is no chimney, but large earthenware stoves, heated with turf, the only combustible in common use in Denmark. There is another remarkable domestic arrangement; instead of beds proportioned to the age and size of the children, which become useless in succession as years pass on, we find beds which grow at the same time as those for whom they are intended. Side-pieces, fastened by hooks, keep the whole together, and lengthen or shorten them; small mattresses are fitted in by the side of each other, or placed one on another as they may be required. The bed of a child may thus be adapted to a grown-up person, and *vice versâ*.

The furniture resembles very much that to be found in our provincial towns thirty or forty years ago. Instead of chimney-pieces there are consoles, on which are usually displayed vases with artificial flowers covered with a glass shade, and sometimes a zinc timepiece of Parisian manufacture. There are no luxurious appliances, no great elegances or refinements for the sake of comfort, but an excessive neatness, and almost always natural flowers or green branches.

The windows have double sashes, the frames being of wood; and these do not open all together, with sash-fasteners (*espagnolettes*), but in small compartments of scarcely sufficient size to allow the head to pass through. Between these two sashes flowers are placed, with a thick layer of fine sand, and paper cornets filled with salt to absorb the damp vapor, which would otherwise cover and obscure the panes of glass; and oftentimes we may see there the profile of some fair young girl, with eyes fixed on the distance, and her mind still farther away.

We had to present a letter of introduction to some one who resided in one of the avenues of Frederiksborg. We soon found the house to which we had been directed, — a charming place, surrounded by clumps of rose-bushes. Instead of an enclosure of walls, there were railings covered with climbing plants. Through a small open garden we could see the entrance door, and the façades of red and white bricks, with some parts filled in with granite. The window-panes were bright and glistening; green creepers were clinging to the corners, and hanging down without restraint. The whole aspect was so gay and cheerful, that the passer-by would be tempted to push open the door and enter.

We present ourselves; a servant-girl, with a roguish look about the mouth, came to open the door to us. She had scarcely heard a few words of our language, when she ran off, with her hands resting on her hips, and shouting with laughter.

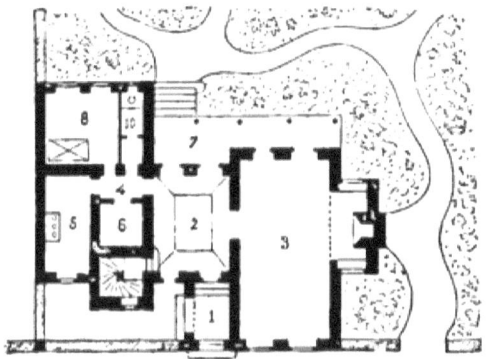

Fig. 202.— Ground-plan of Private Residence.

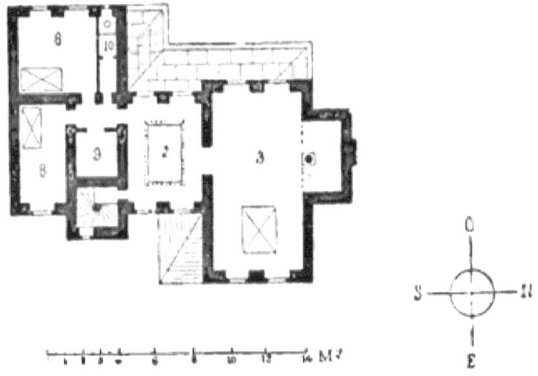

Fig. 203 — Plan of First Floor.

1. Porch.
2. Hall.
3. Drawing-room.
4. Passage.
5. Kitchen.
6. Private room.
7. Covered gallery.
8. Bedrooms.
9. Sitting-room.
10. Closets.

She returned, in a few moments, with a fellow-servant, who joined in her mirth; and there stood the two silly women, pointing at us with their fingers, and exchanging merry remarks, of which we were evidently the subject, thus placing us in a somewhat undignified position. We were, indeed, looking rather foolish, not knowing whether to laugh or to be angry, when the master of the house appeared, and soon found, from the explanations of the servants and the letter which we presented, how matters stood.

The next instant we were in the drawing-room. Our host, who had some difficulty in expressing himself in French, received us in the most polite and cordial manner, and begged us to consider the reception of which we had been victims, as a matter of course, justified by our *strange language*. He introduced us to his family, insisted on our sitting down to table with them, and then offered us every facility to carry out the object of our visit, which was to see his house. He served as our guide, and, as we proceeded, made observations more adapted to give us an idea of the habitation which he had planned in his own mind, rather than that which the builder had realized.

The small porch, which we have already mentioned, leads into a hall communicating with all the rooms (Figs. 202 and 203), similar to that in English houses, occupying the height of two stories, with a gallery on the first floor. From this hall we enter the drawing-room, a large apartment used as a family room, receiving light on one side from the front avenue, and, on the other, from the garden. In one of the sides there is a projecting bay with a fireplace; this forms a smaller room within the larger one, and in winter, during severe weather, thick leather hangings close the entrance, protecting it from the draught which rushes towards the fire. The furniture and decoration of this room partake of that of a dining and drawing room. The walls are painted, the ceilings show the fir-wood beams, left exposed, and adorned with stripes of color.

On the first floor (Fig. 204) a bedchamber is over this drawing-room, having the same form and dimensions, and decorated in the same style. A large square bed, raised high above the floor, occupies a part of the room. At the end of the projecting bay stands the traditional chest, always to be found in old provincial Scandinavian mansions. In this chest are kept the family treasures, the old jewels, the bridal crown, the mother's wedding-dress, and the infant's baptismal robe, — precious relics which go down from generation to generation, and are never

Fig. 204. — Interior of two Rooms.

brought out except on grand family occasions. But they are now, alas! already despised by the young people, who prefer dresses made in the Parisian or London fashion.

On the other side of the hall, on the ground-floor, are the staircase, the kitchen, with its offices, and a bedroom. On the first floor there are secondary bedrooms. On the garden side a veranda is built out, a useful shelter during the summer, for we must not forget that, though the northern climates are rigorous during the long months of winter, the inhabitants are exposed, during the summer, to some days of intolerable heat.

Fig. 205. — External View.

The façades of this house (Fig. 205) are bold and decided; the lines of the building, carried round in a regular and distinct manner, give a clew to the scale of the whole; no cement conceals the nature of the materials or the manner in which they are employed.

Under a Northern climate, more than anywhere else, outer coatings of cement are unsuitable, and very expensive to keep in repair. There is nothing in the external appearance of this building which suggests ideas of false luxury or a vain desire of mere show.

We must especially notice the manner in which the bricks are laid as far as the first floor. They are placed so that their joints intersect each other only at intervals of two rows, thus producing cubes with the angles levelled off, and giving them the appearance of polygons of eight sides, interrupted by a continuous line of bricks of a different color. The effect thus produced is original, and corresponds, much better than a level surface would, with the ornamental parts of the string-courses and of the upper cornice.

This dwelling-house is agreeable in appearance, and comfortable within. It would not satisfy our wants, or the requirements of our worldly and out-door life, but it must be exactly suited to people accustomed to remain at home and enjoy themselves there, and not to seek elsewhere amusements which they can find in the bosom of their family; in fact, persons who think more of the conveniences and comfort of their dwelling than of making a grand appearance and dazzling others.

There was a time when the Danes, being under the influence of French manners of that period, endeavored to copy them, and had succeeded in resembling us; at least, so far as a Dane can resemble a Frenchman. The relics and the traces of that far distant time are still to be found in the large mansions of Bredgade or Amaliengade, — rich dwelling-houses, habitations which required a large household of servants, and involved costly arrangements and expenses, such as people of fortune at the present day can with but few exceptions meet. These mansions, except some still possessed by great families who seldom inhabit them, have for the most part lost their original appearance. The façades have altered in character; the interior arrangements have been modified and adapted to the necessities and requirements of our more simple and moderate modern life.

We may, however, even now ascertain what some of them formerly were, and sketch out, not the façades, the exaggerated rococo of which was their greatest defect, but the ground-plan, which will afford a curious study for an architect, not only in its general distribution, but in the details.

We give, in Fig. 206, the plan of the ground-floor of one of these interiors.

Two large carriage entrances open into the principal courtyard (1); the carriages pass under a porch before the door, which can be closed at each end, and then the coach or sledge, according as the season may be, leaves the court by a second door, and passes in a passage (23) leading to a covered space (25) where both horses and drivers are sheltered from the cold. The visitors enter the door of the vestibule, before which there are no steps, so that when they quit their carriage they pass into the house on the same level. When the guest comes on foot, or leaves his carriage in the street, he enters the door (2), goes through a covered passage, where he is out of the way of the carriages, and, ascending a few steps, meets in the vestibule those who have driven. The servants assist their masters to take off their furs, and wait for them in a cloak-room (7), while the ladies arrange their toilet in a private dressing-room (8), furnished with wash-hand stands and conveniences (13). Two large doors open from the vestibule to the drawing-rooms (10). If there is a fête or a grand reception, the hosts remain in the first drawing-room to receive their guests, who enter this drawing-room and pass through the smaller one into the ball-room (9), at the farther end of which is a bay projecting into the garden, which serves for the orchestra, and is approached by a separate staircase. The dining-room (11) is close by the drawing-room used on ordinary occasions. These three apartments, — the dining-room and two drawing-rooms — communicate with each other, and with a conservatory opening to the garden, to which you may

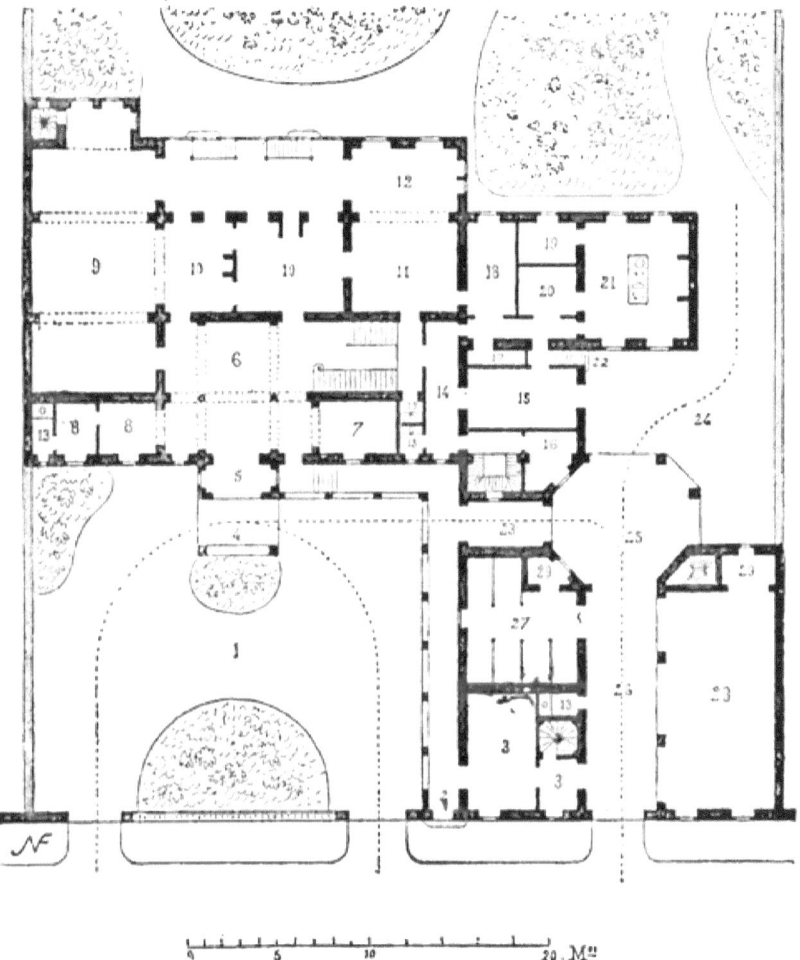

Fig. 206. — Ground-plan of a Private Mansion.

descend by an inner staircase. The grand staircase opens to the vestibule. By passing under the second flight you reach a passage (14) separating the apartments destined for the use of the family from the part allotted to the servants, which comprise an office (18), a kitchen (21), with the scullery (19), and pantry (20), the lamp-room (17), the servants' hall (15), a room for

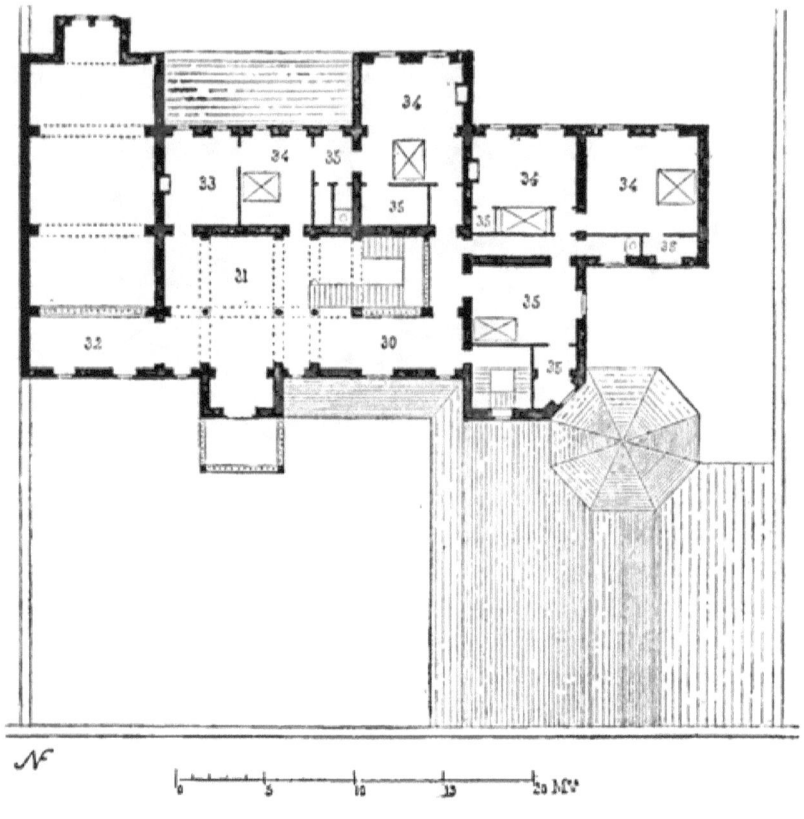

Fig. 207.—Plan of First Floor.

cleaning shoes and brushing clothes (16), as well as the back staircase leading to every story. A door (22) leads from the kitchen to the stable-yard, so that tradesmen and servants do not use the principal entrance.

The side building includes the porter's lodge (3), placed so as to command the principal courtyard and the stable-yard; stabling for six horses (27), a coach-house (28), a harness-room (29), and closets (13); the garden is at the back.

The first floor (Fig. 207) contains the upper part of the hall or vestibule (31), from which you gain access to the gallery of the ball-room (32); then comes a suite of apartments composed of a work-room (33), a bedroom (34), dressing-room (35), and a small room beyond; an open gallery passing round the staircase leads to the bedrooms (34), with dressing-rooms (35).

The upper story contains the still-rooms, the secondary apartments, and the servants' rooms.

Fig. 208.—Interior of Drawing-room and Anteroom.

It can easily be seen by these plans how well a mansion, constructed in such a manner, is suited to the requirements of a wealthy and luxurious family, and how its resources would satisfy all the expensive tastes, and contribute to the enjoyments, of those who inhabit it. How many of our private hotels in Paris are less conveniently arranged, and how much more confined and insignificant they appear in comparison with it!

The decoration of these interiors is in keeping with the general arrangements which we have described. Fig. 208 gives the view of a drawing-room and of its anteroom. The ceilings are formed of open rafters connected by transverse joists, so as to form compartments, each having a centre-piece of carved wood touched up with gold and color. The walls are covered with tapestry, and on the floor there are rich carpets. All the outlines and details are heavy; the ornaments are deficient in grace and delicacy; the wood, which forms the principal part of the construction, is by no means stinted; it is varied in a hundred ways. We find here the decorations of our Louis XV. architecture, applied by those who strove to exaggerate their effects.

Other buildings at Copenhagen are worth visiting, but they are too often only souvenirs of foreign habits and forms, and we only wished to notice those whose internal arrangements and external appearance showed something different from our own, which it would be useful to particularize. There, as elsewhere, however, commonplace buildings are by no means rare, and we did not think it would be interesting to describe them.

ELSINORE (HELSINGŒR).

THE COPENHAGEN STATION. — THE COUNTRY. — ELSINORE. — THE TOWN HALL. — THE KROONBORG.

WE scarcely looked at the Copenhagen station on the day of our arrival; but to-day we had time to examine it, and we made great use of the opportunities that were afforded us to go in and out as we pleased, for before the hour of departure unfortunate travellers are not obliged to spend some time cooped up within a waiting-room.

The building is ninety-two feet long; it is covered with large timber vaults resting on granite pillars, raised thirteen feet above the level of the ground; this arched roof is formed of many boards nailed round the arches on the flat, while other small bevelled planks forming voussoirs are fastened edgeways to these. This double combination of boards, both edgeways and on the flat, offers great resistance, which is still more increased by a succession of ties in the shape of a St. Andrew's cross, connecting the different parts so as to enable them to resist the force of the wind, and to bind them firmly together.

Doors and windows give means of access to the various offices along the bays on each side. On the upper part of the roof is placed a lantern, resting on the spandrels of the arches, and affording at the same time sufficient light and ventilation; a narrow pathway running round the base of this lantern is convenient for necessary repairs.

The waiting-rooms, refreshment-buffets, ticket-offices, and cloak-rooms are entirely lined with varnished deal, touched up with colored stripes. The joists of the ceiling are exposed, and the whole building has an air of order and neatness, which it gives one pleasure to see.

The travellers and their friends crowd on the platform; the former take their seats, while the others, who remain behind, cling on to the doors and the steps. Scarcely can they make up their minds to get down, when the train moves on, and even then they strive to keep up with it, rushing as fast as they can, and crying "Favel! Favel!" (a pleasant journey and good luck to you). When their breath fails, they stop, and we go on our way.

In a few moments we notice that our presence excites the curiosity of our travelling companions. They had previously ascertained by our guide-books that we were not Prussians, but Frenchmen. Those who were next to us made known this discovery to the others at the farther end of the compartment. They addressed us in Danish, and seemed disappointed that they were not understood. Then they spoke to each other, and clubbed together their French to form the sentence that they wished to say; and at last the orator of the company, after having several times repeated his speech to himself in a low voice, said, with an expression which would have been laughable if it had manifested a feeling less flattering to us and less sincere on their part, "We Danes all like the French very much." "And we Frenchmen," we replied at once, "like the Danes very much." And then they began to shake hands with us, and to utter protestations of friendship and affection in Danish, the meaning of which our imagination enabled us to guess, though our ignorance forbade us to understand. These good people alighted, each in his turn bidding us the warmest and most touching farewells. The last who left us was a young officer, with a heavy and constrained gait and manner, perhaps a little shy, who understood a few words of French. He asked us what business brought us into his country. "Nothing," we replied, "but to see and know it." He made us repeat this answer, which seemed to surprise and flatter him. We asked him in our turn if he knew Paris, and if he would not soon visit it. The supposition that he would go to Paris made him laugh exceedingly, but he would not listen to such a proposal. "The French would laugh at me too much," he said more than once. It was impossible to divest him of this notion, and he left us with the conviction, alas! too often entertained, that we are all in France unmerciful quizzes.

As we approached Elsinore, the landscape changed, and assumed a character of entire sadness and solitude. The plains of peat-bog, strangely intersected by narrow ditches cut for the sake of irrigation, and resembling lines of ink, and the naked and barren plains, give place to gloomy and mysterious forests of beech-trees. The first north-winds of autumn bring down the leaves from the trees, and drive them along the ground with a low rustling sound. Seen here and there among the scattered trunks is some peasant's cottage, either red or blue; some charcoal-burner's hut, dark and smoky; and in a hollow road, sunk deeply in the mud at the foot of an ash, a heavily loaded cart is struggling. The sunbeams penetrate through the branches; the rays brighten the tops of the trees, and gild the faded leaves heaped on the ground beneath. A few birds pass over our heads, uttering long shrill cries; but in all this district there is no song, no human voice; nothing is heard but the wind among the trees and the waves on the shore. An indefinable sadness, a sweet melancholy, comes over us before we are aware, and we feel how profound must be the impression made by the continual sight of such scenes as these, — a feeling so true and so deep, that even the inhabitants themselves are not unaware of it, and the word *reemod*, by which they express it, cannot be translated into any other language.

We alighted from the railway before we reached Elsinore, that we might lose nothing of the scenes and landscapes that were passing before our eyes in a succession which is not fatiguing, in spite of its monotony. The distance was short, and yet we were a long time in traversing it. At last there appeared before us a little town, looking bleak and silent, with glittering red roofs. It is almost entirely surrounded by water, and terminated in the distance, at the narrowest part of the strait, by the gloomy Kroonborg.

Three things attract the traveller to Elsinore; the tomb of Hamlet, the river in which "Ophelia with her weedy trophies fell in the weeping brook," and the inscription scratched on a pane of glass by the unfortunate Caroline Matilda: "My God, let me be innocent, and others great."

Hamlet's tomb is no longer in existence; Ophelia's river is dry; and Caroline Matilda's pane of glass is broken.

Notwithstanding this threefold deception, perhaps on account of it, Elsinore has left recollections which it is pleasant for us to retrace.

It consists of a large street parallel to the sea; secondary roads lead on one side to the harbor, and on the other to the country. In one of the most important of these are the houses of the consuls. Large escutcheons fastened to the front of these buildings give them an unusual appearance; you might almost imagine yourself to be in Spain. A little farther on the road widens, and forms a narrow square, in which is the Town Hall. There was not depth enough in the space allotted for it, so that it was necessary to extend the building lengthwise, so as not to encroach upon the square, and to preserve in front sufficient space and ventilation.

The building has undergone modifications in many parts, though it appears never to have been completely finished; but still we can easily understand its appearance and general plan (Fig. 209).

It is built of bricks and red granite, the tone of which matches most happily that of the bricks. The external arrangement of the structure perfectly agrees with that of the interior, being clearly indicated by well-defined lines on the outside. There is considerable variety in the size of the win-

Fig. 209.

dows, which are small and narrow when intended to give light to a room of little importance, but large, high, and double when they open on a hall of greater dimensions. It is deficient in its details and in the ornamental portions, but it is an edifice intended to brave a severe climate, frost, snow, and frequent rains. Delicate sculptured ornaments would have had little chance of withstanding these, and it was wiser in the architect to give all his attention to the choice of materials, the method of employing them, and the study of the due proportions of the different parts of the building.

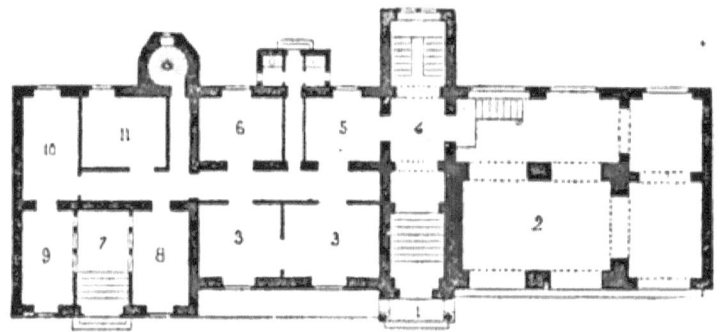

Fig. 210. — Ground-plan of Town Hall, Elsinore.

We notice in the interior the same moderation and the same combinations quietly and well carried out.

We have thought it best to preserve, in our description of the various apartments in this Town Hall, the same terms as are used among ourselves, instead of those common in Denmark, which would not perhaps be equally intelligible.

The principal entrance (Fig. 210) is under a porch (1) sheltering two of the steps, the rest being within the vestibule. No. 2 is a large room serving for election meetings, for political assemblies, and markets of a special nature. A small staircase connects this room with the inner hall (4). The hall-keeper's apartments are in No. 3. No. 5 is the police-office, and in No.

6 an office for the relief of the poor. There is a private entrance (7) for those who wish to transact business with the post-office and the telegraph; a small waiting-room (7) is attached to it. On one side is the telegraph-office, No. 8, and on the other the post-office, No. 9. No. 10 is for the clerks, and No. 11 for the director. A principal and a back staircase lead to the first floor (Fig. 211), on which is a robing-room (12) for the use of the communal councillors. This is of large dimensions; for during the winter they hang up there their furred robes and long pelisses, which are used instead of our more moderate overcoats. Above this room is a gallery reserved for certain clerks whose

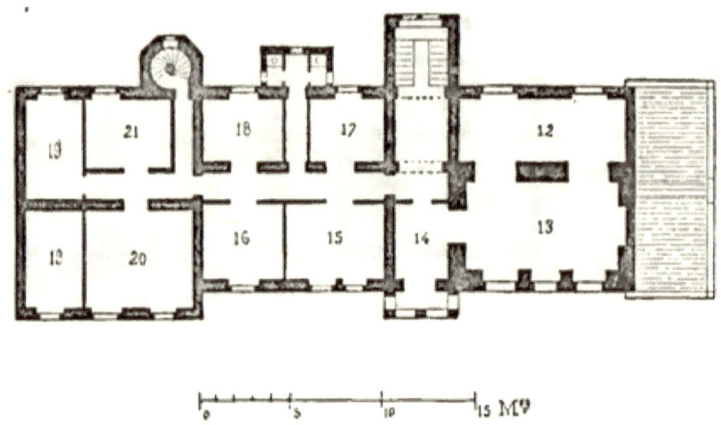

Fig. 211.—Town Hall, Elsinore. First Floor.

presence is necessary during the sittings in the council-chamber. This large room (13) is covered by a ceiling formed of planks of fir, the junctions of which are concealed by unions; the exposed surfaces are varnished and surrounded by bands of color. By the side of this hall opens a smaller one (14), serving as an anteroom, in front of which is a balcony built over the entrance-door. This balcony is used for official addresses to the public, and as a speaker would lose much of his prestige if he were exposed to the sun or protected by an umbrella, a small projecting roof screens him from the weather. The cabinet of the first minister is in 15, his secretary's office is in No. 16, the civil-service offices (17), and the tax-offices (18). A very long

Fig. 212.—Interior. First Floor.

and rather dark passage, although it receives borrowed light from each end, leads to the clerks' offices (No. 19), to those of the architect (No. 20), and to the muniment-room (No. 21).

This is the only public building within the town. The dwelling-houses resemble those which we have already seen at Copenhagen, and it would be of no use to describe them; but there is one point to which we ought to allude,—the difficulty which a foreigner finds in making himself understood. As for ourselves, had it not been for a few English words which a sailor of that nation, who was sleeping off the effects of his gin in the corner of a tavern, was able to translate for us, we ran a great risk of dying of hunger, and of not being able to procure food and shelter in the Hôtel du Nord, the French sign placed outside of which is the cause of many a bitter deception to the unfortunate traveller who is compelled to knock at the door.

An illusion, of which all Frenchmen are too readily the victims, is to fancy that "our beautiful language" is everywhere spoken and understood. This is a great mistake. French is, in fact, in all countries, the language of men of the world, of diplomacy, and of elegance; and it is very rare for a Frenchman to find himself in any drawing-room, wherever he may chance to be, and not to meet with those who can converse with him; but in a foreign country the traveller who wishes to see and to learn passes most of his time in the street among persons of an entirely different character. If, therefore, he cannot readily comprehend what is said by those about him, and if he cannot make his wishes known, he is liable to great inconvenience and unpleasant mistakes, and is often exposed to serious embarrassment if he can express himself only in his mother tongue.

When we have passed along the long street which runs through the town, we reach the harbor,—that is to say, the point where the street is narrowest, and is, at its extremity on the Danish side, terminated by the Kroonborg.

The navigation of the Sound is dangerous. The coasts of Sweden and those of Denmark, on each side, bristle with reefs, and rocks at the water level, and abound in fearful shoals, which are difficult to avoid during foggy nights, when the winds blow from the icy lands of Norway. In order to prevent shipwrecks and disasters, — formerly so common here, — the Danish government erected lighthouses on the coast at the most dangerous points; and, to cover the expense of their first construction and of repairs, they demanded from all ships passing through the Sound a toll, which was paid till 1857, when the maritime powers united to redeem it. In order to compel the payment of these dues, Frederick II. built in 1574, at the narrowest part of the strait, a fort, whose guns might command the entrance of the Sound.

This fort, surrounded by fortifications formerly very formidable, is the Kroonborg (the castle of the crown), Fig. 213.

We enter the Kroonborg, which has some resemblance to an inn. The sentries allow us to go wherever we please, to look at the guns, to count the balls, to mount on the ramparts, and go down into the ditches. This fortress, formerly so formidable, is much changed in appearance, and no longer to be feared. An ironclad, armed with guns of long range, would easily silence it. The Danish government is so convinced of its weakness that it no longer pretends to conceal the fact. It prefers — a far wiser plan — to study the best means of remedying it. The Kroonborg can never have been so formidable as it was said to be, for, being commanded by the neighboring hills on the land side, it could not have provided against a surprise; and enemies who wished to take possession of it might, instead of attacking it by sea, have landed some troops a little farther to the westward, on the shores of the Cattegat, and thus carried it by assault in the rear.

The Kroonborg, therefore, possesses no longer any interest except that which arises from its picturesque situation and its historical claims.

We ascended to the top of the high tower. At the farther end of the Strait, lost in the fog, was Copenhagen; somewhat nearer, the island of Hveen, where the illustrious astronomer, Tycho Brahe, built his observatory and passed twenty years of his life. Still closer, and resembling immense black spots, almost lost in the horizon, are beech-forests, whose lofty branches are incessantly swaying hither and thither in the wind, with a grand, monotonous, and regular sound. Opposite are the coasts of Sweden, bordered by a fringe of white foam, which clearly defines their outlines; the Sound, with its innumerable ships, some surmounted by a crest of smoke, which loses itself in the clouds; others, hidden under their sails swollen by the wind, reminding us of the wings of some gigantic bird. Close at hand, Elsinore, with its red houses scattered along the shore, its lively harbor, and the flags of the consuls flapping in the air; and then, directly beneath us, the enormous dark-brown roof of the castle, and its innocent works, which Nelson braved, without danger, in 1801, when he went, with his fleet, to bombard Copenhagen. The sea is of a greenish blue; the sky is gray, but the transparent and limpid gray of the North. Nature has here impressed upon it a character of grandeur and severity that cannot be described. These Northern countries produce effects entirely different from those to which we are accustomed in the sky of the South. Everything is more calm, sweet, and sad. The contrasts are less striking; they harmonize in tones less intense and more softened down; but the emotion which they cause is not less vivid, and leaves traces as lasting and deep as those produced by the aspect of a country more highly favored and more richly endowed.

In the interior of the castle are a chapel, used for a long time as a store for hay, and some large rooms, for the most part in bad repair, in which Hamlet's ghost no longer wanders. One of these served as the prison of the beautiful Caroline Matilda. Here she was confined, after having been carried off, in the midst of a fête, from her palace of Christianborg; and she remained a prisoner in this gloomy castle, exposed to the blasts of every wind, in front of that dark Northern sea covered with ice and snow; and here she passed long months in the sad recollection that she had been a queen, and that, alas! she had also been a woman.

On that day, say the chroniclers of the time, the sun had, for a few minutes, pierced through the chilly winter mist. The queen wished to go out, mounted on horseback in man's dress, as was her custom. She wore riding-boots, and a long pelisse, and had her beautiful hair hidden under a fur cap. Never had she looked so high-spirited or so charming. As usual, Struensee attended her. When they passed the palace gates, a hand, the queen-mother's, raised a curtain, and pointed out to Christian this gay, young, happy pair.

Christian and his mother exchanged a dark glance. Without a single word having been spoken, they understood each other.

Struensee and his mistress, when once at liberty, dashed off at full gallop along the avenues of Frederiksborg. The hair of the queen, unfastened by the rapidity with which she rode, flowed down upon her shoulders. Struensee secured it again, and on the hardened snow, over which they were riding, there were to be seen, the next day, the traces of their horses' shoes close together confounded with each other. Then they returned, thinking only of their love, and paying no heed to the dark and angry looks of the common people whom they met in the way, who were enraged at the queen's disregard of appearances, and the favor which she lavished on a foreigner.

In the evening there was a ball at the palace; one of those fêtes then given at the Northern courts, where the love of pleasure and sensual gratification knew neither restraint nor limit. Caroline Matilda was radiant with grace and beauty. Struensee, always at her side, confident in her favor, saw on the features of the king no trace of the terrible passions which agitated his mind. The assembly came to an end. Then there was a great tumult, followed by a deep silence. The queen, dragged from her apartments, was hurried along the road to Elsinore, and shut up in the fortress. Struensee was arrested and carried before his judges.

Shortly after, a scaffold was raised on the esplanade of Vesterbro. Struensee was beheaded, and the queen went as an exile to Hanover, to die.[1]

The weather is so fine, and the air so pure, that we are about to make an excursion by sea. We embark at the extremity of a small fjord, near a house which can be distinguished from a distance by a flag floating at the top of a mast.

This is a life-boat station, where brave men are always at hand to carry assistance to vessels in peril on this coast, so dangerous during the foggy days of spring and autumn. Skilful fishermen and hardy sailors, they live here alone, without any other amusement than fishing, which is their main support.

We find the house occupied by its usual inhabitants, who come forward eagerly to do the honors. A veranda serves as a place of shelter for the life-boat, with the rigging and their nets. The outer door opens on a large room (Fig. 214). All round it are low, wide seats, covered with furs; while hanging on the walls are fishing utensils and garments for daily use. In the middle is a large stove, open on all four sides, filled with blazing turf, a good supply of which is stored without. In this hall the men meet before their expeditions, and hither they bring their fish and prepare it. In this room they pass those long days, when the storm roars without, and tells that their assistance may be needed. A man must, indeed, be vigorously constituted, both in body and mind, who can pass his life in such a solitude, without any other excitement than the remembrance of past dangers and the apprehension of those that are to come.

From this hall — whose height extends through the ground-floor, the first story, and a part of the roof — an inner open staircase leads to the story standing only over that portion of the house above the veranda. This contains two bedrooms. The occasional guests, who are brought hither by the storm, sleep in the large room, on camp-beds arranged there.

---

[1] Caroline Matilda was sister to George III. of England. After her divorce the British Court gave her a residence at Celle, in Hanover, where she died in 1773. — Tr.

The building is solidly constructed. Blocks of granite, thrown up by the sea, form the masonry of the walls, the thickness of which defends the interior from the high winds so common on this coast, and the damp, which, in these latitudes, is so dangerous. On the roof are to be seen the traditional carved beams, with ends formed like the prows of a ship, a souvenir of those

Fig. 214.—Life-boat Station, Elsinore.

maritime people who wished to have, even in their dwelling on dry land, a remembrance of the vessels in which every day they risked their lives.

We returned on foot, to pay a last farewell to the Zealand landscape; and, when the evening came on, we found ourselves at the foot of the Kroonborg, at the end of the cape which projects into the strait. The country all around was infinitely sad and melancholy; under our feet was a bed of fine, rose-colored sand, glittering with particles of mica as the stormy waves dashed over it, the crest of each sparkling in the rays of the setting sun.

Fading in the distance, on the Swedish coast, were the mountains of Kiœlen, formerly considered the extreme boundaries of the world; the nearest are low and verdant at their base, but soon become rough and craggy, defended by lofty crests of red granite. The Sound was covered with ships hastening to accomplish their voyage before the approach of winter. The cold, white sky, streaked with sharp and strongly defined lines of brightly colored clouds, contrasted strongly with the greenish tints of the sea. Large birds were sporting on the waves, uttering sharp and shrill cries. Immensity opened before us; beyond us was the new, the unknown, with the seduction, the attraction, the unrealizable dreams which arise in the imagination of every traveller.

Night was coming on, — one of those strange Northern nights, full of soft splendor and indefinite forms. The coasts were streaked with tints graduated from the most intense violet to the softest opal. The sea alone was still bright, and its hoarse murmur silenced all sounds upon the shore. One by one the sails disappeared, and the sea-birds returned rapidly to their nests. The moment of our departure was come; and soon, standing on the deck of the vessel that was bearing us away, we watched the last faint outlines fading into the darkness. The lighthouses shone out along the coast, and we soon lost sight of the Island of Zealand, the extreme point of Denmark, a land which we quitted with that indefinable impression of sadness, with which the heart of a man is always filled, when he is about to leave a country which, in all probability, he beholds for the last time.

THE END.

Cambridge: Electrotyped and Printed by Welch, Bigelow, & Co

www.ingramcontent.com/pod-product-compliance
Lightning Source LLC
Chambersburg PA
CBHW032138010526
44111CB00035B/607